The God Experiment

Can Science Prove
the Existence of God?

RUSSELL STANNARD

Foreword by
PAUL DAVIES

HiddenSpring

Jacket design by Mark Horton

Jacket photo by Adam Chinitz

First published in Great Britain in 1999 by
Faber and Faber Limited
3 Queen Square London WC1N 3AU

Library of Congress Cataloging-in-Publication Data

Stannard, Russell.
The God Experiment : can science prove the existence of God? /
by Russell Stannard ; foreword by Paul Davies.
p. cm.
Originally published: London : Faber and Faber, 1999.
Includes index.
ISBN 1-58768-007-6 (cloth)
I. Title.
BT102.S68 2000
212′.1—dc21
00-057249

Published in North America by
HiddenSpring
an imprint of Paulist Press
997 Macarthur Boulevard
Mahwah, New Jersey 07430

www.hiddenspringbooks.com

Printed and bound in the United States of America

Contents

"I came to know God experimentally"

George Fox, a leading figure in the founding
of the Quaker movement

Foreword

Imagine a faraway planet on which a species of intelligent beings had evolved. Over time, communities of these beings developed organized societies and rudimentary technology. Somewhat later, a group of bright aliens stumbled across the basic laws of physics. Soon what we would call science began to flourish. The aliens realized that with this new knowledge of the world they could improve their technology and understand more and more about the physical universe.

Some centuries passed, and the scientific project reached its culmination. The aliens understood just about everything in their environment, near and far, in terms of scientific principles. A complete "theory of everything" was formulated, involving elegant and abstract mathematical expressions that embodied all fundamental physics. To be sure, some systems remained too complex to study in detail, but the aliens were confident that all the basic principles of nature were thoroughly understood.

Much later, historians would regard this scientific golden age as the easy phase in the attempt by the aliens to make sense of the world. With all the formulas established and all the experiments completed, some curious aliens began asking altogether harder questions. Why, for example, were the laws of nature what they were, rather than something else? The beautiful laws of physics, captured so succinctly within the theory of everything, clearly could have been different. What determined, from among the set of all possible laws of physics, those laws that actually applied to the real world? And where did these laws come from anyway? In addition to asking "Why this Universe?" and "Why any universe?" the aliens began wondering about where they themselves fit in. Did the emergence of life, consciousness, and understanding of the physical world signify a profound link between the nature of the universe and their own abilities to unravel the secrets of nature, or was it just a lucky fluke? Was there any deeper meaning to physical existence? How could the remarkable coherence and consistency of the natural order be explained? Might the universe be unfolding according to something like a scheme? Could concepts such as purpose and design be applied to nature as well as to alien activity? A new project was duly begun to tackle these thorny issues.

Most of the aliens were highly skeptical about the new project, not because they thought the questions were pointless or stupid, but because they were hard - much harder than the scientific questions. In approaching them, scientists had to go beyond physics, rooted as it was in experiment and observation, into the realm of metaphysics. Progress was likely to be slow, consensus difficult. Even the best alien minds were baffled in the face of such daunting mysteries. My description of a hypothetical alien community serves the purpose of contrasting with the history of human civilization. In our case, metaphysical questions were tackled long before science arose. Early human communities constructed a wide range of mythologies, superstitions and religions to make sense of their world. To modern eyes, many of these early attempts at explaining reality look childish and fanciful. Later, when the great world religions developed, more intellectual rigor was brought to bear on these fundamental questions of existence. Leading thinkers in the monotheistic tradition, such as Augustine and Thomas Aquinas, developed a systematic approach to metaphysics and attempted to relate features of the physical universe to theology. Scholars in Judaism and Islam pursued similar projects.

Then, in the seventeenth century, modern science began to flourish. Scientists had an altogether different agenda. Their methods could, with effort, lead to explanations for physical phenomena, but they were ill suited to dealing with metaphysical questions. To be sure, most early scientists were deeply religious, and they saw their scientific investigations as a way to reveal God's handiwork in the cosmos. The laws of nature that underpin the scientific enterprise they regarded as God's way of ordering the world. But principally scientists were preoccupied more with how than with why questions. Over the succeeding three hundred years, science became so successful that its theological underpinnings were largely abandoned. Many scientists began to regard the ancient questions of existence as either misguided or unanswerable, and therefore pointless. They looked back with derision at mankind's early fumbling attempts at metaphysics and presented the scientific enterprise as an antidote to such primitive musings. Once the public was properly educated in the scientific method, it was claimed, they would stop asking meaningless why questions and simply accept the physical universe, with its manifold wonders, as a brute fact.

It is fascinating to speculate whether, had human history resembled that of my hypothetical alien community, this contempt by scientists for matters metaphysical would have been so strident and entrenched. I suspect that had it been the scientists rather than the priests who first addressed the great metaphysical puzzles, then the topics concerned would have been regarded as extremely difficult but entirely respectable to contemplate. Such is scientific hubris! In fact, something of a sea change is occurring in the scientific community. Perhaps it is inevitable that those scientists working at the frontier on topics like the origin of the universe cannot avoid encountering the age-old metaphysical questions that were formerly the exclusive preserve of theologians and philosophers. Those scientists have been drawn, through their scientific work, to revisit the earliest and deepest riddles of existence: why the world is as it is and what the place of human beings might be in the great scheme of things.

Russell Stannard epitomizes this new breed of thinker. He is a physicist by profession, with a long-standing interest in deep problems such as the origin of the universe, the nature of time, the fundamental structure of matter, and the role of conscious observers in nature. He approaches the subject of God and science through the Christian tradition, although his work will be of interest to adherents of all religions and none. In this book he sets out a comprehensive agenda to bring scientific methods and concepts to bear on theological and religious issues, and also to help science rediscover its theological roots. He argues that with the benefit of our scientific understanding of the world, it is now profitable to go back and reexamine those early prescientific attempts at explaining the universe in God-related terms. Remarkably, in spite of their more limited knowledge of the physical universe, many early religious thinkers nevertheless seem to have identified profound and enduring truths.

Stannard does not restrict his analysis to abstract theological and scientific topics. Indeed, he is not afraid to confront mainstream religious problems head-on. He begins his account with a critical assessment of miracles and goes on to consider the significance of Biblical narratives, especially those that relate to the life and death of Jesus Christ. Nor does he shy away from thorny problems, such as the existence of evil, human free will and life beyond death, which have exercised the minds of some of the world's greatest thinkers over the centuries. He brings a refreshing new scientific perspective to bear on these contentious issues, and while he makes no claim to have solved them, readers will discover many fresh analyses.

Unusually for a scientist, Stannard strives to build bridges between ancient religious traditions and modern science. Rather than dismissing many of the Biblical stories as myths, he reexamines them in the light of modern science and finds much of enduring value. One of his key themes, which I strongly endorse, is that theology is not a static discipline, but continually evolving in the light of new knowledge. Thus the concept of God in the Old Testament develops chronologically. He starts out as a tribal warrior deity and gradually evolves into the Christian God of love and forgiveness. But who is to say the process ends there? As Stannard points out, the universe revealed by science opens up whole new vistas that went unnoticed by the Bible writers. There is an urgent need for theological reevaluation in the light of discoveries about the birth and death of the universe, the genetic revolution, and the possibility of extraterrestrial life, to name but a few fashionable areas of research. We should not just look backward to the remote past for religious inspiration and neglect future developments.

The idea of progress in religion may seem strange to some people, but to a scientist it is natural to think of our understanding advancing with the aid of new discoveries. One can still respect the Bible and other sacred texts for building the foundations of faith, but that does not mean they should be the last word on the subject. Stannard's achievement is to garner the core message of the Bible and move on to enrich it with scientific insights.

One of the most exciting areas of theological enquiry at this time concerns the reemergence of what used to be called natural theology - the belief that God is revealed through the workings of nature as well as through personal religious experience. For example, vigorous debate is taking place between scientists and theologians about the significance of the so-called anthropic principle - the discovery that the existence of conscious organisms depends rather sensitively on certain delicate features in the basic laws of physics. Does this point toward some sort of design in the structure of the universe or to the existence of an infinite variety of alternative universes - a multiverse - in which just a tiny fraction possess by chance the favorable circumstances for life to emerge? In universities and at conferences around the world, theologians can be found talking to computer scientists and mathematicians, physicists and cosmologists, geneticists and evolutionary psychologists, discussing complexity theory, the foundations of mathematics and logic, the evolution of altruistic behavior, and many other challenging topics.

Perhaps it is too soon to talk of the new theology, as one does of the new physics or the new biology, but there is certainly a new theological agenda, and this book by Russell Stannard provides an excellent guide to the sorts of issues likely to engage theologians and religious organizations in the coming decades. Einstein once wrote that science without religion is lame and religion without science is blind. I can think of no better emblem for the chapters that follow.

Paul Davies

South Australia

The Prayer Experiment

Does prayer work?

You are suffering from heart disease – in need of coronary artery bypass surgery. At the hospital someone asks whether you are prepared to take part in an experiment. Not, I hasten to say, an experiment involving some novel surgical technique; the operation will be perfectly standard. No, it is an experiment to test whether prayers for the sick are effective.

On agreeing to participate, your name is to be randomly assigned to one of two groups. Patients in one group will be prayed for by special teams of intercessors drawn from a variety of religious denominations, each team being given a particular batch of patients. Patients in the second group will *not* be prayed for. The second group is identical in all respects to the first, with the sole exception of its not being the subject of prayer. There will, of course, be the inevitable statistical differences between the groups, but these should be small, given that each group consists of 600 patients drawn from the five major hospitals participating in the experiment. The second group is the *control* group.

Over a period of two to three years, the patients' case histories will be followed up to see if there are any differences in recovery rates between the two groups. Indicators will include measurements of the physical functioning of the heart, the frequency of death from all causes, length of stay in hospital, and whether patients discharged from hospital return to their homes or enter a nursing home.

As a participating patient you will not know to which of the two groups you have been assigned. You might be prayed for, or you might not. That is all you know. Likewise, the medical staff tending you will have no access to this information. Those doing the praying will know only the Christian names of the people assigned to them, together with some details of their condition – not sufficient to reveal the identity of the individual. Only at the very end of the experiment will all the data be collated. The project has been designed as a rigorously controlled scientific experiment.

I first came to learn of this experiment through being a trustee of the John Templeton Foundation, a charitable organization devoted to supporting projects promoting progress in religion. It was our foundation that agreed to fund this experiment. When I recently spoke of the project in a radio broadcast in the UK, I was inundated with queries from newspaper reporters and radio and TV interviewers; the telephone did not stop ringing for a week. Everyone seemed totally amazed – and intrigued – at the thought that one might apply scientific principles to investigate a religious question.

But why? Several other fields of academic activity have tried – admittedly, with varying degrees of success – to turn themselves into sciences. We have seen, for example, the rise of the social sciences; we have heard Sigmund Freud and Carl Jung claiming on behalf of psychology that it too was a science. So why not theology?

One objection stems from the idea that theology is fundamentally rooted in Scripture. The starting-point is that one accepts, in faith, that the Bible, or some other set of sacred writings, is the inerrant Word of God. This set of writings, interpreted in a literal manner or in some more liberal way, is the ultimate authority on all matters relating to God.

If that is the stance adopted, then it is clearly unlike anything that holds in science. Science is fundamentally based in experimentation and observation. It is an approach where one's theories are in a constant state of flux as they adapt themselves to new empirical findings. No matter how cherished one's hypothesis might be, it must always yield in the face of contrary evidence. The ultimate authority lies with the data. The idea that the truth was set in stone at some earlier time, and is not to be questioned, has no place in science.

But that is just one approach to theology. There is another – one that resonates much more closely with the scientific approach. One of the tasks of this book is to explore to what extent this second approach to theology can be regarded as a science.

I suppose most people's idea of the way scientists go about their work is of an investigation conducted under carefully controlled laboratory conditions. A situation is set up in which, as far as possible, the particular effect under investigation is isolated, and all other extraneous background effects are reduced to a minimum. That is indeed the aim in many scientific studies. As regards religious investigations, the best attempt to apply such a methodology is to be found in the experiment I was talking about just now – the so-called *prayer experiment*. That will be our starting-point. So let us take a closer look at it.

The prayer experiment

Belief in the power of prayer is widespread. One hears the claim, for example, that the collapse of atheistic communism was an answer to prayer. It had long been held that, because of the totalitarian nature of communism – the lack of free elections – once a country went communist there could be no going back. Religion in those countries would become a thing of the past. And yet it was not to be. Against all the odds, communist regimes have toppled, and the churches in those countries, suppressed for decades, are now coming back into their own once more.

Or take the case of South Africa. It was an almost universally held belief that apartheid in South Africa could end only in a bloodbath. In the event, the transition to majority rule occurred relatively peacefully. This is also claimed to be an answer to prayer.

Though such examples might strike believers as highly persuasive, they are not, of course, conclusive. We are unable to rerun history – once with the benefit of prayer, and once without – to see if it makes a difference. No, to try and see whether prayer "works," one has to turn away from the big one-off world events, and concentrate on situations that are repeatable – frequently occurring situations where we have a chance of varying the conditions.

Prayers for the sick appear to offer just such an opportunity. If miraculous healings happen, then this would seem on the face of it to be evidence for God – God directly intervening and having an effect in the world. There is a widespread acceptance of the efficacy of intercessory prayer. This might be evident in the spectacular, highly charged, emotional rallies held by the evangelist Maurice Cerullo, or in the more sober practice of making pilgrimages to holy places such as Lourdes in France or Guadelupe in Mexico. More commonly, faith in miracles manifests itself in the intercessions for the sick offered up in every church on a Sunday, or in the daily private devotions of millions when praying for the recovery of sick loved ones. But do such prayers work? That is what the prayer experiment hopes to discover.

The project's chief investigator is Dr. Herbert Benson of the Mind/Body Medical Institute, New England Deaconess Hospital, Boston. This is not the first time an experiment of this sort has been carried out. Results published in 1988 of an intercessory study at the San Francisco General Hospital performed by R. C. Byrd appeared to show a significant difference between the two groups of patients. Those who received intercessory prayer appeared to have a less complicated hospital course and required fewer medications and procedures than those belonging to the control group who did not receive prayer. However, the results have not been widely accepted, in part because of concerns over the details of the methodology involved.

The current project is a considerable improvement on the original in a number of respects. The sample sizes have been increased from the 200 characteristic of the first study to the 600 involved in the present experiment. Secondly, whereas the Byrd study included anyone admitted to the coronary care unit, the patients involved this time are more homogeneous in that they are all undergoing the same surgery (thus facilitating tighter medical definitions of evaluation points or endpoints of treatment). The follow-up period has been extended from one year to two/three years. Five sites are involved instead of one. More sophisticated statistical techniques will be employed to analyze the data.

In addition, the Benson study includes a third group of 600 patients. Like those in the first group, these are prayed for, but unlike the first, they *are* informed that they are to be the subject of prayer. The intention here is to examine whether there is any additional benefit to be gained (of a psychosomatic or placebo nature) from knowing that one is the subject of prayer. This part of the study will test hypotheses to do with "patient expectation."

Possible outcomes and interpretations

And what of the results? It is too early to say. Final results are not due out before 2002. Meanwhile, there will be no interim progress reports. This is to ensure that early indications do not feed back into the experiment and possibly affect its outcome. So, you might be wondering, why bring up the subject now? Are we not being premature? The reason is that, long before it was agreed to go ahead with the experiment, much thought had been devoted to considering the possible outcomes, and what significance might be attached to them. Even without knowing the actual outcome, it is highly instructive to think through the various options.

As regards the first two groups – those unsure whether or not they are being prayed for – should the project eventually yield a statistically significant positive correlation between prayer and good recovery from the operation, that would of course be fascinating. Doubtless such a discovery would trigger a whole series of follow-up experiments. In the first place one would want to establish, beyond all reasonable doubt, that the positive correlation was no mere statistical freak. Different prayer techniques would be tried to see whether some were more effective than others. One would want to investigate whether other medical conditions yielded to this form of treatment – cancer, perhaps. Clearly an important field of study would open up.

However, it must be noted that none of this would amount to proof of God's existence; persuasive evidence in favor, maybe – but not out-and-out proof. Both the investigators themselves and the funding agency make it clear from the outset that the project is *not* to be thought of as an attempt to prove God's existence. An alternative explanation of a positive correlation might involve, for example, some form of direct transference of thought between the mind of the person praying and that of the patient, presumably of a telepathic nature. There would accordingly be no need to invoke God as an "intermediary" in the process. The beneficial effect would pass directly from intercessor to patient.

As for the other possible result – *no* measurable difference between the two groups – what might be the implication of that?

Doubtless many will jump to the "obvious" conclusion: intercessory prayer does not work – perhaps because there is no God. But again one must be careful. In the same way as a positive result does not necessarily vindicate belief in God, so a negative result does not have to be damaging to belief. There are alternative explanations of a null result:

For instance, when it is said that one of the groups will not be prayed for, that simply means there will be no special prayer team at work on their behalf. That of course will not stop the patients praying for themselves, nor their loved ones and friends from praying. The investigators refer to this (somewhat tongue-in-cheek) as the "unwanted background noise." What the experiment is trying to do is to measure whether there is any *additional* benefit coming from the prayers of the special team. It could well be that the efforts of these strangers will be swamped by the heartfelt prayers of those directly involved with the patients.

There is another concern: when scientists investigate the physical world, provided they ask the right questions and adopt good, sound scientific methodology, nature has no alternative but to yield up its secrets. But applying that methodology to God (or to anyone else with a will of their own) is *not* a guarantee of success. God might simply decide not to cooperate. It could be argued that a loving God might indeed be reluctant to penalize patients merely because some strangers deliberately choose not to include them in their prayers.

Not only that, God might well appreciate better than we ourselves some of the drawbacks of allowing us to probe too deeply into his* manner of working. By the very nature of the clear-cut way in which the experiment has been designed, the result will be a quantitative one. That means it becomes possible to put a price on whatever benefit might be gained from this type of prayer exercise. Do we *really* want some treasury official to use a positive result as an excuse to close down hospital wards – because vicars can be hired to pray more cheaply? While we are doubtless all in favor of a cost-effective Medicare system, it seems a far cry from what many would regard as the true nature of prayer: a natural expression of a loving, trusting, personal relationship with God. For this reason, it would not altogether be surprising if God decides to frustrate the best efforts of the investigators – for their own good. We would do well to recall that it does say in the Bible: *"Thou shalt not put the Lord thy God to the test."* So, we can't say we haven't been warned!

Important and intriguing though this experiment might be, it is necessary to keep it in perspective. The experiment is concerned solely with intercessory prayers; there are many other aspects of prayer. Moreover, it deals only with prayers offered up on behalf of strangers. Like many others, I reckon the central core of intercessory prayer has more to do with the agonizing, involved prayers of loved ones and intimate friends – the so-called "noise" – than with those of distant strangers.

Nevertheless the Benson experiment has aroused enormous interest, it has been beautifully designed, and it deserves to be done. I for one await with great interest both the outcome itself, and the heated discussions that are bound to ensue as to what interpretation should be put on the result – whatever that turns out to be.

Limitations of solitary investigations

In view of the ambiguities that will inevitably attend the result of this experiment, you may be wondering why I have chosen it as the starting-point for our discussion of the evidence for God. The reason is simple. It is to bring home that even when we are able to set up conditions of our own choosing, under thoroughly scientific constraints, it becomes surprisingly difficult to arrive at any firm, incontrovertible conclusion as to whether or not a supernatural intervention has taken place. If we cannot get knock-down proof when we are controlling everything, it is surely unreasonable to expect *any* single, decisive proof of God's existence, and of his influence in the world. Those who make such a demand are likely to be disappointed.

So does that mean that the whole idea of trying to apply scientific thinking to the study of God is ill-conceived? Is it doomed to failure from the outset? No. It is important to recognize that the kind of difficulties encountered over the interpretation of the outcome of the prayer experiment are nothing unusual; they are to be found all the time – even in hard-core physical science.

Take, for example, my own field of research: high-energy nuclear physics. This is the study of the behavior of sub-atomic particles. These particles are so small they cannot be seen directly (under a microscope, say). They are to all intents and purposes invisible – much like an invisible God. Instead, one has to observe their *effects*, and from these draw inferences. The usual effect is that they leave a trail or track behind them marking where they have been. (The track might be in the form of a string of tiny bubbles in a transparent liquid, or a series of small sparks in a gas subject to a high electric voltage.) As the subatomic particles collide with each other, or as they spontaneously disintegrate, so they leave behind characteristic patterns of tracks marking out the paths followed by the various particles involved.

The trouble is that for any given pattern of tracks, there might be a number of competing interpretations. If all one has is a single event, there might be very little that can be deduced from it. Many examples might have to be collected, perhaps using a variety of detection techniques; statistical analyses have to be carried out as to the likelihood of the various rival explanations. Only after a period of time might a consensus emerge as to which is the more likely interpretation. Throughout this process there will not be any well-defined point at which the interpretation is *proved* correct. Rather, the evidence progressively accumulates; the odds become stronger in favor of one particular explanation. Eventually, the controversies die down, and the scientific community as a whole finds that it is no longer seriously questioning the conclusion.

As another example, we can look to cosmology. This will figure prominently in our discussions later, in Chapter 9. There we shall be examining the evidence for the Big Bang origins of the Universe. According to this theory, the Universe began with a great explosion. Why do we think that? For a start, we find that the Universe is expanding; it is still expanding in the aftermath of that explosion. At least, that is the interpretation put on it. But there is another possibility. According to a rival theory, new matter is continually being created throughout space. As fast as matter moves away, the gaps left behind are filled by the newly created material. Thus, the overall picture remains essentially unchanged over time: in particular, there was *no* explosive beginning. This "Steady State" theory used to be a serious rival to the "Big Bang" theory. And that is how the situation would have remained, had not other indications come along.

As we shall be seeing later, the Big Bang theory holds that the initial conditions in the Universe would have been very hot; the explosion would have been accompanied by a fireball. It is argued that the cooled-down remnants of that fireball ought still to be about in the Universe today. Indeed, this radiation has now been discovered. At least, it has all the hallmarks expected of it. But of course there are many sources of radiation in the Universe. It could well be argued that, just as the expansion of the Universe on its own was not proof of the Big Bang hypothesis, neither is this form of radiation, on its own, clinching proof. Rather, it is to be seen as helping to strengthen the overall case.

The expected conditions of the Big Bang also allow one to calculate what kind of atomic particles were likely to emerge from it. The calculated abundances of the different kinds of atom are found to be in good agreement with those of the atoms that make up the gases from which the stars formed. This constitutes yet further confirmatory evidence.

Finally, we note that it takes time for light to reach us from the far depths of space. Examining distant objects through a telescope is like looking back in time. We are able to see directly how the Universe was long ago – and it looked different then to what it does now. The density of matter throughout space appears greater then than it does now – in agreement with the Big Bang theory, and contrary to what would be expected on the basis of the Steady State theory. But in saying that, it has to be recognized that there are difficulties involved in trying to estimate distances to far-off astronomical objects. Systematic errors could creep in, and if present, would distort one's estimates of density. For this reason, the evidence, once again, is not by itself conclusive.

What one discovers from a discussion like this is that acceptance of the Big Bang theory does not rest on any single decisive piece of evidence. Instead, the case has to be based on the examination of a range of indicators, all of which point to the same conclusion. The Big Bang hypothesis is an economical and elegant way of accounting for a wide variety of disparate phenomena. The evidence is cumulative; it is *persuasive* rather than clinching. And different scientists need different degrees of persuasion in order to be won over.

One lesson we can draw from this is that, when trying to establish the reality of God, rather than looking for one decisive experiment –

say, the prayer experiment – we perhaps ought to be broadening our horizons. We need to examine a wide variety of indications to see whether, *taken together*, they add up to a compelling case.

When conditions are not under our control

A further reason one might have for believing it inappropriate to associate scientific methodology with studies of God is that, apart from the prayer experiment, it is hard to think of situations that would lend themselves to the establishment of controlled investigations into God.

This, in fact, is not a problem peculiar to theology. An inability to control the circumstances of an investigation is quite common in science too. Take, for example, cosmology – the study of the Universe on the largest scale. We have just been discussing the scientific evidence for the Big Bang. But, of course, there was never any question of us controlling the circumstances of the Big Bang. The cosmos cannot be contained in a laboratory. In fact, the whole subject of cosmology and astronomy is one where we control virtually nothing. We are reduced to observing, in a purely passive manner, whatever radiation signals happen to come our way.

And yet no one would deny that cosmology and astronomy are "sciences." They gain that status from the systematic and scrupulous way the data are gathered, and the manner in which the theories are always open to modification in the light of those empirical findings.

The same holds in certain branches of the biological and earth sciences. In Chapter 10 we shall be examining Darwin's Theory of Evolution by Natural Selection. We shall see how we humans, in common with the other animals, have descended from more primitive ancestors – stretching all the way back to the inanimate chemicals to be found on the surface of Earth soon after it formed some 4,600 million years ago. This is the generally accepted scenario for human origins.

But how has this assessment been made? The evolution of humans is not a repeatable process. Indeed, we shall later be pointing out that if evolution has taken place on other planets in the cosmos, giving rise to intelligent life-forms, these are most unlikely to end up looking like us humans. And yet evolutionary biology is most definitely a "science."

The reasons are the same: the systematic collection of a wide range of different types of data (the fossil record, anatomical comparisons between species, genetic comparisons, etc.), together with a willingness to allow the weight of that empirical data to be the final arbiter on the success or otherwise of the theoretical hypotheses. Nor is it necessary for that data to be so overwhelming as to convince everyone. There are many professional biologists, let alone lay persons, still unhappy about various aspects of the conventionally accepted evolutionary theory.

Finally, we might mention the earth sciences. These have been transformed in recent times by the theory of plate tectonics – the manner in which various parts of the Earth's crust move about the surface of the globe causing earthquakes, and the building of mountains. Once again, these are processes that are not under our control.

Thus, the ability to control the circumstances under which an experiment is conducted, together with the possibility of repeating the experiment under the same or different conditions, though desirable, is not a necessary prerequisite for that field of study to be regarded as scientific. For that reason we speak of the social sciences – despite the strong limitations that exist on the extent to which it is acceptable to manipulate social groupings. We might also speak of psychology as a science, even though there are strict ethical limits on the degree to which a therapist might seek to "experiment" on his/her clients.

Opening out the prayer experiment

The same kind of situation confronts us over the study of God. God is not some object we can control. We cannot expect God to submit to repeated experimentation under conditions of our choosing. There will be no single, definitive proof of his existence and of his manner of working. Instead, we have to examine, as objectively as we can, a whole range of experience – a multitude of diverse indications – whatever happens to be on offer. We have to ask: given the totality of the data presented to us by our experience of life, does it make better sense in the light of the God hypothesis? Does it all hang together better if we assume there is a God? If so, what kind of God are we dealing with?

Thus, the line of investigation that began with a narrow experiment into the effectiveness of intercessory prayer is opened out. The prayer experiment becomes just one piece of the jigsaw puzzle. The whole of life – every aspect of our experiences – has to be drawn into what I call: *the God experiment.*

Note
*Occasional usage of "his" and "he" not to be taken as implying the assignment of a specific gender to God.

2

Do Miracles Happen?

The prayer experiment is investigating requests for God to intervene in the normal course of events. Essentially the prayers are asking for a miracle. But, of course, there have been many, many claims of miraculous happenings – especially in the Bible. So, is this where we ought next to be looking for evidence of God's intervention? Indeed, were we wise to begin our investigation with examples of healing? Perhaps less ambiguous evidence is to be found in other types of miracle – nature miracles – those that do not involve the complicated inner workings of the human body, with all its psychological ramifications.

The Bible appears to lay claim to many such miracles; it is to these that we now turn for our second source of evidence for God. But note that in so doing, we are *not* looking to the Bible as an authority – a source of unquestioned integrity. We examine it in exactly the same critical frame of mind as we would any other potentially fallible written record.

Definition of miracles

But first we need to clarify what exactly we mean by the term "miracle."

Originally a "miracle," or a "marvel," was meant to refer to *any* event that was held to be especially revelatory of God. God is revealed in various ways. On a starlit night one might sense an awesome presence and power; on contemplating the physical laws some would claim to glimpse a divine sense of order; God's purpose might be discerned through the history of a nation (such as the Jewish nation), as well as through the pattern of one's own individual life. Perhaps even more importantly, God is felt to be revealed to the individual through the medium of prayer and meditation.

But having said that, certain events stand out as being especially revelatory of God. For example, a plane crashes, there is no loss of life, a newspaper headline reads "miracle escape." To say that it is a "miracle escape" does not necessarily imply that a law of physics has been violated. The newspaper reporter is merely saying it is an amazing occurrence. Some would put this down to luck; others would say it was God's providence – evidence that one was under divine protection. Such events can be regarded by the faithful as so revelatory of God that they have the power to change the whole course of their subsequent life.

Clearly, there is no difficulty in accepting miracles if this is all we have in mind – events that are out-of-the-ordinary, but do not violate any law of nature. But this is *not* what most people mean when they question the possibility of miracles. For them, a miracle is specifically a violation of a law of nature – God interrupting the smooth flow of the working of nature by a one-off, supernatural input.

From now on we shall stick to this narrower definition of a "miracle." We ask: are there such exceptions to the laws of nature? Do miracles of *this* kind happen?

Biblical miracle accounts; a variety of explanations

Many religious believers regard miracle stories as a package deal; you either accept them, or you don't. But most Biblical scholars would hold that this is too simplistic. It is certainly not the case that in order to be a religious believer you have to accept all the miracles lock, stock, and barrel. The miracle accounts are a very mixed bag.

In the first place, some of the events described can be covered by the normal laws of nature: they are not miraculous in the narrow sense in which we are defining the word "miracle." For example, Moses feeding the Israelites on manna in the desert. Manna is a syrupy secretion given out by insects called *Trabutina mannipara*. It forms in sugary drops the size of peas which harden on the leaves of tamarisk plants overnight and then fall to the ground in the morning. Bedouin Arabs use manna as part of their normal diet between the months of May and July. So, although the faithful might well offer thanks to God for his providence in supplying such needed sustenance in unlikely circumstances, there is nothing here that is against any law of nature.

Similarly with the casting out of devils. Today these might be regarded as the work of a good psychiatrist rather than a miracle-worker.

Next, we note that one or two miracle stories appear to have been generated by mistake. Compare, for example, the following two stories:

(i) The disciples are in a boat on the Sea of Galilee. They see Jesus walking on the water. Impetuous Peter gets out of the boat to go to him, but sinks into the water;

(ii) The disciples are in a boat on the Sea of Galilee. They see Jesus walking on the seashore (this being soon after his resurrection). Impetuous Peter gets out of the boat to go to him, swimming in the water.

Essentially the same story – apart from Jesus in one instance walking on the sea, and in the other walking on the seashore. It is at this point we note that, on going back to the original Greek, there is an ambiguity between the phrases meaning "walking *on* the sea" and "walking *by* the sea." This observation gives rise to the theory that originally there was but a single story – one in which Jesus was walking by the sea. In the repeated tellings of the story, someone got hold of the wrong end of the stick. Through a simple mistranslation, they unwittingly created the story of Jesus walking on the sea. This explanation appears to me to make a lot of sense. It has always been difficult to understand why Jesus would refuse the temptation in the wilderness to defy gravity by throwing himself off a building, but would then, to no particular purpose, defy gravity by walking on water.

So, we are able to dispose of a few miracle stories either as naturalistic occurrences, or as mistakes in translation. But not many succumb to such easy explanation. What of the others?

A miracle-story-telling culture

We need a background against which to judge them. This is provided by the books that did *not* get into the Bible – such as "The Infancy Gospel of Thomas," or "The Arabic Gospel of the Childhood." In such writings we find a wealth of miracle stories. For instance, Jesus as a schoolboy supposedly got bored during his lessons and made clay models of birds; these then promptly flew out of the window. Again at school, Jesus on one occasion cursed a boy who had run into him by mistake, and the boy fell down dead. We read of a young man who had been turned into a mule by witchcraft. Mary placed the infant Jesus on the back of the mule, whereupon the mule was transformed back into the young man.

Similar extraordinary stories are told of the apostles in writings such as "The Acts of Peter," "The Acts of John," and "The Gospel of Peter." On one occasion, for example, a contest took place between Peter and a magician. The magician had at one stage managed to levitate himself to a great height above the city. Peter pointed out to God that this feat was not doing the cause of Christianity much good. God cut off the magician's power; he fell to earth and broke his leg in three places. Everyone present was converted – and celebrated their conversion by stoning the magician to death!

Clearly such stories are blatant invention; we do not believe a word of them. It is no wonder they were excluded from the canon. But these stories are instructive. They show us that people in those days delighted in miracle stories and tales of wondrous happenings. For us, brought up in a pragmatic culture largely dominated by scientific thought, we find this hard to comprehend. For us, miracle stories can be something of an embarrassment. But for those living in a culture dominated by story-telling, they were a source of delight. They were a recognized and accepted way of conveying to others something of the exceptional nature and quality of the person being referred to.

If this invention was going on in the books lying outside the Bible, can we be sure that the same influences were not at work *within* the canon?

The accretion of miracle accounts in the Bible

We answer this by looking at stories that are dealt with in more than one gospel; we compare the earlier version with the later one.

Firstly, we look at the call of the fishermen to become disciples. In

Mark (the first of the gospels to be written), Jesus simply says to the fishermen, "Follow me and I will make you fishers of men." In the later gospel of Luke, we have the same words of Jesus – but only after a miraculous haul of fish has taken place.

As a second example, we take the arrest of Jesus in the garden of Gethsemane. Mark describes how one of Jesus' followers cuts off the ear of the high priest's servant. That is all that happens: the ear is cut off. By the time we get to the later writing of Luke, however, Jesus performs a miracle: he puts the ear back on and heals it. If this truly happened, it is difficult to understand why Mark, telling the same story, omits the punch-line. Luke's version seems to betray evidence of accretion.

Further indication of the proliferation over time of miracle stories comes when we make a general comparison of the gospels and Paul's writings. Paul's epistles are the earliest writings in the New Testament. Apart from the resurrection, he mentions *none* of Jesus' miracles. This raises questions. For example, in trying to convince people that Jesus was the Son of God, why did he not refer to the Virgin Birth? Surely this is the "proof" beyond all others that Jesus was uniquely divine. It makes for a strange omission – assuming of course that he had heard of the Virgin Birth. If he hadn't, why was that? Could it be that at the time he was writing, the story had not yet come into circulation?

By the time we get to Mark, the first of the gospels, we read of the stilling of the waters, the raising of Jairus's daughter, the feeding of the multitude, the walking on water, and various healing miracles. Most of these are to be found in Matthew and Luke (who used Mark as a source), but in addition there are now to be found the miraculous haul of fish, the ear of the high priest's servant being healed, the raising of the young man of Nain, and the Virgin Birth. Finally, when we come to the last of the gospels to be written, that due to John, we find for the first time the raising of Lazarus, the healing of the man born blind, and water being turned into wine.

We cannot be certain, but there does appear to be a process at work whereby miracle stories were increasingly coming into circulation with time. So, what is going on? Are these attempts to deceive us?

The nature of a miracle story

We can answer this only by coming to grips with the true nature of a miracle story.

The Jews lived in a story-telling culture. What does that mean? In ancient times, stories were much used to convey the wisdom of a nation, including timeless spiritual truths, from one generation to the next. One thinks here of the great myths of Genesis: the creation myths and the story of Adam and Eve. As we shall be seeing in more detail later in Chapters 9 and 10, what matters in these mythical stories is not the six days of creation, or the making of Eve from a rib taken from Adam's side, or the serpent, but the deep spiritual truths that lie behind the stories: the dependence of ourselves and of the world upon God; the nature of marriage as uniting a husband and wife as one flesh; our relationship to planet Earth and how we are to tend it; our potentiality as having been made in the image of God; our tendency to fall short of that potential and to succumb to our desires rather than be obedient to the will of God. It is these deep spiritual truths that matter to us, and the conveyance of such truths was the original intention of those who put these stories together in the first place.

The same idea of conveying truths through stories was continued by Jesus much later in his parables. There might well have been a man on the road from Jerusalem to Jericho who fell among thieves; there might have been a Good Samaritan. But possibly not. It does not matter. The point of the story was to get across to Jesus' questioner the message concerning whom he should regard as his neighbor, and how he ought to behave towards that neighbor.

The prevalence of story-telling in ancient cultures leads us therefore to ask the question of whether the conveyance of deep spiritual truth was the prime motivation underlying the miracle stories.

To answer this question, we turn to John's gospel. John wrote mainly for Gentile readers – those who could perhaps not be expected necessarily to be in tune with Jewish thought, and therefore required the underlying truths to be spelt out rather more explicitly than we find them in the other gospels. Let us take a look at some of the miracles recorded by John:

(i) *The feeding of the multitude.* It is an occasion where Jesus describes himself as "the Bread of Life." Although he is feeding people physically, what he is talking about is spiritual hunger.

(ii) *The raising of Lazarus.* Jesus says on this occasion, "I am the resurrection. If anyone believes in me, even though he dies, he will live, and whoever lives and believes in me will never die." Thus eternal life, we are being told, is not something we have to wait for, as Martha had thought when, earlier in the story, she had replied to a question from Jesus on the subject. Again we are presented with a spiritual truth.

(iii) *The cure of the man born blind.* Jesus, on this occasion, says, "I am the Light of the World." Here the thrust of the incident is the truth about spiritual blindness, as Jesus makes abundantly clear in his subsequent conversation with the Pharisees who were looking on.

(iv) *The miraculous haul of fish.* This is a gloss on the idea of the disciples being fishers of men.

(v) *The Virgin Birth.* Jesus' uniqueness as both God and man is what this story is about – the joining together of the divine and the human in one seamless union. What more graphic imagery could there be to illustrate this truth than a virgin being overlain by the Holy Spirit?

A miracle-story case study

To bring home just how complex a Jewish miracle story can be, let us look at a particular narration in more detail. We ask: what might be the spiritual content of the story of Jesus turning water into wine?

It is an account that appears in John's gospel alone (*John 2*). It speaks of a transformation involving wine – water changed into wine. For Christians, the transformation of something lowly into something higher – involving *wine* – has about it an unmistakable allusion to the Holy Communion service. Such services were well established at the time John was writing. So, is reference being made here to that form of service? The answer is almost certainly yes. We read (in English translations) how Jesus told the servants to bring him water – the water that was later to be turned into wine. However, if we go back to the original

Greek, the word he uses is *not*, in fact, that meaning "servant"; he uses the word for "deacon." He told a *deacon* to bring him water. The deacon is the person in the Holy Communion service who brings the water and wine to the celebrant in order for them to be transformed into the blood of Christ. So there definitely is an allusion here to the Holy Communion service.

What is the function of the water that is brought to Jesus? We are told in the story that it is water used for purification – ostensibly for washing the guests' hands and feet before the feast. But in the Jewish mind the only way one can truly be purified is through the Law of Moses. So, symbolically the Law of Moses is being brought to Jesus. What is Jesus' relation to that Law? He himself was to declare that he had come to fulfill it. It was not a case of him setting aside the Law, but of him fulfilling it, or transforming it. And that is what he does to the water; he transforms it – elevates it.

We next read that the guests are already well drunk. So how much wine does Jesus produce? Between 120 and 180 *gallons*. That is the equivalent of 60 to 90 watering-cans full – and for people already well and truly over the legal limit! And, naturally, it is the very best wine – the steward affirms this. This is meant to symbolize God's *overwhelming* beneficence – the sheer extravagance of his response to our requests.

Let's go back to the beginning of the story. It gets off to a strange start. When Mary comes to Jesus pointing out that the wine is running out, Jesus replies, "Why turn to me? My hour has not yet come." On the face of it this sounds as though he is saying, "Sorry, but I don't want anything to do with this, my time for doing that sort of thing isn't here yet." But then he goes straight ahead and does it. How are we to understand that?

The occasion is a wedding. Jesus sometimes referred to *himself* as the bridegroom. He was once asked, "Why don't your followers fast in the same way as those of John the Baptist?" He replied by saying that when the bridegroom is with them that is the time for feasting. But when the hour is come for the bridegroom to be taken away, then is the time to fast. So it appears that when Jesus says to Mary in our story, "My hour has not yet come," he is speaking as that bridegroom. In effect he is saying, "My hour to be taken away has not yet come, and therefore it is indeed a time for feasting and celebration." In other words, he is saying "yes" to Mary.

We close this study of the story by noting its very first words: "On the third day. . . ." Supposedly this refers back to a conversation with Nathanael. But nobody living in the post-resurrection period could possibly fail to get the allusion of the "third day." The reference is obviously to the resurrection, and to the joy and celebration that attends the resurrection.

Thus, what at first sight might appear to be a rather trivial, fanciful story, is revealed under closer examination to be nothing of the sort. It is in truth a remarkably complex account, encapsulating within it an abundance of spiritual meanings.

In summary, there can be no doubt about the spiritual content of Biblical miracle stories. In this they contrast starkly with the silly, empty stories in the New Testament Apocryphal books about clay birds, the cursing of schoolmates, and the transforming of mules into young men. But this still leaves open the question of whether these spiritually deep stories also refer to physical events that actually happened. Are at least some of these stories also meant to be read as accounts of events that literally occurred as described? Or can we, without delay, summarily dismiss such a possibility?

Can miracles be ruled out as impossible?

Remember we are defining a miracle in the restricted sense of an event that violates a law of nature. But what do we mean by "a law of nature"?

The world presents us with a seemingly breathtaking array of phenomena. Controlled experimentation and close observation, however, reveal that behind this rather bewildering facade, a few general rules of behavior are at work. The situation is not as chaotic as it might at first seem. Given enough information, and a knowledge of the rules of behavior, the future course of events can be anticipated.

This in itself need not mean that everything, under all circumstances and at all times, *must* obey these rules. Certainly it is an empirical observation that those events we happen to have studied do appear to obey them. But it has to be an article of *belief* that the laws apply under *all* circumstances. It is not something a scientist can prove as such.

Of course, this is a belief we all tacitly subscribe to most of the time – even those who entertain the possibility of the occasional miraculous exception to the general rule. But there are those who take it on trust that the laws of nature are without exception inviolable. If they are right, then there is no possibility of miracles.

Others have a different starting-point. They begin from the premise that the rules have to come from somewhere – they can't just happen. There has to be a reason why the world is run on these particular lines, rather than some other. A choice has to be made, and the one who makes the choice is the Creator God. They are *God's* rules; they owe their existence to a divine origin. That being so, there seems little problem in accepting that the originator of the laws could suspend their operation, given sufficient motive for doing so. It is not a question of whether God *can* perform miracles; more, it is a question of whether, as a matter of historical fact, God *chooses* to perform them.

A possible hierarchy of laws

Suppose we tentatively accept that miracles might, from time to time, happen. Does that mean we have to regard such occurrences as "violations" of physical laws?

Jesus, in his temptations in the wilderness, declined to use miraculous power for turning stones into bread, or, as already noted, for defying gravity by throwing himself off tall buildings. In working out what form of ministry he should undertake, he seemed to be choosing one that showed respect for the laws of nature. Some would claim that this in itself was a reason for dismissing subsequent accounts of his supposedly performing miracles.

But we have to bear in mind that Jesus was bound by a higher obligation. He was to be the embodiment of God's perfect love for humankind. At various points in his ministry he was to be faced with people who were ill or in distress. In similar circumstances we know what we would do; out of our love for those people we would do whatever we could to alleviate their suffering. Jesus, as the perfect embodiment of love, could do no less. What was he capable of doing for them?

As the Son of God, he could cure them – miraculously if necessary. It can thus be argued that it would have been less than perfect love wilfully to have withheld such healing power.

Might he have had to decline to perform the miracle because the exercise of such power would have forced the recipient into belief in him – a form of coercion incompatible with freely offered love? Not necessarily. Most of the people involved in these incidents had already declared their faith in him verbally, or had demonstrated it implicitly by coming to him in the expectation of a healing.

Thus, it could be argued, in obedience to the all-embracing law of love, he was *bound* to perform miraculous cures. Such cures would not have been in accordance with the physical laws, but they would have been in accordance with the *higher* law of love.

Something similar to this already happens within physics itself. When it comes to looking at our laws of physics, we find them arranged in a hierarchy. In Chapter 13, I shall be introducing you to Einstein's theory of relativity. There we shall discover that at high speed, time slows down and space contracts. A mission controller at Houston would conclude that an astronaut in a spacecraft traveling at nine-tenths the speed of light would be ageing at half the normal rate; his spacecraft would be reduced in length to half its normal size. The mission controller and the astronaut each have their own space and their own time.

Such seemingly bizarre conclusions are totally beyond the power of classical Newtonian physical law to describe. According to Newton, we all inhabit a common space and a common time, so we ought always to arrive at the same measurements for times and distances. Does that mean whenever a spacecraft travels fast, it "violates" Newton's laws of motion? That, in fact, is *not* how we would customarily describe the situation. Rather we would say that Newton's laws have limited validity, and in particular do not apply to circumstances involving excessive speeds.

It is at this point we have to recognize that the laws of physics are arranged in a hierarchy. The laws characteristic of relativity theory are hierarchically superior to those of Newton. It is not that Newton's laws apply at low speed, and Einstein's at high speed. Einstein's law applies at *all* speeds, including everyday speeds of, say, thirty miles per hour. *All* observers in uniform relative motion occupy different spaces and times. It is just that at speeds low compared to that of light, the differences between the various times and spaces are so small as to make them indistinguishable. Under those conditions, it is far simpler to treat the situation as if there were only the one space and time, and hence use Newton's laws. For most purposes they are a more than adequate approximation. But in our present context, it is important to recognize that they are nevertheless but an approximation to the more comprehensive and superior laws of relativity – laws that cover not only the realm where Newton's laws are useful, but also those situations that the classical laws are powerless to handle.

In the same spirit, one might postulate that, although relativity rules the roost as far as the hierarchy of physical laws is concerned, it might not be the last word. It could be argued that even that set of laws is subservient to a further law: the truly all-embracing law of *love*. According to the religious point of view, love is the very reason for the existence of ourselves and the Universe. As we shall be seeing in Chapter 7, one of the prerequisites for being able to lead a meaningful, purposeful life based on love, is that one lives in an environment that, by and large, operates in a predictable manner – hence the need for physical laws. But the absolutely *strict* observation of those physical laws, at *all* times and in *all* circumstances, is not necessary. In particular they might not necessarily cover untested situations like those involving the actions of the Son of God in human form.

In this way, one could argue that miracles are not maverick occasions where God capriciously and arbitrarily intervenes in the working of the world. Instead, when due regard is paid to the all-embracing law of love, and the exceptional circumstances that sometimes obtain, they can be regarded as part of a law-like, orderly approach to everything that occurs within the world. The physical laws are not "violated"; it is simply that their domain of applicability does not embrace all situations.

When is a law a law?

A further thought: you might – quite understandably – feel uncomfortable over the idea of mixing up laws of a physical nature with a so-called "law" of another kind. I would therefore like to conclude this discussion by pointing out that it is not always clear what one means by a "physical law."

Suppose, for example, you have dropped something, a book or a cup, on the floor and there it lies at your feet. On an impulse you declare, "I command you to rise." Lo and behold, the object jumps off the ground and lands in your hand! Would that be a miracle – a violation of a physical law?

It would certainly fly in the face of the evidence of countless observations that when objects have fallen to the floor they stay put until they are picked up. But in fact, it would not be impossible. We can understand why when we consider that the floor upon which the object lies is made up of atoms. Atoms jiggle about and vibrate by virtue of the heat energy they possess. Normally these motions are in random directions. But imagine for a moment, by some weird coincidence, they all happened to vibrate in unison. This is highly unlikely, given that it would require billions upon billions of atoms all to do this purely by chance. But just suppose it did. And suppose this briefly coordinated motion happened to be in the upwards direction. The cup would be flung into the air. No law of physics would have been violated – only a so-called law known as the *Second Law of Thermodynamics*. This states that such events are so improbable, we can for all intents and purposes say that they never happen. But note, it is only a statistical statement involving probabilities. And because it is statistical, given enough opportunities, you would expect the unusual occasionally to happen – in the normal course of events. So I ask: is the Second Law of Thermodynamics a physical law? If one can envisage situations where, in the *natural* course of events, it could be disobeyed, then it is clearly not a physical law with the same status as the others. (Unless, of course, we are mistaken in according *any* physical law more than a statistical significance.)

Incidentally, the idea that statistical fluctuations could lead to violations of the Second Law of Thermodynamics is one of the explanations that have been advanced to try and explain certain of the miracles. God, at the time he created the world, set up the initial conditions such that at some later point in time, the atoms in the Sea of Galilee, for example, were due to vibrate preferentially upward for a while, so allowing

Jesus to walk on the surface. I personally prefer the explanation I gave earlier for that so-called miracle.

Conclusion

In summary, it can be held that miracles are not intrinsically impossible. Which is not to say they necessarily happen – merely that belief in miracles is not irrational. Such a view does not, of course, entail accepting all the Biblical miracle stories as having a literal content – for the reasons I have given. For us today, the prime importance of the Biblical miracle accounts lies in the deep spiritual truths they illustrate – truths that are applicable and relevant to our own lives. Perhaps we can remain agnostic over whether these accounts did, in addition, refer to actual physical events.

Personally, I am inclined to accept certain acts of healing, and others that are clearly motivated in accordance with what I have been calling the higher law of love. But at this distance in time, we are never going to be able to prove one way or the other what happened. If the "prayer experiment" described earlier, conducted in our own time, and under controlled conditions, is unlikely to come up with an unambiguous interpretation of its outcome, we can hardly expect a firmer conclusion regarding events that occurred long ago and in a culture markedly different from our own. In the end it has to be a personal conviction. For some people, reports of miracles in the Bible will be taken as indicative of the work of God, and thus as evidence for his existence; others will not see it that way.

3
Life Beyond Death

A non-literal understanding of the resurrection

The greatest miracle story of all is that concerning the resurrection of Jesus. It lies at the very core of Christianity. The gospel – or good news – is precisely this: Jesus has risen from the dead. Paul says that if Christ is not risen then our faith is futile. It is to the Biblical accounts of the resurrection we must now turn.

As with the other miracle accounts, it is possible to take this purely as a story illustrating a deep spiritual truth: the idea that death is not the end of everything; there is life beyond. The story of the empty tomb and of the subsequent appearances of Jesus are to be taken as allegories – something concrete for the mind to get hold of as it tries to come to terms with an eternal life that is really beyond human imagining.

With the resurrection occupying such a central place in Christian belief, such an interpretation of the resurrection accounts is bound to stir up controversy. This was famously demonstrated over the sermon by the former Bishop Jenkins of Durham when he spoke on an Easter Sunday of a "conjuring trick with bones." Some would hold that it is impossible to regard oneself as a proper Christian unless – unlike Bishop Jenkins – one does accept that the tomb was physically empty.

I certainly would not say that. The importance of Easter is that it testifies to Jesus having conquered death, that he is in some sense alive now, and present everywhere. He is aware of what we are saying and thinking. His presence is as real as the presence of you and me. Christianity is all about having a loving relationship with that living Lord Jesus. As far as I am concerned, anyone who believes that, believes in the resurrection – at least the resurrection as it affects us who live here and now. This being so, such people can rightly claim to be fully Christian.

As with the other miracle accounts, it is of secondary importance whether the tomb was literally empty – whether Jesus rose physically.

And yet it is a fascinating question. As we shall be seeing, the Biblical accounts of the resurrection provide us with probably the most persuasive documentary evidence for a supernatural occurrence. For that reason, I propose to examine the evidence in some detail.

The structure of Jewish miracle stories

The first question to address is whether the accounts of the resurrection are to be read in the same way as one might approach a more mundane miracle (if *any* miracle can be regarded as "mundane"!).

Jewish miracle stories traditionally conformed to a pattern. They were divided into three parts:

(i) *An introduction.* The purpose of this was to set the scene, ensuring that what was to follow was indeed regarded as a remarkable event. Thus, for example, the man who was to be cured of blindness is described in the introduction to that story as having been *born* blind, i.e., this was no temporary attack of blindness which might have worn off in the normal course of events.

(ii) *The main part of the story.* This is the account of the miracle itself. Often it involves a description of actions taken and words spoken. Thus, for instance, Jesus spits on the ground and makes a mud pat which is then applied to the blind man's eyes. He tells the man to go and wash at the Pool of Siloam.

(iii) *An epilogue.* This usually describes the onlookers as being astonished, and there are often actions on the part of the person cured demonstrating that something wonderful has indeed happened.

Such then is the overall pattern of the typical Jewish miracle story. As one might expect, the most prominent and important section is the middle one – the description of the miracle itself.

With this in mind we turn to the account of the resurrection of Jesus. What do we find?

The first part of the story is there: we have a description of all the events leading up to Jesus' arrest, trial, scourging, crucifixion, and burial. And it is exceedingly detailed: what Jesus was wearing at various stages, who said what, his being offered a drink while on the cross, etc.

The third part of the story is there: the accounts of the many resurrection appearances, which in themselves purport to demonstrate that Jesus had risen from the dead.

But what of the all-important middle section – the very heart of the narrative – the description of the actual miracle itself? It is entirely missing. This alone alerts us to the fact that this is no ordinary Jewish miracle story. No Jew would have dreamt of concocting a miracle story without describing the event itself. If the whole point of the story was to give hearers a concrete image of Christ's victory over death – a picture to carry in the mind – why is there no picture?

We get a hint as to how "scandalous" this omission must have seemed to the early church, through the way attempts were made to fill in the missing details. Mark's account of the discovery of the empty tomb mentions the presence of a man dressed in a white robe. In Matthew he is called an angel (perhaps not too surprisingly as, in those days, angels were not thought of as having wings). Then, in Luke and John, this angel is joined by a second. Matthew goes in for further embellishment; whereas the other gospels describe the stone as already having been moved, Matthew describes the angel in the act of coming down from heaven, and to the accompaniment of an earthquake, rolling aside the stone – with the women onlookers there. The writer seems to be giving way to a temptation to fill in the gap in the narrative – the missing details which his readers would undoubtedly be expecting.

But this is small beer compared with what we find in the New Testament Apocrypha – those books that didn't quite make it into the canon of accepted writings. In the Gospel of Peter, for instance, the writer really goes to town. He describes how two men encircled by a great light descend and roll the stone aside. In full view of the assembled throng, three men are seen coming out of the tomb, one being supported by the other two, with a cross following them, "and the heads of the two reached as far as heaven, but that of him that was led overtopped the heavens. And they heard a voice from heaven saying, 'Hast thou preached to them that sleep?' And the response was heard from the cross, 'Yea.'"

In *The Book of the Resurrection of Christ* by Bartholomew it is claimed that Philogenes witnessed the whole act of resurrection (Philogenes being the father of the Simeon who was cured by Jesus when he came down from the Mount of Olives). He had been to the tomb at midnight to find the heavens opened and filled with Cherubim, Seraphim, Powers and Virgins. The sight was so tremendous, if he had not been supported by the apostle Peter (who was also supposed to be there) he would have died. In this version of the resurrection, Jesus appears in a chariot!

It's obvious what's going on here. The writers are desperately trying to fill in the missing center portion of the narration – so as to force it to conform to a traditional Jewish miracle story. But from our point of view, what matters is that in the earlier versions – the more authentic ones that we find in the Bible – the center section was absent. This alone tells us we are dealing with something radically different.

Characteristics of eyewitness reports

The Biblical narratives are supposed to be based on a set of eyewitness accounts of events that actually happened. So let us now change tack, and examine whether they do indeed have that quality about them. A good deal of work has been put into examining the authenticity of accounts describing events that are alleged to have taken place. These form the basis of psychological tests, and the procedures for sifting through testimonies given to the police regarding crimes and accidents.

The first thing to note is that eyewitness evidence is rarely presented in a neat logical sequence. Rather, one tends to get a kaleidoscope of impressions with irrelevant details mixed up with the important facts. One is left wondering whether the witness will ever get to the point!

Secondly, moments of shock or surprise are remembered particularly vividly. It is almost as though the unexpected scene has been indelibly imprinted on the witness's mind.

Thirdly, one expects there to be aspects of what people have witnessed that they are unable to explain – perhaps even aspects of the way they themselves reacted at the time. Typically one has them saying, "I don't know what came over me. I don't know why I didn't think to call the police straight away. It seems sensible now, but at the time – I don't know, I just didn't."

Lastly, if more than one witness is involved, then it is highly unlikely that their various accounts will agree in all details. In broad outline, yes, you would expect a general consensus – but not over details. It is when the schoolchildren march into the principal's office and trot out exactly the same story, word for word, that one knows their testimony needs to be taken with a pinch of salt.

The resurrection accounts as eyewitness statements

So, with those criteria for assessing the authenticity of eyewitness accounts in mind, let us examine the accounts of the resurrection as we find them in the gospels.

We begin with the two disciples going to the tomb. They start out together, but one outruns the other and gets there first. But he doesn't go straight in; he waits for the other to arrive. And it is the second disciple who enters first. This in itself is quite unimportant; it has no bearing on anything. Why bother to mention it? Presumably because that's just the way it was; witnesses do throw in extra information for no good reason.

They enter the tomb, and to their surprise it is empty. But that's not how it is described. They don't just say, "The body's gone." Instead we get a description of the way the cloth that had been round Jesus' body was still lying there, and the smaller cloth that had been round his face was also there but lying separate from the first one. Why mention this detail? Because it is a moment of shock. The scene is etched into the mind. They are describing a picture they can still see.

How about the followers of Jesus who were walking along the road to Emmaus? They are joined by the risen Jesus. They don't recognize him. They walk together and talk together; they still don't recognize him. They go in the house together and eat together. They still don't recognize him. Not until he breaks the bread. Then their eyes are opened. Why? Something particularly characteristic in the way Jesus did it – some mannerism? Perhaps they had been told by the disciples how Jesus, on breaking the bread at the last supper, had spoken of the bread being his body and the wine his blood. Now, in this house on the road to Emmaus, they see exactly the same action, the breaking of the bread – a very special moment, recalling for them those strange words. But it still must have left those disciples feeling foolish when later they related the story of their encounter with the risen Jesus, and had to admit that, for some unaccountable reason, they hadn't recognized him. It was an aspect of behavior that the genuine witness is unable to explain. It doesn't make for a neat, tidy, rehearsed exposition. It's just the way it happened to be.

We get exactly the same kind of thing with Mary Magdalene's encounter with Jesus. At first she mistakes him for the gardener, and she enquires whether he knows where Jesus' body has been put. Then comes the flash of recognition – when he speaks her name. What was so special about him uttering her name? Mary had been a prostitute. Men had used her; she had been a sex object. Then Jesus had come into her life, and had treated her, not as a thing, but as a person; he took a personal interest in her. He had called her by name. We can imagine what her feelings must have been on hearing for the first time this remarkable man address her by name. She would never have forgotten that – how he said it, the tone, the inflection of the voice. It all came back to her when Jesus once again spoke her name in that garden.

Next, we address the inconsistencies in the different gospel accounts. Matthew and Mark would have us believe that all Jesus' post-resurrection appearances were confined to Galilee; Luke has them occurring in and around Jerusalem; John has them happening in both locations. It is a small thing; it could easily have been sorted out. And if it were a made-up story, a conspiracy, doubtless the gospel writers would have taken the trouble to get the details straight – so everyone was telling the same story. But they didn't; one suspects because they were simply relaying fallible, somewhat careless eyewitness accounts, rather than some carefully crafted invention.

Perhaps of more concern is the description of Christ's body after his resurrection. An obvious question on everyone's lips on hearing about Jesus' appearances would have been, "What kind of body did he have? Could you touch it?" This would have been important in establishing whether it was merely a vision, or something more substantial.

We note in this connection that doubting Thomas was encouraged to put his finger into the imprint of the nail marks in Jesus' hands, and to thrust his hand into the wound in Jesus' side. Then we recall that Jesus broke bread – he could exert physical pressure – and on occasion he ate. These incidents point to a tactile body.

That being so, what are we to make of Jesus' injunction to Mary in the garden, "Touch me not; for I am not yet ascended unto my Father"? Does this constitute a serious inconsistency? Actually, no. The original Greek can be translated either as "Do not attempt to touch me," which is the sense that has usually been given to it, or alternatively as "Stop touching me," implying that Mary was already touching him – perhaps clinging to him. The latter translation would be consistent with the descriptions of other encounters with Christ's body. Our preference for the latter translation is enhanced when it comes to the phrase "for I am not yet ascended unto my Father." It would be a curious state of affairs if embracing were not allowed now, but would be later on. According to the latter interpretation, this phrase could simply mean that there will be plenty of opportunity and time for loving embraces in Heaven, but for now he has other things in mind for her; he has an urgent errand for her to run; she is quickly to go and tell the disciples what has happened. It is the second translation, "Stop clinging to me," that modern versions of the Bible prefer.

Mention of the women who were first to find the tomb empty raises a further point. They were *women*. Women lacked the status of men in society. They were regarded as not being qualified to act as legal witnesses. If the resurrection were a made-up story, and the disciples wanted people to take it seriously, they would never have had women as the principal witnesses. Another thing: how do the men fare in this story? Why weren't they at the tomb alongside the women? Because they were in hiding – behind locked doors – for fear of their fellow Jews. They were cowards. The only courageous people in this story – the only ones to emerge with any credit – were the women. Can one really imagine Jesus' disciples sitting down and concocting a story which cast themselves in such a bad light?

In short, one can conclude that the gospel narratives pass the tests expected of eyewitness accounts of actual events. They are clearly meant to be taken at face value.

Alternatives to a resurrection

That of course, still leaves us with the problem of whether or not to believe them. So, finally, what are the alternatives to a resurrection?

The tomb was empty; about that there can be little doubt. If it weren't, the chief priests could simply have produced the body and instantly put a stop to the rumors of a resurrection. Some people have conjectured that perhaps there was a muddle over which tomb had been used. But again, the motives for the priests to find the body were too great for it to be plausible for them simply to have "lost" the tomb.

So, with the tomb empty, who could have taken the body? The priests? Yes. But they had no motive. Suspicion therefore has to fall upon the disciples. But what might their motive have been? What could they have gained from such a deception? A dead leader shamefully martyred would have been a much more powerful rallying cry than a silly made-up story of a resurrection. Sure enough, there had been stories of temporary resuscitations (for example, that of Lazarus), but these people died again. Resurrection to eternal life was a totally different matter. Though some people in those days believed there would be a resurrection, that was to be at the end of time. It was certainly not expected to take place within the course of history, in one's own day. Not surprisingly, even some of Jesus' closest followers could not at first accept the report that Jesus had risen.

Such a theory of theft and deception calls for a conspiracy of massive proportions. Not only were all Jesus' closest friends involved – the twelve disciples and all the women – but a crowd of five hundred. And it was not as though Jesus' supporters were the kind of people who were habitual liars. They would all have had to have acted totally out of character. It would have to have been a conspiracy which held up even in the face of torture and death. Such tremendous pressures were brought to bear, but not one of the supposed conspirators ever confessed to a plot.

The subsequent behavior of Christ's followers

Finally, we look at the transformation wrought in the disciples. At the time of the crucifixion, they were a defeated, demoralized rabble, hiding for fear of their lives. A few days later, they were unrecognizable. They were *triumphant* – ready to lay down their lives for the cause. There is not a hint of anger or indignation against the terrible wrong done to their leader; instead there is unalloyed joy. This is *not* the natural reaction of people who are supposed to have just come out of a meeting where they have devised some cock-and-bull story, that no one is going to believe anyway, and moreover is going to land them in trouble with the very authorities from whom they had previously been hiding. Clearly, something dramatic must have happened. Could it be they were telling the truth?

Conclusion

In the end, of course, it has to be a matter of personal conviction – based either on an analysis of the weight of the evidence – or on one's own personal experience of the risen Christ. As with the other Biblical miracle accounts, it is not possible at this distance to arrive at any universally acceptable evaluation. Even if we ourselves were to witness a resurrection today, how would we convince others who had not seen it? Suppose some figure from the past, such as Winston Churchill, were suddenly to materialize in the room where you are at present sitting. The two of you talk together, you eat together. Then the manifestation disappears. How would you go about offering proof of what had happened to others? You wouldn't be able to. That being so, it is unreasonable for a skeptic to expect proof of Jesus' resurrection. All we can note is that the evidence in favor of a physical resurrection of Jesus is as strong as it could conceivably be – given the circumstances. It can be regarded as a further incremental corroboration of the God hypothesis.

For the record, I myself accept that there was a bodily resurrection. But I do have to add that if somehow it could be proved that I am mistaken, it would not to any significant degree adversely affect my faith. Regardless of what exactly happened 2,000 years ago, I still find the presence of Jesus today a very real presence – and that is what I believe to be crucial.

4

Staying Within the Law

What if one finds it quite impossible to accept that there might be exceptions to physical law? Does that mean God has no effect on anything happening in the world? If that were to be the case, it would be largely immaterial whether there is a God or not, and we could draw our "God experiment" to a premature conclusion. Even if one does believe that God can, and does, intervene on occasion in miraculous fashion, we are still left with the problem of whether that is God's *only* type of interaction. If so, it would appear to be a very occasional, intermittent type of interaction.

So it is we now turn to the question of whether the physical world can provide intimations of God's presence – through its *normal* operation.

God as the ground of existence

We begin with the question: "Why is there something rather than nothing?"

Normally we take the existence of the world for granted. It is simply *there*. Given that there is this world, it is the job of the scientist to investigate what kind it is. But a theologian would say this is jumping the gun. Before examining the details of the world, we ought to be enquiring why there is a world at all. What is *responsible* for its existence? What can be said about the ground, or source, of all being?

Some are inclined to dismiss this as a meaningless question. But to many of us, it appears perfectly sensible and reasonable. The fact that it might be difficult, or impossible, to answer conclusively need not affect the validity of the question itself.

The theological answer is that the world and ourselves owe our existence to God. In saying that, we do not have in mind a God who created the world long ago, and since then has had no further part to play. God's responsibility was not limited to a single act of creation – the world from then on being able to continue in existence on its own. Theologians customarily couple talk of God the Creator with that of God the Sustainer. It has long been held that God's creativity is required equally at all points in time.

If that is the picture one has in mind – God continually upholding the world in existence – then, in a sense, God is involved in absolutely everything that goes on in the world. It is not that God performs this miracle and that miracle, but is otherwise not involved – when nature is running smoothly. Rather, it is the case that nothing at all happens without his direct involvement.

That then is one sense in which God is thought to have an effect. It is not something that can be experimentally tested, of course. We cannot momentarily switch off God's sustaining power – if there is such a thing – and see whether, in fact, we promptly disappear! So it remains a defensible position to claim that no such influence is required; existence is just a natural state of affairs calling for no explanation. But for the faithful, it is a way in which they see God relating to the world.

Stacking the cards

Secondly, there has been the suggestion that God brings about effects through the way he originally set up things at the very beginning. The effects we see at later times come about through their causal links to those initial conditions. According to this idea, God could have fixed the motions and positions of all the fundamental particles initially so that, through the natural outworking of the laws of nature, the divine purpose was achieved.

We have already mentioned a possible example of this: Jesus walking on the Sea of Galilee. From the very start, God could have arranged things so that, by the time Jesus later stepped on to the water, the atoms in its surface were all due to vibrate synchronously in the same direction at the same time. In this manner, Jesus could have been prevented from sinking. Such an occurrence, in the normal course of events, would be exceedingly unlikely, relying as it would on pure chance. But in the present context we are not dealing with chance; we are envisioning God deliberately tampering with the initial conditions to ensure that "the unusual" actually did happen.

Nor does this procedure have to be confined to miraculous events. It could account for any normal event where God wanted to have an input. In fact, we can liken the situation to that of the card player who deals a pack that has been prepared in advance to ensure the desired outcome.

Although it is an interesting idea, it strikes me as being somewhat contrived. Devising the unique set of initial conditions necessary for bringing about a detailed multitude of desired outcomes, occurring at widely different locations, and at different times throughout history, all interlocked and needing to be coordinated – that would surely be a monumental task, even for God!

The missing links in the causal chain

The approach just described relies on the idea that from any given cause it is possible to predict what its effect will be. That effect, in its turn, then becomes the cause of the next effect – and so on down the causal chain. All the events linked by this chain are fully determined by what has gone before. It is a picture of events that appears to be fully confirmed by our everyday experience, and indeed much scientific experimentation is based on that belief.

But such a state of affairs does not always apply. When scientific studies are extended to include the behavior of matter at the sub-atomic level, it is discovered that, from any initial behavior of the particles at a given point in time, it is *not* possible to predict what will happen next – at least, not with certainty. Why should this be?

In order to predict the future, one needs to have precise information on both the position and the motion of every particle taking part. Given such information, and knowing the forces between the particles, one would then be able, in principle, to calculate the future positions and velocities of the particles. The problem is that the constituents of the sub-atomic world are exceedingly small and delicate. It is impossible to have any interaction with them without disturbing them. One cannot even *look* at them without destroying features of what one is trying to see. This arises because in order to see something one obviously must illuminate it. But light itself carries energy. As the light strikes the tiny sub-atomic particle, some of that energy is transferred to the particle, thus altering the very motion one is trying to observe.

This is the realm of quantum theory. Later on we shall be saying a good deal more about it. But for the time being we simply note that, according to quantum theory, one is denied simultaneous knowledge of both the precise position and precise velocity of any particle. To have precise knowledge of position, say, one must be prepared to sacrifice all knowledge of its velocity; alternatively, precise knowledge of velocity can be bought only at the price of loss of all knowledge of position. In between, there are the intermediate cases where *some* knowledge can be obtained of both the position and the velocity, but not precise knowledge of either. This is all summed up in Heisenberg's famous uncertainty relation.

(If you are interested, the relation is: $\Delta x.\Delta p = h$, where Δx denotes the range of uncertainty in position, Δp the range of uncertainty in momentum [momentum being the mass times velocity], and h is a constant called the Planck constant.)

For example, we might know that the position of an electron lies between, say, 23 centimeters and 29 centimeters. The uncertainty of position is therefore 6 centimeters. Corresponding to this, the relation specifies a range of possible values for the velocity (or momentum) of the electron. In order to improve on the determination of the electron's position, one would have to use a different form of illumination. This might, for instance, allow one to reduce the uncertainty from 6 centimeters to 2 centimeters. However, because that new illumination would have to be of a more energetic type, it is liable, on bouncing off the electron, to give it a more severe knock; this will increase the uncertainty in momentum. Heisenberg's Uncertainty Relation tells us that a reduction in position uncertainty to a third of what it would otherwise have been, must necessarily be compensated by an increase in momentum uncertainty by a factor of three. Alternatively, any improvement in the precision of the momentum determination must be accompanied by a corresponding increase in the uncertainty of position.

Thus, according to the uncertainty relation, we are denied all the information that would be necessary to predict the future precisely. The best we can do is state the probabilities of a variety of possible outcomes.

Now, you might be wondering what all this might have to do with God's action in the world. Earlier we raised the possibility of God setting up initial conditions such that the tight chain of cause and effect would eventually produce the desired outcomes. This second approach is quite different. It makes use of the fact that there is no such thing as a tight chain of cause and effect – at least, not at the sub-atomic level. One *cannot* be absolutely sure what is going to happen next. That being so, it is argued, God could take advantage of these quantum gaps in our knowledge – the missing links in the causal chain. God could use the quantum uncertainty to push things in the required direction – while still staying within the probability limits allowed by the uncertainty relation. By making use of what would appear to us to be merely statistical fluctuations, God's input would remain undetectable.

An apparent problem with this approach is that we are talking of very small uncertainties – those significant only on the scale of individual sub-atomic particles. What possible effect could that have on the macroscopic scale of normal everyday life? John Polkinghorne, ordained minister and former Professor of Physics at Cambridge University, invokes chaos theory. Chaos theory alerts us to the fact that there are many circumstances where the slightest alteration to the initial conditions can lead to marked changes in the final outcome. How a situation develops on the large scale can depend sensitively on the smallest details of how it was originally set up. An often quoted example of chaos theory in action concerns the weather. If a butterfly in Britain decides to flap its wings, this could conceivably set in motion a whole train of events eventually culminating in a hurricane in Florida. This arises because weather patterns are exceedingly unstable.

So it is we form this picture of God using random quantum probabilities at the atomic level, these slight effects being subsequently magnified by the chaos theory mechanism to produce significant changes at the macroscopic level where we humans operate.

Nor do we have to regard chaos theory as the only way of magnifying the effects of the underlying quantum events. Think, for example, of biological genes. The physical characteristics of our bodies, and those of other animals, are largely dependent upon the genes inherited from parents at conception. The genes are based on a molecule (a particular combination of atoms) called the DNA molecule. DNA is, if you like, the blueprint design for our bodies. Changes, or mutations, to the DNA – perhaps affecting but a single atomic constituent – can have profound effects on the overall structure of the resulting body. As we shall be seeing later, it is these random changes to the physical characteristics of animal bodies that provide the variations upon which the process of evolution by natural selection gets to work. Thus, the development of the different species we see today can be attributed in the first instance to what was happening at the atomic level. So, again, minimal inputs at the quantum level can give rise to significant effects at the macro-level.

The idea that God might make use of quantum uncertainty as a means of having an effect on the world is an intriguing one. But it has to be admitted, such a proposal raises a niggling concern. Such a mechanism, so subversive and undercover, might strike one as being unseemly and inappropriate. Are we really supposed to believe that the great Creator God has been reduced to this somewhat sneaky, half-apologetic mode of operation?

Ourselves as agents in the world

If one likes neither the idea of a fixed causal chain based on specially set-up initial conditions, nor the use of the flexibility allowed by a probabilistic quantum chain of events, what else is left to God?

At this point we turn to the question of how we ourselves, as human agents, have an influence on the world. If we could sort that out, perhaps it would give us a clue as to how God operates.

We influence things through the actions of our physical bodies. These in turn are governed by impulses coming from the brain. There is some relation between what goes on in the brain and the mental experiences one has as a *conscious* human being. We know that following the mental experience known as "making a decision" (for example, to raise one's arm), this is followed by the appropriate physical action (the raising of the physical arm). What the connection, or the relationship, is between what goes on mentally in the mind and what goes on physically in the brain, nobody knows. Perhaps we shall never know. The so-called mind/brain problem has proved so elusive, many have come to regard it as a mystery of ultimate significance.

One of the features we encounter in mental experience is that we appear to possess free will; we arrive at freely chosen decisions. We do not regard ourselves as automatons blindly having to follow the dictates of our fate. But how does this arise? After all, if we are asked how the brain works, I suppose most of us would be inclined to describe it as operating like any other physical assembly of atoms – in accordance with the laws of nature. But if that is so, doesn't that mean that the future flows of chemicals and of electrical currents in the brain are predetermined? From that, one would expect that whatever conscious thoughts might be associated with those particular physical flow patterns would also be predetermined. On that picture, there is no need of any conscious decisions – what will be, will be.

But that is not how we live out our mental lives. Even if we were intellectually convinced that our brains operate in a deterministic fashion, and hence our thinking is determined, none of us conducts our lives on that basis; we do not *behave* as though there is no need to make decisions. Even were we to try to follow such a policy, the mere fact of deciding in future not to make conscious decisions would in itself be a conscious decision.

Here we come across an extraordinary dichotomy. In many ways the life of the mind closely mirrors the life of the physical body. Thus we get the physical raising of the arm being accompanied by the mental sensation of feeling it go up; the physical act of taking aspirin with the alleviation of a mental headache; the racing of the heart with the experience of fear; the burning of the skin with the feeling of pain, etc. But the apparent "openness" of mentally taken free-will decisions does not seem to be reflected in a corresponding openness in what we presume is happening at the physical level in our brains.

This raises the issue of whether quantum theory has anything to contribute here. We have already noted an openness, a quantum indeterminism, at the atomic level. The future progress of brain events is *not* expected to be determined on the micro-scale. Could this be the answer?

The trouble with invoking quantum uncertainty is that one is not replacing determined outcomes by chosen ones. Quantum processes are based on random chance, not conscious decisions. When in ordinary life an issue is settled by the toss of a coin, we are not making a decision; we have in fact abandoned the conscious decision-making process and left the matter to chance instead. So, I for one do not see how invoking quantum uncertainty can offer a satisfactory account of decision-making as we know it.

Free will as an illusion

Of course, what this might be telling us is that we are not as free as we like to think we are. Our thoughts *are* determined in the same way as the physical processes in the brain are. We are under the illusion of being free and unconstrained in our decisions simply because the part of the brain associated with thinking is not fully aware of what else is going on in the brain; the so-called "openness" is just another name for ignorance.

One might at first object to this idea on the grounds that if our thinking, like the corresponding physical processes, were required to run along predetermined lines, we would be aware of having to operate under such a constraint; there would be a tension between what we *wanted* to think and do and what we *had* to think and do. But this does not necessarily follow. Just as the physical outcome arises in a perfectly natural way from what physically went before, so the corresponding mental outcome (the "decision") will arise in a perfectly natural way out of what mentally went before (the mind-set). The mind-set and the resulting decision will be wholly compatible with each other. The outcome is identical to the "choice" such a mind would have made had it had "free will" in the normally accepted sense. There is therefore no reason why there should be any perceived sense of having to act under constraint.

Alternatively, if it is the quantum realm that is relevant to decision-making, then our so-called decisions are in truth derived from pure chance. Once an outcome is realized, the mind immediately "owns" it – in other words, feels responsible for it in some way. But this sense of "ownership" is a delusion; the outcome has not arisen from any deliberate decision made freely and consciously.

Thus, we have the possibility that free will is an illusion – either because the outcome of the supposed decision was determined all along, or because it was a result of mere chance – without our knowing it.

Mind over matter

One way to defend the notion of a genuine free will is to adopt an interventionist approach – the mind, as an entity in its own right, intervenes in the working of the brain.

Unlike less complicated physical structures, the brain is accompanied by consciousness. As we said earlier, we do not know why this should be. For the time being at least, we must simply accept it as a brute fact. This leads to the suggestion that when the mind reaches a decision on a certain course of action, there is an interruption to the normal flow of activities in the brain. A mental decision to raise the arm is accompanied by a physical change in the brain state that is different from what it would have been had the mind reached some other decision, or taken no decision at all. That altered brain state then leads to a chain of events throughout the body resulting in the arm being raised.

What this means is that if, at the time the decision was made, a scientific study had been in progress on the behavior of the subject's brain, the investigators would have observed a change in the processes that was completely unpredictable on the basis of a knowledge of what had been going on immediately prior to the decision's being made. The processes occurring in the brain would be observed not to follow the same rigid pattern as that which governs the behavior of inanimate matter. In effect, they would have witnessed a "miracle" – an interruption to the normal running of the laws of nature. This is the so-called "dualistic" approach to the mind/body problem. The mind is thought to be capable of acting on the brain in a manner not too dissimilar to that of some external physical agency.

It has to be said that this is a solution that is currently out of favor (not that there are any scientific investigations of brain processes to disprove it). It is a widely held assumption that nothing goes on in the brain that is markedly different from what happens in inanimate matter. Although the processes occurring in the brain are undoubtedly more intricate because of the extreme complexity of the physical structure, they are nevertheless all to be held accountable for – in principle – through the operation of the well-established laws of nature. As I say, whether this is so or not, we simply do not know. In the absence of any decisive studies, the interventionist solution to the free-will problem remains an option.

The holistic approach

One final assault on the problem I wish to mention is that based on quantum "wholeness." From the outset, it has to be admitted that this is something not at all well understood. But briefly the situation is this:

Imagine two electrons approaching each other, colliding and then separating. They end up so distant from each other that there is effectively no longer any physical interaction between them. It is natural to suppose that with no physical force operating between them, we are now dealing with two separate and distinct physical systems – each consisting of an isolated electron.

And yet it is not so. This can be demonstrated in the following way: All electrons spin like miniature earths rotating about their north/south axes. Once the electrons are well separated from each other after the collision, we arrange for an experimenter to carry out a measurement of the "north/south" direction in which one of the electrons spins. The extraordinary thing is that, whatever the result of this measurement, it immediately affects what a second experimenter will discover on carrying out a similar measurement on the orientation of the spin axis of the second electron.

But how is this influence conveyed across space from one location to the other? It cannot be by any known physical force, electrical or gravitational; the two electrons are physically isolated from each other. Not only that, since the advent of Einstein's theory of relativity, we have come to accept that nothing can travel faster than the speed of light – be it matter or energy. And yet, the "information" about the direction of the spin axis appears to be conveyed instantaneously from one electron to the other; it is not subject to the same restriction. As "Dame Edna Everage" might put it – this action at a distance is all rather spooky!

The resolution of the problem (if indeed it can be regarded in any sense as a resolution) is that, contrary to appearances, we are not dealing with two separate isolated physical systems, each consisting of a single electron. Instead we are dealing with a *single physical system* consisting of two electrons. When the measurement of spin is made on the first electron, it is in reality a measurement made on the entire two-electron system. The whole system is simultaneously affected. In this way, the second experimenter, although situated at a distant location, operates on the *same* physical system as the first experimenter. The results of this second measurement will therefore be dependent on what the first experimenter has already done to that system.

I have to say the situation reminds me somewhat of a form of witch-craft practiced long ago. It was customary for those fearful of witchcraft to take very good care to keep their possessions to themselves. This was in the belief that a lock of hair, or nail clippings, or worn clothing, or a used menstrual pad, were they to fall into the wrong hands, could be used to inflict what was called "contagious magic." Thus it was held that things that had once been physically connected to a person, in some sense *remained* connected to that person. Contagious magic was then founded on the idea that what was done to the part was done to the whole.

Of course, today we would regard such beliefs as the fanciful super-stition of the ignorant. But somewhat to our embarrassment, we find exactly the same kind of thinking has now been incorporated into respectable modern quantum theory! The two electrons we have been considering are subject to "quantum wholeness." Although there is no longer any recognized physical force operating between them, they are nevertheless components of an integrated system. All this because, for one instant in the past, they fleetingly encountered each other. That brief, casual meeting, long ago, continues to hold them fast with invis-ible bonds, their destinies mutually entwined.

With this being true of the simplest combined system one can imagine – two electrons that are so far separate from each other that no physical force operates between them – how much more must this apply to a system consisting of the human brain, the most complex object in the known world. Can anyone seriously imagine that we can account for the workings of the brain without taking into account the "spooky" effects that *must* be going on up there?

I hasten to say that quantum wholeness does not in any discernible way provide an explanation of how we come to have free will. There could conceivably be a connection, but what that might be is beyond us at present. No, the reason for raising the subject is to sound a warning – a warning against trying to apply simplistic methods of reasoning to an understanding of the brain. And if an understanding of the brain in purely physical and chemical terms is likely to remain beyond our grasp for a very long time, what hope have we of widening that study to include the phenomenon of consciousness?

Conclusion

Our discussion of how we, as conscious agents, have an effect on the world – either through the exercise of free will, or in its absence – has ended inconclusively. Given the state of current knowledge on the subject, this is inevitable; we are bound to feel dissatisfied with the outcome. For the time being, there simply is no intellectually or philosophically competent explanation.

So, where does that leave us? I believe there is nothing for it but to adopt a more pragmatic approach. This holds that, even though we have no coherent understanding of what goes on in our physical brains, and how this relates to what goes on in our minds, we nevertheless have to get on with our lives. In that context, at least, we can safely assert that it makes no sense to assume anything other than that we do possess free will. Day-to-day living can only be conducted on the basis of having to make a stream of decisions, each of which affects the world we live in, and for which we are to be held responsible. Furthermore, if we do not see ourselves as supernatural miracle-workers – our decision-making minds intervening miraculously in the working of our brains – then presumably we believe that somehow or other we are able to bring our influence to bear on the physical domain in a manner compatible with the smooth running of the laws of nature.

That being so as regards ourselves in relation to the world, then it does not strike me as sensible to rule out the possibility that God could have a somewhat analogous relationship to the world. If we humans do not make use of supernatural interruptions to the running of nature whenever we wish to exert our influence, then I don't see why God should have to rely on such means. This is not to say that miracles *never* happen. But miracle-working would not have to be God's exclusive, or indeed main, ongoing interaction with us and the world.

5

A Meeting of Minds

Looking inward

The physical world is not the only place where one might search for evidence of God. Indeed, many would say that the main focus of the God experiment ought to be on the mental, rather than the physical. After all, one asks, "Is there a God?" not merely to satisfy some disinterested academic curiosity, but as a prelude to entering into a personal relationship with that God – a relationship founded on love. The most convincing evidence for God, therefore, is likely to be found in the exercise of that relationship. Religion is nothing except outward show and ritual if it is not accompanied by a deeply felt inner religious experience. This being psychological in character, it directs us to examine the life of the mind, and in particular, the nature of prayer.

Earlier we discussed an experiment investigating the effectiveness of prayers for the sick. But, as we noted then, there is much more to prayer than intercessions. Prayer in its totality is multifaceted, consisting as it does of worship, thanksgiving, contrition, self-dedication, contemplation, meditation, etc. Intercession is but one component. These different forms of prayer are various aspects of the relationship with God. It is in these acts we are confronted with the sense of the numen – a great power that is other than ourselves. We become exposed to a wisdom that is not our own – a wisdom that can take us by surprise. These experiences have an "otherness" about them – we are encountering another mind.

Or are we? Is the perceived "otherness" of this experience genuine evidence of God impacting directly on the human mind? Perhaps we should be seeking some other explanation. For example, might not the sense of "otherness" derive from the unconscious – the unconscious mind impacting on consciousness in a way that mimics an input from a supposed God?

Ideally, of course, we would like some scientific means of deciding the issue. But from the outset, the prospects do not look hopeful. The contents of an individual's mind are not open to direct public scrutiny, in the way a biological specimen, say, can be jointly examined, and experimented upon, by a group of scientists. Except that Sigmund Freud, the founder of modern psychology, did in fact regard his work as a science.

In his defense, it can be argued that open access to the data is unnecessary, provided that the description given by the individual faithfully and truly relays to others the nature of the psychological experience he/she has had. Again, when it comes to the repeatable nature of scientific investigations, there is no problem; the psychological experiences reported by many individuals can be collected and compared, these leading to the identification of reproducible, repeated patterns of common experience. Of course, one does on occasion come across aberrant experiences – perhaps of individuals convinced that they are Napoleon or God. Rogue results are to be expected in any scientific study. But these are easily sifted out, leaving a reproducible set of psychological experiences common to large sections of the population, and hence requiring some universally applicable, overarching explanation.

As with many other scientific investigations, it is the *interpretation* of the raw data that can prove problematic. To illustrate the problems encountered over the interpretation of religious experience, this chapter is devoted to presenting the conflicting views of two great psychologists: Sigmund Freud, whom we have already mentioned, and Carl Jung. As we shall be seeing, they came to markedly differing assessments as to the origin and significance of the inner religious experience.

Sigmund Freud

Freud was not the first to discover the unconscious, but he certainly played a major role in systematically uncovering many of its contents and its workings, and how it can impact and affect conscious experience.

Freud drew attention to how, in childhood, we repress shameful, disagreeable, painful, alarming thoughts. We push them out of our conscious thinking, and from there they lodge in the unconscious.

Freud held that these thoughts were mostly of a sexual nature.

Though repressed, they can yet express themselves. They give rise to neurotic behavior – that is to say, behavior arising when one is at odds with oneself because of some conflict between basic instinctual urgings and the demands of one's perceived individual and collective obligations. Such behavior can give rise to unreasonable fears and compulsive actions. One of the aims of psychoanalysis is to bring the repressed features into consciousness where they can be identified for what they are and dealt with.

As regards religious belief, Freud was of the view that it arose from wish-fulfillment. This is a process whereby the unconscious takes something that is devoutly wished for, and causes the conscious mind to believe that the wish has indeed been fulfilled. In particular, Freud claimed that as one grows up, one becomes anxious and fearful of losing the fatherly protection one has enjoyed in childhood. One wishes that it would continue into adult life. So the unconscious invents a heavenly father-figure to take the place of the earthly father. The idea of there being a God out there is thus just a projection arising out of this unacknowledged infantile fear.

Wish-fulfillment has a second effect. We fear death, and would like to have life prolonged. So, again, the unconscious gets to work and convinces us that there is indeed life beyond death.

Freud accepted that there was within us an inner moral authority, or ethical complex, monitoring the individual's behavior. He called it the *superego*. (We might loosely think of it as conscience.) But whereas a religious person would think of this as originating with God – the promptings of the Holy Spirit, if you are Christian – Freud claimed that it was nothing more than whatever code of behavior was instilled into one by parents and society during early childhood.

Thus, according to Freud, belief in God and in eternal life is an illusion. It is immature and mentally unhealthy. Far better to face up to the realities of life, harsh though these might be, and learn to stand on one's own feet. One should spurn the false comfort and support of this fictitious figure in the sky, with his empty promises of life beyond death.

Such then are Freud's views on religion. They are set out in his books *Moses and Monotheism*, *Totem and Taboo*, and *The Future of an Illusion*.

When they first appeared, some regarded them as having conclusively explained away religion. Today, among professional psychologists, they are among Freud's most neglected works. Why should this be?

In the first place, the theory appears to be based on straight, dogmatic assertion, with no evidence offered. The philosopher of science Karl Popper was among those particularly scathing about the *ex-cathedra* statements Freud so often made.

Secondly, it has to be said that those of us familiar with the *quality* of the religious experience – the sense of awe and wonder, the sheer beauty and nobility of the numinous – find it quite impossible to understand how something of that nature is supposed to have arisen out of the dustbin morass of repressed shameful and frightening responses to feelings of sexual inadequacy, which is what Freud would have us believe are the main contents of the unconscious. There seems to be no connection between the two.

Thirdly, it is obvious that simply because one wishes for something to be true does not in itself say anything about whether the thing wished for is the case or not.

Next we note that if Freud were correct, we would expect all religions to be based on a father-figure God. This is far from the case. Such a figure is not there in Buddhism. You would expect it to have been there at the start of the Judaeo/Christian/Islamic tradition, but it was not. As we shall be seeing in the next chapter, the idea is almost non-existent in the Old Testament. It takes on its prominent role only in relation to Jesus and *his* Father – we being merely "sons by adoption." Indeed, traditional Christian theology then goes far beyond the simple Heavenly Father idea of God with its doctrine of the Trinitarian nature of God (more of that in the final chapter).

As for dismissing religious practice as a manifestation of neurotic behavior, here Freud seems to have been misled by a superficial similarity between compulsive actions of certain neurotics, and religious ritual performed in church services. But this is to neglect an important distinction between the two: neurotic behavior consists of actions performed unconsciously; religious ritual is performed consciously and deliberately.

This is not to say that there aren't neurotic people whose obsessions have a religious content. There are. But this is not surprising. Neuroses can be associated with anything and everything. There are people with scientific delusions. For example, they might be obsessed with the idea that there is some force field adversely affecting them, or they might claim to be getting telepathic messages from space aliens. There can be delusions with a political content, where the victim believes he is being hounded by government spies and agents. And there are those delusions of a broadly social nature, where the subject believes that everyone is involved in a plot against them. The fact that a small minority have delusions of a religious nature is only to be expected.

Another point to note is that the idea of religion being just a prop, a comfort for the weak, is far from the mark. Though it can indeed be a comfort in that sense – and there is no harm in that – when one speaks of the Holy Spirit as the Comforter, that designation carries an altogether different connotation; it means the Strengthener. The Holy Spirit gives one the wherewithal needed to stand up to the challenges and demands of the religious way of life. The religious life is one of self-denial and self-discipline – not self-gratification. It can in some circumstances even lead to martyrdom. There is so much in religion that could not possibly have anything to do with wish-fulfillment. Note that, among the great religious figures such as Moses, Elijah, Jeremiah, and Jonah, none wanted to assume the roles chosen for them by God. They knew that such vocations would inevitably embroil them in dangerous confrontations with the authorities of the time.

Yet another point about wish-fulfillment. Wouldn't one expect religion to be more prevalent among the poor and needy – those denied the most in terms of worldly goods and esteem, and therefore with the greatest scope for wishing? But survey after survey reveals this not to be the case; one has only to compare the well-attended churches in relatively affluent suburbia with the empty ones in the inner city to know this.

As for the desire to prolong life, is that wish really a potent factor in promoting religious belief? For early Judaism it was not. References to descending into Sheol seem to refer to an unpleasant state of non-existence rather than to fullness of life. This lack of anything much after death was one reason why for Jews it was so important to have male children as a means of perpetuating the family name. Buddhism seeks annihilation rather than life eternal. And even many Christians, if closely questioned, do not actually believe in life beyond death, despite their recitation of the creed on a Sunday morning.

In fact, the whole thesis of wish-fulfillment can be turned on its head. If the religious life can be so demanding, cannot one claim that it is atheists who are more prone to indulge in wish-fulfillment – through their wish to avoid religious obligations and duties to God.

Finally, why don't we probe into the possible workings of Freud's mind – given what we know about *his* childhood – in the same way as he attempted to psychoanalyze others? What do we find in his background, and what would we expect his subsequent attitudes to be – based on his own theories?

Freud came from a free-thinking, non-observant Jewish family. In Vienna 90 percent were Catholics and there was much anti-Semitism. Freud's father, Jacob, once told of how he was walking down a street wearing a new fur hat. "A Christian came up to me, and with a single blow knocked off my cap into the mud and shouted, 'Jew, get off the pavement!'" Freud asked his father what happened next. "I went into the roadway and picked up my cap," he replied. At the age of forty-three, when Freud recalled that incident, it was clear that he was still overwhelmed with feelings of shame at his father's passive behavior. He wrote:

> I contrasted this situation with another which fitted my feelings better: the scene in which Hannibal's father . . . made his boy swear before the household altar to take vengeance on the Romans. Ever since that time Hannibal has had a place in my phantasies.
>
> (*The Interpretation of Dreams*, SE IV, p. 197)

He had earlier written:

> Hannibal, whom I had come to resemble in these respects, had been the favourite hero of my later school days . . . . To my youthful mind Hannibal and Rome symbolized the conflict between the tenacity of Jewry and the organization of the Catholic Church.
>
> (ibid., p. 196)

We can but guess what part the passive response of his father to an overt act of anti-Semitism, by a supposed Christian, played in shaping his attitude toward religions based on father-figures, and toward Christianity in particular. Jacob was never able to provide adequately for his family; they were desperately poor. Freud dismissed him as "always waiting for his boat to come in." His contempt for his father came to be incorporated within his psychological theorizing:

> In the second half of childhood a change sets in in the boy's relation to his father – a change whose importance cannot be exaggerated. From his nursery the boy begins to cast his eyes upon the world outside. And he cannot fail now to make discoveries which undermine his original high opinion of his father and which expedite his detachment from his first ideal. He finds that his father is no longer the mightiest, wisest and richest of beings; he grows dissatisfied with him, he learns to criticize him and to estimate his place in society.

> (*Some Reflections on Schoolboy Psychology*, SE XIII, p. 242)

Freud's first encounter with religion came through his nanny, the maid-servant of the household, Thérèse Wittek. He was later to describe her as "the prehistoric old woman," and "an ugly, elderly but clever woman." She was always taking him to church and instructing him about God and hell. But then, with Freud still only about two and a half years old, she was dismissed from the household for stealing money and encouraging Freud to do the same. She was jailed for ten months. Again one can but conjecture what lasting impression this "Christian" woman's hypocrisy left on the boy.

Given the poor example of the nanny, the general anti-Semitism of so-called Christians in Vienna, and the low esteem Freud had for his father, it is little wonder he grew up wishing to reject religion and anything that smacked of adulation of father-figures. He became an atheist from his earliest years.

So much for the deficiencies of Freud's attempts to explain away religious experience. But before leaving the subject, one ought to sound a brief conciliatory note. Though his theory of religion was unsound for a number of reasons, it would be foolhardy to dismiss it entirely. Wish-fulfillment projections based on childhood experience might not be the explanation of belief in God, but they nevertheless do have a part to play. Surveys reveal that the view held by religious people as to the nature of their heavenly father can be significantly colored by the relationship they have had with their own earthly parent. If one has had a severe upbringing, then one is inclined to emphasize the sterner, more judgmental aspects of God. On the other hand, if one has enjoyed a more free-and-easy relationship with one's father, the inclination is to think of God as being correspondingly more benign. In general, it seems true to say that the old Victorian idea of a strict disciplinarian type of God has now given way to a contemporary notion that in some cases borders on the idea of a God who takes the line: "Let's talk this thing over together man to man, shall we?" The emphasis now is on love and forgiveness rather than punishment. It is rare indeed today to hear a sermon on hellfire and damnation.

Clearly, what is going on in these different perceptions of God is projection – one is projecting on to the figure of God aspects drawn from one's own personal experience of earthly relationships. It is unavoidable. But that by itself is not to say that belief in a heavenly father is *nothing but* a projection of one's earthly father – as Freud would have had us believe.

So much for Freud. It is now time to turn to the work of our other psychologist – one who came to radically different conclusions.

Carl Jung

Carl Jung studied under Freud, and was always generous in acknowledging his debt to him. But in time they fell out. Jung grew disenchanted with what he regarded as Freud's dogmatism – his authoritarian stance. He did not think Freud was right to place so much emphasis on the unconscious as being just a repository for the unconscious repression of shameful thoughts – mostly those regarding sex. He thought of the unconscious as containing much more besides that. In general, he was not so much interested in the first years of life and in how repression dating from those years affected one's later psychological development; he was more concerned with the second half of life, and the achievement of a fully rounded personality.

While accepting that the unconscious does indeed contain repressions of thoughts derived from one's own individual experience of life – what he called the *personal unconscious* – he held that there was in addition a *collective unconscious* that we all share from birth. To understand what he meant by the latter, it is perhaps best if we approach it from the standpoint of genetically influenced behavior.

We saw in the last chapter how our genetic make-up is contained in a molecule called the DNA molecule. Essentially it consists of a chain of smaller base molecules, the sequence of which constitutes a set of codes. These determine our physical characteristics, but also certain behavior traits – what one might loosely regard as inherited instincts. As we shall be seeing in more detail when we come to consider evolution by natural selection in Chapter 10, these were fashioned in the so-called struggle for survival. According to Darwin, certain individuals by chance acquire codes leading to either physical characteristics or behavior traits that enhance their chances of survival. These individuals are the ones more likely to live to an age where they can mate. In mating, they pass on the newly acquired beneficial genes to their offspring. Those individuals, on the other hand, with characteristics that are less beneficial, are not so likely to survive and mate. This means the less beneficial genes tend to die out over time. Thus, genes that confer some survival advantage are selected in preference to others that do not. It is through this process of evolution by natural selection that we have arrived at today's range of species adapted to survival in their various habitats.

For our present purposes we concentrate on behavior traits. These might include, for instance, what we might loosely call the "killer instinct" of today's domesticated cat. Even though it is not hungry, it will automatically stalk and try to kill a mouse or bird. This is an inbuilt tendency that was essential to the survival of the cat's ancestors; without it the prey would have been likely to get away, and the ancestor would have starved. We see genetically influenced behavior in the way a baby kangaroo, on being born, will automatically head up its mother's fur to find the pouch that is to become its new home; the animal is "pre-programmed" to do this; its behavior is not something it has to be taught. Then we have the mothering instinct, whereby a mother will go to any lengths to protect her offspring.

Recognizing this genetically influenced behavior at work in other species, it is only reasonable to expect that, as evolved animals ourselves, we humans are also subject to similar tendencies. Confronted by a certain set of circumstances, we have a natural inclination to behave in a certain manner – one that did not have to be consciously learned because it was pre-programmed into us.

As with the other animals, such behavior traits are encoded into our DNA, and this was done from the moment of conception as our DNA was being compiled from that of our parents. Over succeeding generations, such survival codes have become a common feature of all members of our species.

Now, if all this is going on in the physical, biological world, we would expect there to be a correlate in the psychological realm of the mind. And this is what Jung discovered. It is called the collective unconscious – the tendency all of us members of the human species share of adopting thought patterns that are common. We have a predisposition to think and act in certain ways when presented with appropriate stimuli from the environment.

Jung, of course, knew nothing of our modern understanding of genetically influenced behavior based on what happens at the biological level of DNA molecules. He arrived at his conclusions by carefully studying the responses of his patients, and identifying from them continually repeated patterns of thought and attitude to given situations. He supplemented this by also examining recurring themes in traditional fairy-tale literature, ancient practices, alchemy, myths, legends, dreams, etc. In this way he identified certain elemental tendencies which he called *archetypes*. Together these archetypes made up our collective unconscious. The archetypes are to be regarded as unseen organizing principles that shape our conscious thoughts and attitudes. One way is to think of them as jelly moulds. In themselves they are empty. But when filled by conscious experience, they shape the form that the experience takes. The word "archetype" in fact means "imprint." And because the archetypes are possessed by us all, we find our thoughts being shaped in similar ways, these in turn yielding common behavior patterns.

Thus, for example, Jung identified a mother archetype and a father archetype – these leading to instinctive attitudes toward parents. There is the "wise old man" archetype, resulting in a tendency to look to some person as the fount of wisdom and authority. Closely allied to that is the "hero" archetype inclining one to worship and follow a leader, perhaps blindly according him allegiance. This can turn out to be very dangerous when the object of this hero-worship is a man like Hitler, or a leader of a fringe religious cult that eventually ends up committing mass suicide. In the man there is the "anima" archetype – the unconscious feminine side of his personality, and in the woman the corresponding masculine "animus" archetype. Then there is the "shadow" archetype. This is the sum of all the personal and collective elements which, because they are incompatible with the chosen conscious attitude, are denied expression in life and therefore coalesce into a relatively autonomous "splinter personality." The shadow personifies everything that the subject refuses to acknowledge about him or herself. These traits nevertheless keep resurfacing; they constitute the dark side of oneself.

In summary, there are, it seems, as many archetypes as there are recurring typical situations capable of engraving themselves on the collective psyche.

And among the archetypes there is a "religious" archetype. The evidence for this is that it appears that all peoples everywhere and at all times have acted religiously. Admittedly, on occasion there have been reports of ancient tribes that were not religious. But on further investigation, these claims invariably have been proved unfounded. Traces of religious involvement manifest themselves in found artifacts, and particularly in the manner of burial adopted in these ancient societies. We thus conclude that there is an all-pervasive tendency to be religious.

In parenthesis, I might mention that Richard Dawkins, well known as a crusader against religious belief, has taken every opportunity to promote the idea that religion is to be likened to a computer virus infecting the human race. Computer viruses are self-replicating; they are based on pieces of software that keep saying "duplicate me." In this manner they proliferate and spread across the internet system from one computer to another. Dawkins sees this as being similar to the way religion is passed on from one generation to another through parents telling their children about it, and instructing them, in their turn, to pass it on to the grandchildren, etc. After a while it gets a firm hold and, like a computer virus, disrupts the normal running of things.

Although superficially persuasive, Dawkins's argument is flawed. What he does not take into account is that religion has been in evidence at all times and in all places throughout the history of the human race. In fact, there is nothing more *normal* than to be religious. If religion is to be regarded as a contagious infection, then most people have for most of the time been sick. No, what is *abnormal* is the current rise in atheism. Why is it that atheism, which initially got a hold in the industrialized West, is now spreading? Would it not be more appropriate to regard atheism as the virus?

The religious archetype is enormously influential. Jung held that if this inner drive did not manifest itself in the worship of God, then it would come to rest on some other object. It is rather like the way experiments have shown how the mother archetype of the newly born gosling can be deflected towards some bizarre alternative object. If, instead of being presented with its real mother, the gosling immediately encounters some human being or a piece of painted wood, then all its pent-up feelings of devotion to a mother will get displaced. The human or the piece of wood is treated as though it were the real mother.

So it is with religion. The religious archetype can get deflected to some object other than God. The individual might come to devote all his or her energies to nationalism, racism, feminism, support for a political party or a football team, campaigning against blood sports or highway bypasses, support for environmental pressure groups, fighting AIDS, and so on. Not that some of these activities in themselves are not worthy and deserving of support and action. What we are talking about here is when a person gets things out of proportion – when the whole focus and rationale of his/her life centers on the cause in question, to the exclusion of other considerations. When that is the case, the cause has become the person's religion.

Above the door of Jung's house, he had carved in Latin a sentence attributed to the Delphic Oracle. When translated it reads, "Invoked or not invoked, the god will be present." Even though we ourselves live in what seem to be particularly irreligious times – in the sense of declining church attendance and formal observance – one has only to go into a bookshop and see the proliferation of books on the occult, to realize that the deep-rooted religious archetype will find its expression somehow.

Again we see its all-pervasive influence at work in attitudes toward death. A person might assert the finality of death, and deny all possibility of life beyond the grave, but will nevertheless feel compelled to speak well of the dead. Or take the way the British people reacted to the death of Diana, Princess of Wales. What could possibly have triggered such an overwhelming display of grief? Jung would surely have had a field-day explaining it to us – in terms of the religious archetype.

Jung, perhaps somewhat confusingly, spoke of this archetype as the *self*. Why should it be given such a name? Let me try and explain. Earlier I mentioned how it was a particular characteristic of Jung that he concentrated on the second half of life; this contrasted with Freud and his special concern for the early years. As Jung saw it, each of us comes under pressure to behave and conform in certain ways. We take on responsibilities for running a house, and supporting a family. This means having a job. Work is time-consuming; it is normally of a highly specialized nature, perhaps requiring lengthy training. Because of the need to specialize in order to become good at one's vocation, there are other aspects of one's potential that have to be neglected.

I myself well remember how at school I had first to give up art, which I had enjoyed, in order to concentrate on studying for the exams I was to take at age sixteen. Then came further specialization as I had to drop English to concentrate on my scientific studies at advanced level. And by the time I got to university, I was doing nothing but physics and the mathematics needed to support the physics. At each stage it was something of a toss-up which way the decision went – which subject got dropped, and which was retained.

We all have similar stories to tell. These life-affecting decisions might be made for quite arbitrary reasons – perhaps related to the personality of a particular teacher, or what one's friends have opted to do.

This means that by the time one reaches mid-life, there are large aspects of one's initial potential that have never been tapped; they remain stunted, while other parts of one's make-up have been excessively nurtured to the extent that they have taken over one's whole life. Each of us reaches the halfway stage of life unbalanced.

Thus, according to Jung, it becomes the task of the second half of life to redress this imbalance. We are to return to the neglected parts of our personality and encourage them to give belated expression to themselves. The overall aim is to become a fully rounded, whole person. This process Jung called *individuation*. It was the process of fully realizing oneself as an individual – not being formed and shaped by largely incidental and accidental outside restrictions and pressures – but being true to one's real self. As such, the process begins in one's earliest years, and carries on in our working career, marriage, bringing up a family, etc. But it is in danger of being left half-done. In the second half of life one must consciously strive to attend to those neglected parts of one's potential; one must learn to give expression to the totality of one's personality – expression to the all-important archetype known as the "self."

Jung then went on to say that just as a round object – like a ball – has to have a center, so the well-rounded person has to have a center. And that center is to be God. The process of discovering the real you is indissolubly bound up with the process of getting sorted out over your relationship to God. For that reason, the self archetype becomes synonymous with the religious archetype. In fact, Jung would speak of the religious archetype as the "God-image." We are reminded that the Bible tells us that we are made in the image of God. So the process of discovering your true self is one where you are confronted with the God-image. The very core of your being, its very center, defines for you the meaning of life – where you stand. That meaning is rooted in God – or if not in God, then in some God-substitute. It is what colors and gives meaning to your whole life, and for that reason all other archetypes relate to this self archetype or God-image – hence its position at the very center of the psyche; the psyche being the sum total of all that is conscious and unconscious.

We saw in Freud's psychology that religion was to be regarded as a sign of immaturity, an inability to stand on one's own feet and realize that there is no protective father-figure. Religion was a neurosis – the state of being at odds with oneself because of unresolved conflicts. Psychologically it was unhealthy and needed to be treated. For Jung it was quite the opposite. A well-sorted-out religion was an integral part of psychological maturity – the epitome of psychological well-being. It was something one should actively seek to cultivate. Jung said:

> Among all my patients in the second half of life – that is to say, over thirty-five – there has not been one whose problem in the last resort was not that of finding a religious outlook on life. It is safe to say that every one of them fell ill because he had lost that which the living religions of every age have given to their followers, and none of them has been really healed who did not regain this religious outlook.

> (*Modern Man in Search of a Soul*)

For Jung, the moralistic God was not a projection of a superego that had been instilled by parents and society. Rather, the superego was to be regarded as an introjected God or, as Jung put it, "a furtive attempt to smuggle in the time-honored image of Jehovah in the dress of psychological theory."

Which brings us finally to the question of the *origin* of the religious, or self, archetype.

I introduced the subject of archetypes by drawing on what has recently been learned concerning genetically influenced behavior fashioned by the process of natural selection. And there is no doubt that we see in the life of the mind the counterparts of those inherited external behavior patterns we all share.

But that is not to say that this is all there is to the archetypes. It does not exclude the possibility that there are mind-sets in the psyche that have little if anything to do with the survival of the fittest. Take, for example, this religious archetype.

One might at first try to dismiss it as simply a chance genetic aberration, which once it came into existence, was subsequently perpetuated because it happened to confer a better chance of survival. After all, a gene that encouraged people to act cooperatively could indeed have survival value.

But there are problems with this suggestion. One is the obvious disadvantage of having, as the rallying point for the shared loyalty, a belief in an invisible God whose existence could not be indisputably demonstrated. Why not make the rallying point a charismatic leader (which of course does happen – in response to the hero archetype we mentioned earlier), or alternatively a shared devotion to a particular country or race – which is also commonplace? What is not good for survival is a belief in a God that leads you to love your enemies, and to care for the sick and disabled – those who, in terms of the harsh dictums of evolutionary theory, one would presumably have to brand as the "unfit."

Certainly Jungian psychologists would be reluctant to accept that the archetypes are limited only to those that are clearly the psychological counterparts of the genetic traits to do with survival.

How the others might have arisen, however, is not clear. With genetically influenced behavior fashioned by evolution through natural selection, we know that the mental character traits relate to a physical sequence of base molecules; those traits can be altered by altering the sequence. But this does not exclude the possibility that there might be additional mental traits associated with other features of the DNA molecule, such as for example its overall helical structure. This presumably did not arise through the same selection process; it is there because the chain of base molecules has to have an overall structure of some kind. Could it be that this overall structure is the physical analogue of the self archetype to which all other archetypes relate? Such an idea would be pure speculation, very hard to prove or refute. Suffice it to say that psychologists might well be right in seeing more to the archetypes than just the mental correlates of the physical features fashioned by natural selection.

These considerations are of particular interest when it comes to the origins of the God-image or self archetype. Jung, having explained that the term "archetype" derives from the word meaning "imprint," once wrote:

> . . . thus an archetype presupposes an imprinter. Psychology as the science of the soul has to confine itself to its subject and

guard against overstepping its proper boundaries by metaphysical assertions or other professions of faith. Should it set up a God, even as a hypothetical cause, it would have implicitly claimed the possibility of proving God, thus exceeding its competence in an absolutely illegitimate way . . . we simply do not know the ultimate derivation of the archetype any more than we know the origin of the psyche. The competence of science as an empirical science only goes so far as to establish, on the basis of comparative research, whether for instance the imprint found in the psyche can or cannot reasonably be termed a "God-image." Nothing positive or negative has thereby been asserted about the possible existence of God, any more than the archetype of the "hero" posits the actual existence of a hero.

("Introduction to the Religious and Psychological Problems of Alchemy,"
Psychology and Alchemy, Collected Works 12, paras 1–43)

So what Jung is saying here is that psychology of itself cannot make claims about the existence of God. In the final analysis, we are left with the problem of whether the source of the otherness of religious experience is God (acting either directly on consciousness, or through the intermediary of our unconscious) or whether, alternatively, that source lies solely in our own unconscious.

What makes this a particularly difficult problem to unravel is that, in talking of prayer, we do not have in mind some ghostly telepathic transfer of thoughts from a source physically situated outside. God is thought to be *in* oneself as well as outside. It is the God within that stirs up thoughts in one's mind. We are called to be at one with God. As we approach that ideal, it becomes increasingly difficult to draw a hard-and-fast distinction between the mind of God and that of the believer.

None of this prevented Jung himself, as a private individual, from having his own personal views on the subject. In a famous TV interview with John Freeman, he was asked whether in fact he did believe in God. He replied: "Difficult to answer. I *know*. I don't need to believe; I know."

Conclusion

This draws to a close our study of what two leading psychologists had to say about religion. Confronted by essentially the same data on recurring types of religious experience, their studies led to diametrically opposed views on how they should be interpreted. Clearly it remains for us as individuals to decide for ourselves where, within this broad spectrum of interpretation, our own response lies. Sufficient to say that, for many, the inner religious experience lies at the very heart of the God experiment, providing the most compelling evidence for God.

6

Getting Acquainted with God

What is God like?

If prayer is to be seen as a meeting of minds – our mind and God's mind – then presumably God has some kind of personal nature. So, what kind of personality – if we can call it that – does God possess?

As in any other type of investigation, including scientific studies, no one is expected to discover everything for themselves; there is no point in reinventing the wheel. Each of us benefits from the experience of others – particularly from that of the acknowledged leaders in the field. When it comes to finding out what kind of God we are supposed to be dealing with, if one is of the Judaeo/Christian/Islamic tradition, then an important source of information has to be the Bible. There we expect to find the accumulated wisdom of the great religious figures of the past. Unfortunately, the picture of God it presents seems, at first sight at least, to be a confusing one.

For a start, we are assuming there to be just the one God. And much of the Bible points to that conclusion. It affirms God as the creator and ruler of the whole world. But elsewhere it refers to other gods, for example, the Canaanite baals. The God of the Israelites was jealous when his people worshiped these other gods.

Next we note that God is supposed to be a God of love and mercy. But there is much in the Old Testament about a God of wrath and vengeance. His anger could be so great as to bring him to the verge of destroying his people.

Then again, God is supposed to be the god of all peoples – loving them equally. In that case, how are we to account for what happened to the Egyptians? We can understand God wanting the Israelites to be freed from slavery, but killing off the Egyptians' first-born children and drowning their army seems somewhat extreme.

I repeat: what kind of God do we think we are dealing with?

Progressive theology

Much of the confusion is resolved once it is realized that theology, not unlike science, is a progressive subject.

All too often we are inclined to think of theology as static – fixed in stone. Our understanding of God was formulated once and for all at some point in the past. Since then, all that has been required is for that original conception to be faithfully preserved and passed down to succeeding generations. Thus, it is held, theology stands in marked contrast to science which is a dynamic endeavor, constantly moving forward, progressively refining and improving its understanding of the world.

Such a view of theology could not be further from the truth. One has only to place the writings of the Bible in chronological order to see this. The Bible, of course, is no ordinary book; it is a whole library of books, written by different people at different times. And, for whatever reason, they are not presented to us in the order in which they were written. Indeed, the chronology is even more complicated than that. Genesis, for example, is not in itself a single book; it is a collection of writings which themselves are not in chronological order. Take the two creation stories: the one beginning at verse 4 of Chapter 2 was written in the eighth century BCE, 200 years *before* the one we find earlier in Chapter 1.

It is no easy matter for Biblical scholars to sort out the correct chronology. But when this is done, to the best of their ability, a truly fascinating pattern emerges. What we discover is that the conception of God (in the Judaeo/Christian/Islamic tradition) has changed and evolved dramatically over the ages. These developments took place largely through the insights of great leaders and prophets. There follows a brief sketch as to how these ideas about God gradually took shape over the course of history.

Originally there were thought to be many gods. They were largely territorial, each being in charge of a particular country or tract of land. On crossing the border from one country to the next, one was expected to worship the god of the country that had now been entered. Much like an earthly king, it was he who was in charge of everything going on in that territory. The god of particular interest to the Bible is one called Yahweh; the god who lived on Mount Sinai. He was a fearsome god; put a foot on his land, and one ran the risk of instant death.

Moses belonged to the Israelite nation, which at the time was enslaved in Egypt. But he had escaped and found his way across the desert to Mount Sinai. He strayed on to the mountain, and met Yahweh in the form of a burning bush. Not only did he survive the encounter, he was told to return to Egypt and lead his people out of slavery. When Moses protested that the King of Egypt was unlikely to grant freedom to the Israelites, Yahweh offered help. He sent plagues and all manner of troubles upon the Egyptians, including the slaughter of their first-born. Eventually the Egyptians capitulated and gave the slaves their freedom. They then had second thoughts and went after them to bring them back. In the course of the chase, their army was drowned in the Red Sea.

Yahweh was a tribal god; he was the god of the Israelites, and only the Israelites. To that extent he was conventional. Where he was *not* conventional is that he had exercised power in a country that was not his own. How was it possible for the god of Mount Sinai to perform acts in Egypt?

Yahweh was different in another respect. Normally one belonged to whatever god was in charge of the land where one's people lived. There was no choice in the matter, any more than one could choose one's parents. But with Yahweh and the Israelites it was not so. They entered into a contract, a covenant. Yahweh proposed that if they conformed their lives to his ways – as embodied in the ten commandments brought down from Mount Sinai by Moses – then he would afford them his protection, and guide them to a land of their own. The Israelites were to become an adopted people. It wasn't to be a matter of birth, but of choice.

The next development was that Yahweh went with his people on their wanderings through the desert. He was no longer exclusively tied to Mount Sinai. We see here a further loosening of the link between a god and his particular territory.

They reached the promised land, but it was already occupied. This posed no problem, however, because Yahweh was still at this stage a tribal god concerned only for the interests of his adopted people, the Israelites; he cared no more for Canaanites than he had done earlier for Egyptians. He installed his people. The worship of the Canaanite gods, the so-called baals, was to be discontinued. Yahweh was now in exclusive control of the country.

And yet old habits die hard. King Solomon had many wives, some of whom were foreign. They wished to continue to worship their own gods, and Solomon permitted this – even building altars to them in the great temple in Jerusalem he had originally dedicated to Yahweh. Not only that, but the people in general surreptitiously took up the worship of other gods. After years of wandering the deserts with their flocks, they had become settled. It was now worthwhile to turn to agriculture and grow crops – because those who planted them would still be around later in the year to collect the harvest. But crops require rain. To whom should the Israelites pray for rain? Yahweh had supplied them with manna to eat in the desert, sure enough, but basically he was a warlike god – good at fighting Israel's enemies. No, the experts at making it rain were the old Canaanite baals.

Here we get another strand of thought contained in old ideas about gods. There was not only the notion that they could be territorial, but also that different gods were associated with different functions. We see this particularly with the ancient Roman and Greek gods – Mars the Roman god of war, Aphrodite the Greek goddess of love, Bacchus the Roman and Greek god of wine, and so on. Yahweh was regarded by the Israelites at this stage as being particularly good at fighting. It was up to the prophet Elijah to demonstrate that Yahweh's powers and influence extended beyond merely waging war. In a time of drought, he went up a nearby mountain and prayed to Yahweh for rain. A cloud appeared. Tiny at first, it grew and grew – and it rained. So it became clear to the Israelites that Yahweh was not simply a god of battle; he could look after their needs in times of peace also.

And note that Yahweh could make clouds in the sky; he controlled the sky. But the sky stretches everywhere. His domain of influence was spreading.

Elijah was prominent in calling the people back to exclusive worship of Yahweh. Under the bidding of the vengeful, jealous Yahweh, Elijah instigated the slaughter of 450 priests of Baal that Queen Jezebel had set up throughout the country.

But then we see a new side to Yahweh. The prophet Hosea had a wife who was repeatedly unfaithful to him. He ought to have done away with her – had her stoned to death. But he could not bring himself to do it. He found that no matter how often she deceived him, when she returned to him he could not help but forgive her. Hosea saw in this a parallel with Yahweh's relationship to the Israelite people. They too were repeatedly unfaithful to him, chasing after the other gods. Although Yahweh would punish them for their wrongdoing – as for example in the way he set the people against each other to the extent that the kingdom became split into two halves, at enmity with each other – he did not destroy them. Why? Because he was not purely a god of justice and vengeance; he had the capacity to forgive. He was a god of mercy.

Then we have the contribution of Amos. He lived at a time when the people had become polarized: the rich and the poor. With the cultivation of the land, some landowners had become very rich. Most were singularly uncaring of the plight of the starving masses. As long as they went through the motions of making sacrifices on the temple altar, they reckoned they had done as much as was needed. It was Amos, a poor shepherd, who had the task of denouncing the excesses of the rich. Yahweh was not a god simply interested in the good of the Jewish nation as a whole, and therefore particularly interested in the leaders of that society – the rich and influential. He took a personal interest in everyone – as individuals. Again this was to be seen as fresh insight.

The next prophet on the scene was Isaiah. He came from a very different background to Amos; he was one of the ruling class. He spent much of his time in the palace of the king. He was used to nobility and splendor. He had a vision of Yahweh in which his glory filled the heavens; he was god of the whole Earth. It was not that he ruled the land of the Jews, and in addition had considerable influence beyond its boundaries: he ruled everything.

And yet the Jews had difficulty focusing their worship on this god. They set up altars to him in each village and town, which was fair enough, but then they got to talking of "the Yahweh of our town," as distinct from "the Yahweh of your town." They had in fact regressed once more to the worship of local deities. King Josiah decided to put a stop to this once and for all. He ordered all altars to be smashed except the one in the great temple at Jerusalem. From then on, there was only one place where sacrifices could be offered. With just one altar it became clear that there was just one god the Jews should worship.

All of this meant that sacrifices could only be made by journeying up to Jerusalem. These pilgrimages were very significant occasions for the faithful. Unfortunately, King Josiah's plan had its down side. Whereas people got a special thrill coming up to Jerusalem to the one and only altar, when it was time to quit Jerusalem and head for home, they felt as though they were leaving Yahweh behind. Although this had never been Josiah's intention, the people got to thinking that Yahweh lived exclusively in the temple at Jerusalem. Out of sight, out of mind. Once they were home, they felt free to live their lives however they wanted to, Yahweh supposedly being none the wiser.

It was against these excesses that the prophet Jeremiah railed, warning the people that if they did not mend their ways Yahweh would punish them by sending in the Babylonians to lay waste their country. The authorities tried hard to stop Jeremiah upsetting the people with his predictions of gloom and doom. His warnings went unheeded, however, and in due course the Babylonians invaded. They captured Jerusalem, and razed the temple to the ground. After 350 years, there was nothing left of it. The rulers and leading citizens were taken into exile to Babylon. It seemed the end of the Jewish nation, and of their god. Having got used to the idea that Yahweh lived in the temple, they had now to come to terms with the idea that their god had been made homeless, or indeed had been destroyed along with the temple.

At that stage, Jeremiah ceased castigating the people and became their comforter. He assured them that after a period of seventy years, Yahweh would bring them back home from exile and they could make a new start; they would be forgiven. As for the loss of the temple, that was not the disaster they had assumed it to be. It was not the case that Yahweh lived in a specific building. He made his home in the hearts of people – wherever they might be – even in exile in Babylon. It is difficult to overestimate just how significant was this particular shift in thinking about Yahweh. He was a god who made his home *inside* the individual person.

Then we have Ezekiel. He had a wild vision that left him in a state of total shock for seven days. He had glimpsed the wonder, the power, and the awesome nature of Yahweh. It was so breathtaking and tremendous, he could not put it into words. Here we have the realization of how pitiful it is to try and describe Yahweh by making analogies with earthly images such as kings. Yahweh is so great, so beyond human imagining, that our descriptions have no chance of doing him justice. Contrast this with earlier accounts of him as someone who walks in the garden in the cool of the evening, or engages in a wrestling match with Jacob – portrayals of him that barely extended beyond a somewhat larger-than-life man.

Then we have the most remarkable revelation of all. Toward the end of the Book of Isaiah (beyond Chapter 40), another writer takes over. We know nothing of him; he is simply known as Second Isaiah. According to him, Yahweh declares:

> As the heavens are higher than the earth, so are my ways higher than your ways, and my thoughts than your thoughts.

> (*Isaiah* 55:9)

This was confirming the message of Ezekiel that we have no way of comprehending fully the nature of God. But then he also says:

> I am the Lord, and there is no other;
> apart from me, there is no other god.

> (*Isaiah* 45:5)

There we have it – at last. There is only the one god. From now on one can refer to him as God with a capital "G" because there is none other with which to confuse him. We can now seen that when in the past Yahweh was spoken of as being jealous, it was not that he wanted the people to worship him in preference to the others. It was more the case that he didn't want his people wasting their time addressing gods that weren't even there.

From this perspective it now becomes possible to understand why he was able to exert influence in Egypt and leave his mountain; he was the God of all the Earth. He not only owned it all, he created it in the first place. Only now, at this late stage in the story, does it become possible to think of God as being the sole Creator God.

Moving on to the New Testament, Christians see there yet further insight into God. He sends his own Son to live the life of a human, to share in our sufferings and to be the ultimate sacrifice on our behalf. We see in Jesus the perfect human life; what we ourselves are called to be. That God would humble himself in this way is the most eloquent testimony there could possibly be as to the inexhaustible depths of his love for us. Christ's prayer for the soldiers who were nailing him to the cross that God would forgive them because they knew not what they were doing, again shows the extraordinary extent to which he is prepared to forgive.

Summary

Reviewing these changes, we find we have progressed:

- from the god who was tied to his mountain retreat – to the creator of the whole world;

- from one god among many gods – to the one and only God;

- from the god of the Israelites who cared nothing for Egyptians and Canaanites – to the one who is God of all people equally;

- from a warlike god of wrath and vengeance – to the God of love and mercy;

- from a god who would strike people down dead if they approached too closely – to the God who dwells in our hearts;

- from the lofty God of the heavens – to the one who comes to Earth and suffers alongside us.

Earlier I warned that this would be but a sketchy, broad-brush approach to the development of theology down the ages. It is crude in the sense, for example, that I have presented the changes as building up toward the climax of monotheism. This is fair enough in terms of the generally accepted religion of the times. But that is not to deny that there had been certain schools of thought that had arrived at that position long before it became the consensus. In a subject this complex, the true story-line splinters down more than one path, some ending in blind alleys, others undergoing a number of detours. But the overall picture that emerges is one of general progression.

Progress still to come

Nor is this progress in theology something that took place solely in the distant past. Before leaving his disciples, Jesus told them that he would send them the Holy Spirit:

> When he, the Spirit of truth, comes, he will guide you into all truth. . . . He will bring glory to me by taking from what is mine and making it known to you.
>
> *(John 16:13–14)*

One way of understanding this passage is to see it as hinting that there was still more that God could reveal about himself, but the people of those days were not prepared for it.

Take, for example, the way we in our own time have begun to recognize and take an interest in the feminine side of God. We are coming to see God not only as our Heavenly Father, but also as our Heavenly Mother. In earlier times, when all positions of power and influence were occupied exclusively by men, it was only natural to think of God in masculine terms. But social change has meant that today the superiority of the male no longer applies – at least not to the same extent. This affects how we can think of God. Our minds have been prepared; we are now able to enrich our conception of God by exploring female analogies as well as male ones. For instance, I am rather taken with the analogy of the created world springing from the womb of God. The act of giving birth can be a useful complementary model to the more usual one of the world being fashioned much as a potter shapes a pot.

Again, with our modern understanding of astronomy we see just how vast and prolific the Universe is. This enhances our sense of the unimaginable power of God, far exceeding what was possible in the past. On planets out there, going round distant suns, are there other civilizations? If so, how does God relate to them? Are they more advanced than we are? Are they more valued by God than we are? How does the Son of God relate to them in terms of salvation?

Then comes the recognition of all the chance processes that are going on in the world, whether we are thinking of the formation of planets with only a few capable of supporting life, or the random mutations to DNA upon which the process of evolution by natural selection gets to work. It is an interesting way for God to achieve his purposes. So what is this telling us about God?

Then we have the aeons of time that the Universe existed before life developed within it, and the infinity of time that lies in the future when the stellar fires will have run their course and all becomes cold – the Heat Death of the Universe – the end of all life. What does this tell us about how God relates to the physical world itself? Are we right in seeing it as nothing more than a home for life, or in the eyes of God does it have a worth of its own – regardless of whether there is life in it?

Make no mistake about it: theology is an ongoing activity; it is far from static – far from being stuck in the past.

Marrying the new and the old ideas of God

If we think of our understanding of God as being so much better these days than it was in the past, you may ask, why do we retain "out-of-date" ideas? Why do we still read those passages in the Bible that refer, for instance, to there being other gods?

One reason is that there often remains a kernel of truth in them; religious people of the past were never entirely wrong in their conception of God. Agreed, we no longer think of there being other gods in the sense of supernatural beings. But as we saw in the last chapter, the psychologist Carl Jung warned that we have a natural inborn tendency to be religious, and if that drive is not consummated in the worship of God, then it will be deflected on to some other object or cause. Some different passion will absorb our energies; it will become a "god" for us, and those passages in the Old Testament about the Israelites chasing after other gods still provide us with salutary warnings of the consequences of chasing after modern "gods."

Or you might wonder why one continues to read passages describing Yahweh as a severe, indeed vengeful, God of justice. Surely we now know him to be a God of love, and mercy, and forgiveness. True, but the element of justice is still there. In the Christian tradition, the price of sin had to be paid by someone – it couldn't just be swept under the carpet as though it had never happened. And the price – a terrible one – was paid by Christ. What happened to Christ on the cross was not the work of the "Big Old Softie" kind of God some people seem to believe in these days. He is made of sterner stuff than that – and references to Yahweh as the God of justice act as an important reminder to us that there is another side to the "gentle Jesus, meek and mild" type of God.

So, on balance, it is right for us constantly to remind ourselves of the earlier ideas of God, provided we do this in the context of the overall development of theology, and don't read into them a significance and interpretation that is no longer deemed appropriate.

Genuine progress in theology?

From the above it would appear that our understanding of God has undergone changes and development as radical as any that have taken place, through science, in our understanding of the world. Moreover, that ongoing progress, as in science, continues in our own time.

But are we sure that it is genuine "progress"? I believe so. One would no more wish to revert to past understandings of God than one would wish to go back to earlier notions of science. In the philosophy of science, it has become customary to speak of "critical realism." This term acknowledges that we can never expect at any stage to be absolutely certain that our scientific theories are correct and will never need further amendment. But at least we are convinced that there is a real world out there (we are not making it up) and that our current descriptions of it are superior to those they have superseded.

I reckon the term "critical realism" can be applied as appropriately to theology. Modern theology does not have to be dogmatic in the sense of its supposedly providing the last word on the ultimate truth about God. Our understanding of God is fallible; it is open to correction and refinement in the light of greater experience. The fact that theology is, and always has been, in a state of flux, is a sign of strength rather than weakness and indecision. Scientists and theologians alike must approach their respective data with humility, fully prepared to change their theories in the light of new evidence and insights.

A dissenting view

Before concluding, it is only fair to point out that there is, of course, a quite different way of accounting for the continually changing conception of God. According to this alternative viewpoint, the changes do not represent genuine increases in our understanding of God; God is not progressively revealing to us more and more of his true nature. Rather, it is a case of people continually recreating God in their own image, and in accordance with whatever might be the current prevailing tendencies in society.

Recall how, in the last chapter, when we were dealing with the psychological inner religious experience, we saw that it was difficult to put it all down to wish-fulfillment – the unconscious tricking us into believing that our wish for a protective father-figure had been fulfilled in terms of a Heavenly Father. This could not be the whole explanation. And yet we noted that there was indeed a *certain amount* of projection going on.

So we have to ask questions like: is it the case that God is a forgiving God, and the only way he could get that message across was through a person who knew, from personal experience, what forgiveness was all about – Hosea in relation to his unfaithful wife? Or was Hosea simply creating a forgiving God in his own image?

Again, is it the case that God wanted to get across to us something of his splendor and majesty, and could only do that through someone used to pomp and ceremony – the rich Isaiah at the king's court? Or again was Isaiah simply projecting into the heavens a God in his own image?

If God is a God who cares for the individual – the poor as much as the rich – does it mean that such a message has to be entrusted to someone who is himself interested in the poor, because that is what he himself is – the humble shepherd, Amos? Or was Amos indulging in wish-fulfillment?

There is no easy way to resolve such dilemmas. In the end it is up to each of us as individuals to make up our own minds on which side of the fence we come down: genuine revelations of God's nature coming to us through minds that are prepared and sensitized to the transmission of that particular message; or those self-same minds projecting on to an imaginary god their own likeness.

As you will guess, I myself side with the first interpretation – that these are genuine revelations of God. Why do I think that? Because if we are to put it all down to making God in one's own image, then only forgiving people would think of God as forgiving, only rich people would think of God as powerful and magnificent, etc. But that is not how it is. Once the prophets said what they did, it was not long before their messages gained *universal* acceptance. One doesn't have to be poor to accept that God loves the poor as much as the rich; one doesn't have to have an unfaithful wife in order to accept that God can forgive. Certainly it takes the soil of a prepared mind for the seed of the idea to germinate in the first place. But once germinated, it could be propagated. Consensus formed around those particular ideas concerning the nature of God that were judged to have the ring of truth about them. It is the same in science. It took the prepared mind of an Einstein to cultivate the theory of relativity. But once this insight had been articulated, it quickly gained universal acceptance in minds that could never have originated it.

7

Why Evil and Suffering?

Does our conception of God make sense?

So much for how we come to have our present-day understanding of God. We can sum it up by saying that there is just the one God; the Creator of the Universe and of ourselves; all-powerful; all-loving; all-good. Because God is everywhere, even within our very minds, he is also all-knowing.

But does such a portrait of God, assembled from the accumulated insights of past ages, tally with our own experience of life as we find it today? All-powerful? All-loving? All-good? How can that be compatible with the evil and suffering we find in the world, to say nothing of death? For many people, the existence of evil and suffering poses an insuperable problem to belief in a benign God.

It is no good us calling our investigation "the God Experiment" if it is aimed solely at finding evidence *in favor* of God's existence. Science doesn't operate like that. Science takes on board *all* the evidence – whether or not it appears to be in favor of, or contradictory to, one's chosen hypothesis. So we too must be even-handed over the evidence; we cannot in all intellectual honesty sweep the problem of evil and suffering under the carpet just because, on the face of it, the evidence does not seem to fit. It is to that problem we must now turn.

But before doing so, I should perhaps make it clear from the outset that I have no ready answers. Anyone who thinks they have cracked this perennial problem once and for all should, I suggest, imagine themselves face to face with someone terminally ill, suffering intense, unremitting pain; or someone who has just lost a loved one; or a survivor of the Nazi Holocaust; or someone whose life has been blighted by the sexual abuse they suffered as a child. Under any of those circumstances, would an intellectual argument about the problems of evil and suffering be of any help? Of course not. In those situations, what is required is the exercise of compassion, understanding, sympathy, and offers of practical assistance.

But that is not to say we just throw up our hands in helpless resignation, declaring it to be a mystery. A mystery it certainly is – using that term in the sense that we are confronted with something that we shall never comprehend in its entirety. But that is no excuse to remain silent. We must at least provide pointers as to where the truth might lie – some measure of rationalization.

Various approaches to the problem of evil

One generally hears talk of the problem of evil and suffering – "problem" in the singular. But I think it helpful to break this down into the problem of evil, and the problem of suffering. Inasmuch as evil can lead to suffering, there is clearly a link between the two. But not all suffering derives from human, moral evil; it can also come from natural causes – floods, fire, earthquakes, etc. For that reason, suffering merits separate treatment.

The first question we have to ask about evil is whether it is *real*? That sounds fatuous, I know. But it is a genuine concern. After all, it could be that the all-good God simply creates goodness, and evil is merely the absence, or comparative absence, of goodness – in certain places at certain times.

An absence can be experienced as something real in its own right. On a cold day, for example, we wrap up in lots of clothes. Why? To keep the cold out. But what do we mean by that? Cold is nothing but the absence of heat. It is not a case of "cold" getting in from outside; rather, it is heat being lost to the outside.

An objection to the notion that evil is nothing more than an absence of goodness is that such a proposed solution does not do justice to the sheer power and depth of evil in some of its manifestations. Can one really account for the deaths of millions of Jews in the Nazi concentration camps as simply an absence of goodness? When a crowd of soccer fanatics meets a handful of rival supporters, and mob hysteria takes over, to the point where they positively relish kicking and beating up the helpless victims, are we to put that down to an absence of goodness?

It has to be said that in extreme cases, an absence can indeed give all the appearance of something highly active in its own right. In the case of coldness, under severe conditions we talk of "frostbite" – the cold actively *bites* our toes. We talk of the scourge of poverty and the ravages of disease – even though these could equally, if not so forcefully, be described as due to an absence of money and an absence of health.

Nevertheless, it is customary to accord to evil a metaphysical status on a par with that of goodness. That being so, we must enquire as to its possible origins.

One solution is to postulate a rival divine power – an evil spirit challenging the goodness of God. The Bible in various places refers to the Devil. Satan is not to be thought of as a rival god, but as an angel created by God who subsequently rebelled against its maker. Though there have always been people who believe this to be literally true – that Satan is as real in the spirit world as God, others see the Devil as more in the nature of a useful fiction. By thinking of the power of evil personified, actively seeking to tempt and lure people into sin, one is placed on one's guard against such backsliding tendencies. It is when we laugh at the Devil, depicting him with red cape, horns, and a tail, that we are in danger of not taking genuine evil as seriously as we ought.

An alternative to thinking of two rival spiritual beings is to postulate that goodness and evil are both to be found within the one deity. In other words, the assumption that God is wholly good is not, in fact, correct. Just as there is a dark side to each of us, there is a dark side to God – a "shadow" side to him, as Carl Jung put it. Indeed, this was the solution to the problem of evil that Jung himself advocated. Goodness and evil both originated with God.

It is a possibility, but one that has commanded little acceptance. It is an understanding of God that appears to be at odds with the kind of God one personally encounters in one's prayer life – the kind of God personified for Christians in Jesus.

Which leaves us with one final possibility: God is wholly good – as traditionally believed – but he is placed in the position where he is somehow forced into allowing evil to have a place in his created world. It is not that he *wants* evil to be present; rather it is the case that there is some logical imperative that demands that it be there.

Is this not doing away with another of the supposed findings about the nature of God, namely that he is all-powerful? Not necessarily. When we say that God is all-powerful, that does not imply he is able to do logically impossible things. An omnipotent God is no more able to form four-sided triangles than we. So, the question is whether there might be some *logical* constraint under which God has to operate.

Love as the supreme principle

If one were to be allowed just one word to describe God's all-important characteristic – just one word – it would have to be *love*. His purpose for making us was that we might enter into a loving relationship with him.

This in itself is somewhat surprising. I don't know about you, but if I were a god intent on creating a world, I suspect my first consideration would be to ensure that the inhabitants of that world were happy and content; everyone would have a good time. The key word to describe my world would have to be "happiness," rather than "love." I would doubtless have been a very popular god!

On mature reflection, however, I might find myself regretting that policy. After all, it is common experience that people who have everything handed to them on a plate – those who live solely for the pursuit of pleasure – become insufferably spoiled and self-indulgent. So, perhaps God got it right when he elevated the concept of love to be the greatest good, rather than human happiness.

In any event, it is not up to us to choose what kind of God we deal with – any more than the scientist is called on to decide how the physical world "ought" to have been. Theologians deal with whatever God they are given, just as scientists are stuck with whatever world they find. Both have to try and understand what is presented to them. And what we are saying is that, for whatever reason, God's prime reason for creating us has to do with the concept of love rather than happiness or pleasure. That being the case, certain conclusions follow.

The necessity of freedom – and evil

One is that God must give us free will. Love is not something that can be forced, or coerced, or programmed into us. By its very nature – in order for it to have any value – it must be freely offered.

So far, so good. But if that will is to be really free, then there must be the possibility of us exercising it in a manner that is not in accordance with God's will. There must be the possibility of our withholding that love. This is a risk God has to take. Nor can it be just a *theoretical* possibility. When dealing with billions upon billions of people, if nobody in practice ever did reject God, then there would be grounds for doubting the reality of this "freedom." In order for free will to be genuine, there must surely be actual examples of people who do decline to respond to God's love; they turn their backs on God. And, in doing that, they turn their backs on the source of all goodness; they embrace evil.

The very manner in which we, as humans, evolved through natural selection, in itself almost inevitably ensures that some will not enter into a right relationship with God. In Chapter 5, we saw how we have inherited built-in genetic tendencies to behave in certain ways. These behavior traits evolved through their being able to confer some survival advantage on our ancestors. It is only to be expected that among these instinctive tendencies will be one inclining us toward selfish, self-centered behavior – a behavior trait likely to be conducive to the survival of our ancestors when food and shelter were in short supply. Note: we have a tendency to be self-centered rather than God-centered; we start life at a distance from God. This being so, it takes a positive, conscious decision on our part to recenter our lives on God in place of ourselves. In religious terminology, this is the act of repentance – the principal meaning of which is "a change of mind."

There are those who will not take that step. Indeed, *all of us* – believers and non-believers alike – from time to time turn our backs on God; we do our own thing; we misuse the freedom God has given us.

But, you might say, why does God make it so hard for us? Why not give us a natural tendency to love him and do his will, rather than the reverse? Just as a hypnotist might place a post-hypnotic suggestion into a subject's mind that on waking she will find herself infatuated with him, so God could have created us with an irresistible tendency to love him. True. But would such a contrived form of "love" be of value? Would the hypnotist think he had genuinely *won* the woman's love?

Obviously not. The same would be true of a falsely induced "love" of God.

In similar vein, one cannot have a God who makes us free, but is constantly overwhelming us with manifestations of his presence and power – for instance, through a never-ending succession of spectacular miracles. That would be another form of coercion. No. For our freedom to be genuine, God *must* adopt an approach to us that is veiled, that is somewhat hands-off. It is an approach that is clear to those of the faith – those who have eyes to see and ears to hear – but one that is open to other interpretations for those who exercise their freedom differently.

Thus, the so-called "free-will defense" of the all-good, all-loving, all-powerful God, is that in order for love to be given a chance, God has to permit the possibility of evil. This is something that is logically required. It is not God who creates the evil. The evil we find in the world is *our* responsibility; we create it whenever we decide to rebel against God.

Various approaches to the problem of suffering

Much suffering is caused by the evil we do. Indeed it almost becomes part of the definition of what constitutes an evil act: a deliberate act that knowingly and wilfully leads to someone suffering. But this addresses only part of the problem. Even without anyone perpetrating deliberate evil acts, there would still be much suffering from *natural* disasters – earthquakes, floods, tornadoes, etc. – as well as from disease and disability. How are we to account for suffering that comes from such sources?

One approach is to regard suffering as a punishment for sin. Accordingly, those who suffer most must have sinned most. From earliest times, this seemed an obvious way of trying to make sense of why some are called upon to suffer more than others. In the great Biblical exploration of suffering, this was the answer given to Job by his friends: all the calamities which befell him must be God's way of punishing him for having been particularly wicked. But Job would have none of it. He knew he wasn't perfect, but he wasn't *that* bad.

The idea of suffering as a punishment for sin was still around at the time of Jesus. But, like Job, Jesus rejected any such explanation. And in our own times, it seems perfectly obvious to us that those who suffer most are in no way more wicked than the rest.

In order to build a more constructive approach to the problem, we return to the question of free will. We have seen how free will is an essential prerequisite for being able to love God or love each other. But free will can only be exercised in an environment that is predictable. One must be able to anticipate the likely outcome of any course of action we might choose to take. That means the environment must be law-like – it must obey set rules. It must be a neutral environment – one that can be used for good or ill.

Not only that, it must be a *common* medium – one through which we can interact with other individuals. We make ourselves known to others through physical bodies operating in an environment that is jointly shared. It must be a world that does not bend its rules to meet the passing whim of any individual – an occurrence that might infringe the interests of some other individual who has just as much, or as little, right to have things *their* way. A gardener might want it to rain; a vacationer might prefer fine weather: there is no pleasing everyone. So the environment has to be even-handed. The world we jointly inhabit has to have a *nature of its own*. And that is how we find it.

But having said that, it follows that the inexorable working out of those laws of nature is bound from time to time to lead to some unfortunate consequences. One of the prices we have to pay for our freedom is that we are liable on occasion to fall foul of those laws.

Another point regarding the integrity of the world and its laws is this: just because we have declared that the greatest good is love – love between conscious living creatures – we must not immediately assume that this has to be the one and only purpose behind creation. Quite apart from its being a home for conscious, living beings like ourselves, the Universe might *in itself* be a source of delight to God. Just as God extends to us a measure of independence so that we can be ourselves, so he extends a measure of autonomy to the world – he lets it be. Natural disasters appear evil only when seen from *our* perspective. They might not be so regarded from God's perspective. They are but the natural outworkings of creation – creation doing its thing – and as such could be seen as good.

Of course, it might be objected that if God *really* loved us the way he is supposed to, he would not let terrible calamities, such as earthquakes and floods and volcanic eruptions, cause havoc to innocent people. He should on such occasions intervene. This brings us up against all the difficulties we encountered when dealing with the question of miracles. How for instance is God to stop an earthquake, or volcanic eruption, without it being obvious that some spectacular intervention to the smooth running of nature has taken place? If God were to intervene on a scale like that, it would not be long before everyone was forced to accept his existence. One would be coerced into a relationship with God, whether one liked it or not; the conditions necessary for freely offered love would be compromised. As we have noted before, it seems incumbent on God to have a somewhat hands-off approach. While he might offer a sign to someone who already has faith in him, and so is not *relying* on such a sign, it is a different matter performing signs and wonders on such a scale that unbelievers are likely to be forced to reconsider their position regarding their relationship to a possible God.

One has also to point out that sometimes – by no means always – but *sometimes*, when people fall victim to a natural disaster, they are not entirely innocent of responsibility for what happens to them. I am as guilty of this as any. As a young research physicist, I took up an appointment at the Radiation Laboratory, Berkeley, near San Francisco in California. Journeying out on the old Cunard ship *Mauretania*, I saw on the wall of the ship's library a photograph of San Francisco in the aftermath of the 1906 earthquake. It was a scene of total devastation – hardly a building left standing. What was I doing going to a place like that!? Geologists at the time were warning, as they do today, of the Big One to come. So, I knew the dangers involved – but still I went and stayed. The work opportunities were too tempting, the climate was inviting, the life so good. But throughout my time there I never completely shook off the sense of unease. I could not help thinking, if I get caught up in an earthquake, I cannot honestly blame the San Andreas Fault; it will be *my* fault, and mine alone. The same goes for anyone who settles in that area; the same goes for anyone who makes their home in Naples, under the shadow of Vesuvius, or in many other locations known to be dangerous.

Of course, it would be glib to say that people should simply avoid such places. Those living in Bangladesh know all about the dangers of living in a place prone to flooding, but they simply cannot afford to move – there is no other place for them to go. Similarly, the inhabitants of Assisi could be pardoned for thinking that the risk of an earthquake in that location was too small to worry about – until it happened in 1997. No, despite the fact that some people can be held responsible for a measure of contributory neglect of the potential dangers, we are still left with the problem of totally undeserved suffering.

The necessity of suffering

At this stage I find that a useful approach to the problem is to ask: what if there were *no* suffering in the world – no suffering whatsoever? What would be the knock-on consequences of such a seemingly idyllic world – the kind of world most people think God *ought* to have set up?

When one talks of "no suffering" one would, of course, have to include mental suffering as well as the physical kind. (Most suicides occur as a result of mental rather than physical suffering.) In such an imaginary world, everyone would have to have everything they could possibly want, otherwise they would suffer feelings of deprivation and inadequacy.

In such a world, how would one demonstrate one's love for another?

A moment's reflection reveals that this would be extremely difficult, if not impossible. Certainly one could have good times together – sex, and that sort of thing. But sex is enjoyable. How is the partner to know that one is doing it out of genuine love, and not just for the sake of one's own enjoyment? The same holds for any other activity that is pleasant.

Proof of love can come only from the way one reacts to the other's *needs* – the way one person puts himself or herself out for the other – how they *suffer* and *sacrifice* themselves in order to alleviate the suffering, and tend to the needs, of the other. In order to be convincing, the loving act has to be costly.

This can be seen in little things: for example, the way a mother will get up in the middle of the night – even though she is herself desperately tired – in order to feed and change the diaper of her baby. Or it is to be found in big things, like the way someone might devote his or her life to the care of a housebound wife or husband suffering from the ravages of multiple sclerosis, rather than going off to seek some other partner. One sees it each time someone gives a big donation (often one they can ill afford) to a charity devoted to the relief of refugees or victims of famine. Such self-denial is a demonstration of brotherly love for people one does not even know and has never met.

These, and countless other examples we can all bring to mind, serve to confirm that, in order for love to be manifest, there has to be self-sacrifice and suffering on the part of the giver, in response to the need and the suffering of the person to whom the love is offered. In a world without *any* suffering, there would be no needs to attend to, no suffering to alleviate, and no one would, in any case, be allowed voluntarily to take on any measure of suffering on behalf of another.

Earlier we saw that in order to have love as the highest principle, there had to be free will – and hence evil. Now we discover that a second condition to be satisfied is that the world must be such as to permit suffering.

The good side of pain

The next point to be made is that, although we naturally do all we can to avoid and alleviate suffering, there are circumstances where a measure of suffering may not in itself be a bad thing.

Take pain, for example. It would be simplistic to think of pain as if it were something *totally* bad. In fact, in its origins, it is a thoroughly positive, good thing – a vital part of our ability as an evolved animal to live and survive in an environment that can sometimes be hostile. Pain is a warning of danger and injury. The pain of placing a hand on a hot object is a warning to withdraw the hand to avoid injury. It needs to be unpleasant so as to make the avoidance of danger immediate and instinctive. Likewise, the prolonged headache we get when we bang our head on an overhanging tree branch provides us with an unpleasant memory to encourage us in future to take greater care to avoid such encounters. Internal pain, like that of appendicitis, is similarly a warning that something is wrong inside and needs attending to; without the pain we might be unaware of the condition.

Certain people have a medical condition that prevents them from experiencing pain. They lead a most hazardous life. Even we in our own small way know that when we have been to the dentist and had a local anaesthetic, it can be difficult, in the absence of feeling, to escape biting our tongue or cheek. Pain does have its uses.

But of course that does not go for *all* pain. Why, for instance, do we have to go on suffering the pain once the warning has been heeded? One grasps a hot object, then in response to the pain signal, lets go as quickly as possible. But if it was not quick enough and one gets burnt, the pain continues long after it has served its useful function. Or take the case of arthritis. What is the point of being continually reminded by the pain that the joints are swollen – when there is nothing that can be done about it?

As for the *degree* of pain, this can often seem out of proportion to the severity of the condition for which it acts as a warning. Toothache can be agonizing – but it is hardly life-threatening. On the other hand, many fatal diseases give no discomfort at all – at least not until the terminal stage. And what good comes from the suffering and pain of childbirth?

Then one is bound to ask questions about the suffering endured by animals – particularly that which arises in the course of evolution by natural selection (which we examine in Chapter 10). This is a process often dependent on predators catching and killing prey. If producing humans by this means is what God had in mind from the beginning, couldn't he have chosen some other way of doing it?

Of course, when talking about suffering in the animal kingdom, we have to be careful that we are not projecting too much of our own human experience on to the lower animals. Is a worm in pain when it writhes about, having been accidentally cut in two by the gardener's spade? Are both halves in pain (they are both writhing about)? Does the worm now have *two* minds – both in pain – or is it not mentally experiencing anything at all? Does the wriggling fish on the end of the hook feel pain? If we think that, why isn't angling banned?

How much of pain is in the *anticipation* of it? Is it not curious that a soccer player can come off the field at the end of a game to discover his leg grazed and bleeding – an injury he cannot even remember sustaining – and yet the same person recoils at the prospect of having a needle stuck in him at the doctor's? In one case the attention was distracted; in the other it was focused on what was happening. If we ourselves respond so differently to injury, depending on our state of mind at the time, can it not be argued that animals – possessing as they do a mental capacity far lower than ours – might feel very little? It is impossible to say. But the problem of suffering in the animal kingdom might not be as pressing as it is generally portrayed.

Other good things from suffering

We have seen that there are circumstances where pain can be a positively helpful warning of danger – not always, but in some cases. There are other good things that can arise out of suffering.

We have already noted that it provides others with the opportunity for ministering and showing love and concern. Suffering can be effective at bringing people together. As Paul says, we "weep with those who weep." People assist each other in all sorts of ways, whether it's helping out at the local hospital, raising money for a hospice, getting in the shopping for the housebound, etc. All these activities forge links between people.

One of the interesting aspects of the prayer experiment we spoke of at the beginning, is the group of patients that *know* they are being prayed for. Regardless of whether such prayers can be shown to bring about physical benefits in terms of improved recovery rates, it is already widely acknowledged that people derive much comfort and inner strength from knowing that they are being upheld in their troubles by the prayers of others.

Or take someone you don't particularly like, or indeed someone who is an adversary of some kind. On learning that they have fallen desperately ill, or that they are dying from some incurable disease, one's feelings toward them immediately change; one feels closer to them – more sympathetic. Suffering, to say nothing of death, can be a great reconciler.

As for the people suffering, there can be additional benefits for them too. If the highest good is to be in a loving relationship with God – that is what we are intended for – then evil is whatever keeps us from such a relationship with God. That being so, we cannot simply conclude that suffering of itself is necessarily evil. Certainly there are those, worn down by suffering, who become bitter, cynical, disillusioned, and turned in on themselves. These are the ones who lose their faith in the face of calamity. Suffering in these cases is truly an evil – a separation from God. But it does not have to be. Setbacks and difficulties can, and often do, lead to a *strengthening* of ties with God – a deeper realization of one's dependence on God, a more profound appreciation of his ultimate protection. That being so, the suffering that brought about this enriched relationship with God can surely not be called "evil." In itself, suffering is neither good nor evil; it is what we *make* of it, how we *use* it that determines whether it works for good or evil – whether we end up closer to, or further away from, God.

I would go so far as to say that all that is best, most valued, longest lasting, is born out of pain and suffering. Human suffering can destroy – or ennoble. Under the pain of suffering, one either becomes a bitter person, or a better person.

Pottery must be fired. Unless the clay pot is subjected to extreme heat, it will remain soft clay – no use to anyone. It has to pass the test of fire before it is transformed into something useful and valuable. Not all clay pots survive this test. An unsuspected flaw – a trapped air bubble – will cause the pot to explode and be destroyed.

So, too, must we be submitted to the test. One speaks of this world as a "vale of soul-making." It is through trials and tribulations that we develop our spiritual souls. And just as every piece of pottery that has ever been fired is still around today, in some form or other, so it seems to me our souls need to be fired in the kiln of suffering in order to become immortal.

Jesus uses the alternative metaphor of the vine being pruned. Just as the gardener prunes the vine to make it even more fruitful, so God prunes every fruitful branch with the pruning knife of suffering, in order that it too will yield yet more fruit.

All of us, from time to time, become so distracted by our daily activities, so wrapped up in the pursuit of our goals and ambitions, that we fail to keep things in perspective; we lose sight of the bigger picture – what life should *really* be about. We need to be jolted out of our routine. Often the only way this can happen is by our being made to suffer in some way. Many a life has been transformed – for the good – by a long, enforced spell in a hospital, or a brush with death. As C. S. Lewis put it:

> God whispers to us in our pleasures, speaks in our conscience, but shouts in our pains – it is his megaphone to rouse a deaf world.
>
> *The Problem of Pain*, C. S. Lewis

If things go well we are inclined to be complacent; it's human nature. It is so much harder to attend to one's devotions when all is well with our world. It is more likely to be in times of trouble that we are driven to our knees in prayer. Too many people regard God in the same way as a jet pilot regards the parachute – something to be called on in emergencies. So be it; if that is the only way God can jolt us out of our ill-considered self-satisfaction, let there be emergencies.

Too much suffering?

There are those who are quite happy to accept that good can come from suffering in the ways I have described. That is not the problem. The problem is the *degree* of suffering that some are called upon to endure. It is all very well saying there has to be suffering in order for there to be a demonstration of love. But why *so much* suffering? Particularly one thinks of the Holocaust; of the appalling suffering and death of many innocent children. Why did God not set *limits*?

In a sense he *has* set limits. Under great pain and torture, the victim is at some stage likely to pass out – to become unconscious. Secondly, there is the limit set by death. The sufferings of this mortal life will come to an end when we pass to the life beyond. We suffer, yes; but only for a time. Thirdly, there is the possibility that he has set limits we do not even recognize. For all we are aware, the "natural" state of affairs – that which would exist in the absence of a loving God – might have more in common with a never-ending, all-pervasive holocaust than the life we know. Only through God's influence is suffering contained within the limits found.

Such suggestions, valid though they might be, nevertheless carry little consolation. In the end, we simply have to face the fact that we are dealing with a God who never does things by half. We shall encounter further evidence of this in the next chapter when we have to come to terms with the vast scale of the Universe, and the seemingly unending stretches of time that had to pass before intelligent life put in an appearance. To our limited human minds, these defy the imagination. It is the same with suffering; what we on our restricted human scale would regard as excessive suffering might not seem so to God.

What we have to learn to accept is that this is no toy world. It is not a playschool, pretend type of world; it is the genuine article. We are not God's pets. As a general rule, pet-owners pamper and spoil their animals; they make sure they come to no harm, and never want for anything. But that is not how God is with us. He has something more challenging in mind. He wants us to be strong, to stand on our own two feet, take responsibility for our own destiny, and to some extent be independent of him – so that we can, of our own free choosing, respond to him in a loving relationship. This is not to claim a loving relationship between equals, but certainly something much richer than the dependence of a pet on its owner. However, in order to acquire this distinctive individuality, we must expect to go through tough times and suffer hard knocks. If a little sacrifice and suffering is a small indication of love, then profound suffering is a sign of a deep love.

In this context, it is important to recognize that there are two distinct types of evil: the sort that causes suffering, and a second sort that leads to *triviality*. We humans are wonderfully complex beings, capable of great depth and spirituality. But it has to be said that many of us live our lives at a very superficial level. Few ever come close to fulfilling their true potential. This has to be seen as a waste of the life that has been given us, and as such it is an evil – an affront to our Creator.

A measure of suffering might be the only way to trigger an exploration of this potential, and hence avoid the evil of the trivial, misspent, wasted life. The greater the intensity at which one lives, the greater the love one has to offer. The other side of the coin, of course, is that an intensely lived life could result in a deeper exploration of one's potential for causing harm – evil of the first kind. The two go hand in hand. But living an *intense* life, rather than a trivial and superficial one must, in itself, be good.

Instinctively we know this to be the case. We have only to think of the way we are prepared to take risks in order to enjoy a more fulfilled life. One cannot ski without running the risk of a broken leg; one cannot learn to ride a bike without the risk of falling off; one cannot climb a mountain without the risk of a fall; one cannot enjoy foreign travel without the attendant dangers of possible plane or train crashes, or the boat sinking. These risks we voluntarily undertake. Why? We do it in order to add zest and depth to our life. A rich life exacts a price – the richer the life, the higher that price.

Take marriage, for instance. There are many advantages to living alone. One can have the house or apartment just the way one wishes; eat what one likes, go out and do whatever one wants. There is no need to fit in with anyone else's plans. One can simply do one's own thing. But that is not what most people choose. Instead, they prefer to be involved in a loving relationship with someone else – even though that entails self-sacrifice, compromise, difficulties, and conflicts of interest. It is a price most of us are prepared to pay. Even having gone through the traumatic upheaval and unhappiness associated with divorce, people are still liable to seek out a new partner with whom to share their lives. This surely testifies to there being something about a loving relationship that is far more rewarding than a life of private self-indulgence – it is something worth suffering for.

In considering whether the suffering in this life is excessive, another point to take on board is that all suffering is relative. If it were all to be scaled down – in response to our protests that at present it is too severe – we would quickly readjust our sense of what was, and was not, "severe" suffering. We would soon end up convinced that the higher levels of suffering, even on this reduced scale, were excessive. Take a small child and the way it yells and screams when it falls down and grazes its knee. To hear it crying one would think it was the end of the world. It is only later, when in adulthood we have been visited with greater pains, that the severity of a grazed knee is viewed in a different perspective.

One final point about the severity of our sufferings. A few unfortunate people are driven to commit suicide. But for most people, this way out of suffering is never a serious option. Indeed, it is our natural reaction to fight tooth and nail to stay alive. For many people the greatest fear is the fear of death – the end of this life. Surely that in itself says something powerful about how we really value this life – despite the many complaints we make about it.

Where lies justice?

The problem of suffering is seen in its starkest form when it involves the plight of children:

> One day when we came back from work, we saw three gallows rearing up in the assembly place, three black crows. Roll call. SS all around us, machine guns trained: the traditional ceremony. Three victims in chains. . . . All eyes were on the child. He was lividly pale, almost calm, biting his lips. The three victims mounted together on to the chairs. The three necks were placed at the same moment within the nooses. . . .
>
> The child was silent.
>
> "Where is God? Where is he?" someone behind me asked.
>
> At a sign from the head of the camp, the three chairs tipped over.
>
> Total silence throughout the camp. . . .
>
> The two adults were no longer alive. Their tongues hung swollen, blue-tinged. But the third rope was still moving; being so light, the child was still alive. . . .
>
> For more than half an hour he stayed there, struggling between life and death, dying in slow agony before our eyes. And we had to look him full in the face. He was still alive when I passed in front of him. His tongue was still red, his eyes were not yet glazed.
>
> Behind me I heard the same man asking:
>
> "Where is God now?"
>
> And I heard a voice within me answer him:

"Where is he? Here he is – He is hanging here on the gallows."

(E. Wiesel, *Night*, trans. S. Rodway, Fontana/Collins, 1972, pp. 76–7)

We are reminded here of the God who dwells inside each and every one of us – the Holy Spirit; the God who suffers when we suffer.

The suffering and death of small children is the single most powerful piece of evidence our God experiment has come up with that appears to refute the idea of an all-loving, all-powerful God of Mercy and Justice. In such cases, there is manifestly no justice to be seen. It strikes at the very heart of the God hypothesis.

At least, it strikes against the God of "half-baked" Christianity. By that I mean a belief that is basically Christian – Jesus was the best man who ever lived, and we all ought to follow his example – but a form of Christianity without the resurrection, without a belief in life beyond death. That kind of religious belief, so popular these days, so apparently reasonable, simply does not stand up to close examination; to me it makes no sense. It is manifestly clear that some people are subject to manifold injustice in this life. I am at a loss to see how a belief in a loving God – one who is supposed also to be a God of justice – can be sustained without there being something beyond this earthly life. God has to have the means whereby he can compensate for all that is wrong with this life. It is for this reason I devoted a whole chapter to sifting the evidence for the resurrection of Jesus. It really does play a key role in the whole scheme of things.

Now, it will be objected that this is simply the "jam tomorrow" scenario – a product of wishful thinking. Remember how Freud claimed that if you wished for something hard enough, your unconscious could trick you into believing it's true. But why shouldn't it be "jam tomorrow"? What kind of pessimism is it that assumes that happy endings must by their very nature be an illusion? If God is all-powerful, and all-loving, and a God of justice, then this is something he *can* do, and indeed is *bound* to do.

How can a life hereafter adequately compensate for the intense suffering that some individuals have to undergo? Intense their suffering might be, but one thing is certain: it is finite; it comes to an end. The life beyond death is *infinite* – and there is no comparing the finite to the infinite.

One point that puzzles many over this Christian belief in resurrection is the way the creed declares: "I believe in the resurrection of the body." How can this be? How are all the pieces of a person's body to be gathered together again once it has decomposed and been eaten by worms and gone to make up the bodies of the worms now – or, alternatively, when it has been reduced to ashes and gases in the fires of the crematorium?

This is to misunderstand what is meant by that credal statement. It is not a question of gathering together the atoms of the old body. When it says that we believe in the resurrection of the body it is not talking about the *physical* body. It means that in the life to come, each of us will retain our *individuality*; we shall not be lost in some kind of anonymous, homogenized spiritual "soup." We shall still be recognizable as ourselves.

Why then talk about "resurrection of the body" like that? It is here we need to remind ourselves that, in this earthly life, it is only through the possession of physical bodies that we distinguish one person from another. We recognize each other from our physical appearance, the sound of the voice, and so on. To some extent that is how it must be in the next life; we shall need a "body" of sorts. Not *this* body – not a physical body, but a body of some kind.

As an analogy, take an encyclopedia. One might conjure up a mental picture of a whole shelf full of books. Alternatively it could be in the form of a CD-ROM disk. All that information – exactly the same information – repackaged in different form. That is what one means by the resurrection of the body. Each of us is to be likened to a bundle of information. At present that information is packaged as a physical body. But it doesn't have to be. It can be passed on and repackaged in a different form – a spiritual body.

I have spoken specifically of Christian belief. Other religions, of course, differ in varying degrees with regard to what, if anything, lies beyond death. Hinduism, for example, speaks of reincarnation – coming back to this world in a different form – rather than resurrection. What *is* remarkable is that all the major religions – East and West – are agreed that there is something about us as individuals that continues beyond death – a persistence of identity – and the quality of that extension of life depends to some extent on how we live *this* life. Death marks a transition, rather than an end. As such it is not to be feared.

God's involvement in suffering

So far we have tended to confine our thoughts to our own engagement with suffering, how we cope with it, and the possible effects it has on us. But that extract from Wiesel's book raises the question of God's involvement.

In the first place it has to be said that God is not one to stand back and let us get on with it alone. Religious believers are convinced that God hears our prayers. That's why we pray to him for the sick. The prayer experiment we mentioned at the start might be able to throw some light on this when the results become available. It is not that we expect such prayers for recovery always to be answered in the way we would like. God is the only one who knows the full circumstances. In his greater wisdom he might realize that the long-term well-being of the person might better be served some other way than by a straight "yes" to our request. Regardless of how he might respond, however, we are convinced that God is not impervious to the suffering. Either he alleviates it, or he strengthens us to help us get through the trial – if there is no other way.

For Christians, the ultimate evidence for God's involvement in, and concern for, human suffering is to be found in the life and the sufferings of Jesus. If Jesus truly were the Son of God, as is claimed, then God has first-hand experience of what we are going through. We look at the figure of Christ on the cross, and we ask: "If that isn't love, what is?" God is not a God who just offers encouragement from the sidelines; he's in the thick of it with us – assuring us, through the resurrection of Jesus, that this is the way to ultimate victory and the accomplishment of his purposes.

Ultimate mystery

That really is as much as I can say about how one might begin to try and make a little sense out of the mystery of suffering. All it amounts to is a few pointers as to where a hint of a solution might lie – why the existence of evil and of suffering is not *necessarily* against the idea of an all-good, all-powerful, all-loving God. The God experiment remains intellectually viable.

But let us be clear, no matter how hard we strive to come up with answers, we are faced with mystery – something that lies ultimately beyond the power of human reasoning. This much is made clear in the story of Job we mentioned earlier. Job, the good God-fearing man upon whom befalls a series of terrifying calamities, in the end comes face to face with God. He has demanded an explanation for his troubles. We are thinking, "At last we are to receive the answer straight from the mouth of God." But no. Instead of an answer, Job is bombarded with a whole succession of questions from God:

> Where were you when I laid the earth's foundation?
> Tell me if you understand.
> What marked off its dimensions? Surely you know!
> Who stretched a measuring line across it?
> On what were its footings set, or who laid its cornerstone –
> While the morning stars sang together, and all the angels
> shouted for joy? . . .
> Can you bind the beautiful Pleiades?
> Can you loose the cords of Orion?
> Can you bring forth the constellations in their seasons or lead
> out the Bear with its cubs?
> Do you know the laws of the heavens?
> Can you set up God's dominion over the earth?
>
> (Job 38)

And so the questions come, thick and fast – over fifty of them – all designed to expose how little humans know about anything. Job can do nothing but humbly accept that in the final analysis, suffering is beyond understanding; it is something we must bear patiently, trusting that the loving, all-powerful God will, in his own time and in his own way, ensure that all will be well.

We are like children in the face of God. How often are children bewildered by, and resentful of, the rules laid upon them by their parents? In later life they might be able to look back with the benefit of hindsight and see the good that came out of being forced to do home-work, being made to acquire tidy habits, clean their teeth, not live on a diet of chocolate, take nasty-tasting medicine when ill, go to bed at a set time, and so on. But at the time, it was simply a case of getting on with it, trusting that one's parents were acting in a loving, caring way.

So it is with us and God. A God who was fully comprehensible to the mind of man would be a product of the mind of man. The fact that we do *not* fully understand God strikes me as the mark of his indepen-dence – his independent reality. He is not the sort of God anyone would have been inclined to dream up out of their own imagination. He is too problematic for that.

8

Our Place in the Scheme of Things

We have seen that a key feature in the defense of a loving, good, and all-powerful God is that the rationale for our existence is founded on a loving relationship with God. Once that premise is granted, we begin to see how there might have to be a measure of evil and suffering. Without them, love would be unable to flourish.

But that in turn raises another difficulty: are we really expected to believe that the Creator of the entire world takes that kind of personal interest in each and every one of us? To put it bluntly, given all that has been revealed to us about the world through modern astronomical investigations, can we possibly regard ourselves as *that* important?

It is interesting that in the answer to Job we quoted just now, God began by directing Job's attention to the heavens. It was God's way of cutting him down to size. So it must be with our God experiment. It is time to resume our study of the physical world, but now to expand its scope to take in the Universe – the grand overall stage on which we live out our lives. What kind of place is it? What are the implications of modern astronomy for the significance of human life?

A quick guide to what is out there

On looking up at the sky we see the Sun, Moon, and stars. They appear to be revolving round us once a day. But looks are deceptive. As is well known, it is really the Earth that is revolving on its axis once a day. Only the Moon actually orbits us. It is our satellite, the Earth having eighty-one times the mass of the Moon. As heavenly bodies go, the Moon is not of great interest.

Much more important is the Sun. Although it looks about the same size as the Moon in our sky, apparent size is affected by the distance of

the object from us. The Sun is much farther away than the Moon –
400 times farther. In fact, the Sun is so large, one million Earths would
fit inside it. It is we who orbit the Sun, not the reverse.

The Sun is mostly made up of the two lightest elements, hydrogen
and helium. It is a ball of fire, its heat being derived from the nuclear
fusion of its hydrogen into helium (as happens in nuclear-fusion
bombs), followed by the progressive fusion of the helium and other
products to produce yet more complex nuclei. The Sun has been burning like this for the past 5,000 million years. It has about another 5,000
million years to go before eventually running out of fuel.

Turning our attention to the stars, we find that a few of them continually change their position against the general star background.
These "wandering stars" are not really stars at all; they are planets. Like
the Earth, these eight other planets orbit the Sun, and shine by light
reflected from the Sun. The planets and the Sun together make up the
Solar System.

Stars (as distinct from planets) are balls of fire just like the Sun. In
fact, the Sun is itself a star – a medium-sized one. The reason the
others look so small is on account of their great distances from us. On
a scale where the distance from the Earth to the Sun is represented by
one meter, and that to the most distant planet in the Solar System
(Pluto) is forty meters, the nearest star to us (Proxima Centauri)
would be at 250 kilometers. Putting it another way: light travels at
300,000 kilometers per second (or 186,000 miles per second). At that
speed, sunlight takes eight and a half minutes to reach us, whereas
starlight from Proxima Centauri takes just over four years.

Recognizing that stars are in themselves suns, it becomes natural to
enquire whether any of them have planets going round them in the
same way as the Sun does. From our understanding of how the Solar
System originally formed out of a gas cloud (more of this later), it
would seem that other stars, forming in the same way, would also be
likely to have planets. In fact, at the time of writing, about forty planets
going round other stars have now been detected.

How many stars are there? A hundred thousand million, gathered
together in a great flattened, swirling disc called a galaxy. That's twenty
stars for each man, woman, and child on Earth. We are positioned

about two-thirds of the way out from the center of the disc. On a clear, dark night, away from the glare of street lights, one can see a faintly glowing band stretching across the sky from one horizon to the other, called the Milky Way. This is the Milky Way Galaxy seen end-on from our position lying in the disc. Looking away from the Milky Way one is directing one's line of sight out of the plane of the disc where there are fewer stars.

What lies beyond the Galaxy? Other galaxies. How many? A hundred thousand million – the same number as the average number of stars in each galaxy. So that is 20 *galaxies* for every man, woman and child on Earth. Adding together all the stars of all the galaxies, the total number in the Universe is approximately the same as the number of grains of sand in a sandcastle five miles high by five miles wide and five miles long. (I had to do some messy experiments on the kitchen table, sub-dividing piles of sand and counting individual grains in order to arrive at that estimate!)

The galaxies occur in clusters. Our own galaxy belongs to one called the Local Group – a collection of about thirty galaxies gravitationally bound to each other. On a larger scale still, clusters are associated into even larger superclusters. These are thought *not* to be gravitationally bound to each other, though clearly their close positions relative to each other must have arisen from their mutual gravitational influence.

Clusters and superclusters of galaxies are found at very great distances from us. Some lie so far from us, it takes almost 12,000 million years for their light to reach us. The Universe is BIG.

The place of humans – the Galileo affair

So much for our whistle-stop tour of the Universe. Where do we humans fit into it?

There was a time when it was thought that we were at the center of the Universe – it had been created exclusively as our home. Just as each newly born baby starts life thinking that everything revolves around it, and has subsequently to learn better, this was a misconception that the human race as a whole had to grow out of. It was a painful transition – one associated above all with the name of Galileo.

Throughout this book I have been at pains to point out that the religious quest has more in common with a scientific investigation than most people suspect. Yet in the case of Galileo, it appears their approaches could not be more different – one doggedly holding on to a traditional, outmoded viewpoint, the other open-mindedly adapting to whatever new data are found. And that is not all. Here we have the church actually trespassing on the other's preserve – in outright opposition to the advance of science. The story is gleefully peddled of how Galileo was imprisoned and tortured for stating that it was the Earth that went round the Sun, rather than the reverse. Some versions of the legend even have it that, having been forced to recant his views, he stamped his foot on the ground, defiantly declaring, "And yet it moves!" Whereupon he was cast into the dungeons and had his eyes put out.

But what *really* happened?

It had been Copernicus who in 1543 had originally come up with the new cosmology based on the Sun being at the immovable center of the cosmos. His ideas did not catch on because they did not seem to make much sense according to the science of his time. For example, if the Earth were moving, why didn't all the loose things on its surface, to say nothing of the clouds, get left behind? Not only that, where was the force keeping the Earth going? We have to recall that in those days, they did not have the benefit of a good understanding of mechanics – something that was later to come from Galileo himself and from Newton. At that time it was not appreciated that no force is needed to keep something moving – provided there is no friction or air resistance. In addition it has to be said that, in terms of mathematical simplicity, the new theory offered no advantage over the old one. Copernicus was still wedded to the idea that the planets had to move in circles. However, the experimental data on planetary motions did not fit with the idea of each planet moving in a simple circle about the Sun as center. So Copernicus proposed instead that each planet moved in a circle, the center of which moved in a circle about the Sun. This motion based on composite circular motions was complicated. Only later was it replaced by the simpler idea of planets moving in ellipses – an insight due to Kepler. For these reasons the ideas of Copernicus caused little stir at the time.

Then in 1609, Galileo built one of the newly invented telescopes, trained it on the sky, and started gathering data on the moons of Jupiter, the phases of Venus, etc. These observations lent weight to the Copernican world-view. At this stage, Galileo's problem was not the reaction of the church, but that of his scientific colleagues. Some of them were so deeply suspicious of the distorting glasses in the newfangled telescope, they refused even to look through the instrument. They were also concerned that the mechanics they had been teaching all their lives now appeared to be jeopardized.

The response of the clerics on the other hand was altogether more favorable. The Jesuit mathematicians of the Roman College were quickly convinced. Galileo, a devout Catholic himself, was delighted with this. Inevitably some church officials were worried that the authority of Scripture was being called into question. They required of Galileo that he speak of his theory as a hypothesis, rather than as an incontrovertible established fact. Galileo had no trouble going along with this. The Pope himself had a great interest in natural philosophy. He wrote a letter of congratulation to Galileo, and even a poem celebrating the discoveries made by the telescope.

With Galileo now getting on in years, his friends, including the Pope, encouraged him to write a book setting out his findings – the very book that was later to get him into hot water. The Pope even asked Galileo to include in it an argument of his own. This was to the effect that God, being all-powerful, could arrange to make it *look* as though the Earth went round the Sun, whereas in reality, the Earth was fixed and it was the Sun, and everything else, that went round it. A rather silly argument, and one that Galileo must have been reluctant to include, but he dutifully complied.

The book, *Dialogue Concerning the Two Principal Systems of the World*, passed the church's censors. In fact two lots of censors were involved, one in Florence, the other in Rome. Unusually, it was written in the vernacular Italian rather than the academic Latin that would have been conventional for such a work. This made it instantly accessible to the public at large. It was published in 1632, and immediately caused a sensation. Everyone was talking about it.

But within a year, Galileo was on trial for heresy. So, what went wrong?

In the first place it has to be said that while Galileo managed to get his book passed by the censors, it was only with difficulty. Galileo was a persistent man. He had badgered the censors unremittingly, winning more and more concessions. He had worn them down. But more importantly, although he had presented the Copernican view as a hypothesis – as had been required – it was hardly a balanced discussion. The spokesman for the theory, a character called Salviati, completely overwhelmed his rival in the dialogue, Simplicio, who had the admittedly unenviable task of defending the earlier cosmology based on the ideas of the Greek philosophers.

Worse than that, though, was the manner in which Galileo had chosen to deal with the argument advanced at the request of the Pope. This he had put into the mouth of the discredited Simplicio. Simplicio introduces it by saying that this was "a solid doctrine that I once heard from a most eminent and learned person, and before which one must fall silent. . . ." No reader could have failed to recognize that this must be the Pope himself. Salviati goes on to demolish the argument with scorn – thus holding the Pope up to ridicule. This was not sensible. From what we know of the character of the Pope – a rather vain and conceited man – this was too much. Not only was he personally being lampooned, but he was doubtless advised that his very Papal office was being treated with contempt. Hence the trial.

Galileo was himself in no doubt as to why he had suffered this reversal of fortune. Years later he wrote in a letter:

> I hear from Rome that His Eminence Cardinal Antonio and the French Ambassador have spoken to his Holiness and attempted to convince him that I never had any intention of committing so sacrilegious an act as to make fun of his Holiness, as my malicious foes have persuaded him and which was the major cause of all my troubles.

As for the later stories of imprisonment and torture, these were but gross distortions. Galileo never saw the inside of a prison; even during his trial he lived in a comfortable five-room suite with a servant provided to attend to his needs. Admittedly, there had been a nominal threat of torture – but this had been merely an archaic form of words, since it was actually illegal for someone of Galileo's age to be tortured. His punishment was merely that of having to recite the penitential psalms. In the event, he was even excused this when his daughter, a Carmelite nun, was permitted to say them on his behalf.

Nevertheless, it has to be said that the church emerged from the whole sorry business with little credit. No one can today read without anger the words of the infamous abjuration by which Galileo was forced to renounce his support for the Copernican view:

> I, Galileo, son of the late Vincenzio Galilei, Florentine, aged seventy years, arraigned personally before this tribunal and kneeling before you, Most Eminent and Lord Cardinals Inquisitors-General against heretical pravity throughout the entire Christian Commonwealth . . . with sincere heart and unpretended faith I abjure, curse, and detest the aforesaid errors and heresies. . . .

But having said that, it is important, nevertheless, to keep things in perspective. The important lesson we learn from this account is that the Galileo affair was not the science-versus-religion conflict it was later cracked up to be. It arose more directly out of a private, personal conflict – one in which a headstrong, tactless Galileo had bruised the feelings of a rather vain, self-important Pope – the latter feeling, with some justification, that his trust had been betrayed by a one-time friend.

The fact that the Copernican shift in understanding of the structure of the world did *not* have any crucial theological significance is more than adequately borne out by the fact that there had already been an *earlier* shift in cosmology. It had been just as significant as that introduced by Copernicus, and yet it had produced no clerical backlash whatsoever. I refer to the fact that the cosmology being defended by the church at Galileo's trial was not in any case the cosmology of the Bible. Interpreting the Bible literally we are presented with a three-tiered Universe. It consists of a flat Earth; above it is the Heavenly realm; below it is Hell. But what the church came later to defend was a cosmology in which the Earth was a sphere, around which circled the Sun, Moon, and stars. It was a cosmology taken over from the Greek philosophers when the new religion of Christianity came into contact with Greek culture and ideas. How did this happen? When did it happen? It is hard to say. It was a process of natural assimilation and gradual change. Of one thing we are sure: it was a change of cosmology that took place without any fuss or bother. This being so, one cannot help but wonder whether, given men of different temperaments, the whole unfortunate Galileo affair might never have happened – thereby making this diversion into history unnecessary.

The place of humans – the present day

What was learned from Copernicus and Galileo, and what has since been confirmed and extended by modern astronomy, is that we are emphatically not at the center of the Universe. We live on one of nine planets circling the Sun. The Sun is just a medium-sized star. It occupies an undistinguished position in the outer suburbs of the Milky Way Galaxy. Our Galaxy is an ordinary galaxy – one of a cluster of galaxies called the Local Group. That, in its turn, is a not very important member of a supercluster – the supercluster being one of many others. These have been observed out to a distance of 12,000 million light years (a *light year* being the distance traveled by light in a year). This is called the *observable Universe*. For all we know, the observable Universe might be but a small part of the *overall Universe* – with galaxies lying beyond the present reach of our telescopes – perhaps out to infinity.

In the face of such immense numbers and size, it is understandable that we ourselves should feel small and unimportant.

We have to accept that on an astronomical scale we have virtually no effect on anything – it is we who go round the Sun; the Sun does not go round us. For all the effect we have on the motion of the stars and planets, we might just as well not exist – we are not important.

But "importance" is a slippery concept. It derives its significance from its context. . . .

The thinking reed

Consider the following question: "We have just agreed that physically the Sun is more important than us. Most of us would like to think of ourselves as being important. Does that mean we would prefer to swap places with the Sun?"

It does not take much thought to realize that the answer is emphatically "No." It is all very well being important, but if you do not *know* that you are important, what's the point? And of course, the Sun does not know that it is important; it does not *know* anything; it is not conscious (at least, we strongly suspect that it is not!).

It is when we introduce the notion of *consciousness* – our ability to be aware of things, and to have thoughts and feelings – that the whole understanding of what counts – what is and is not important – gets overturned. No one put this better than the French mathematician and philosopher, Blaise Pascal, when he wrote:

> Man is the feeblest reed in existence, but he is a thinking reed . . .
> though the universe were to destroy him, man would be more
> noble than his destroyer, for he would know that he was dying,
> while the universe would know nothing of its own achievement.

> (*Pensées*, 1, 6)

We noted earlier that no one understands how consciousness comes about. All we can say is that it appears to have something to do with the complexity of the brain. Our brain is admittedly not big on the astronomical scale, but it is probably one of the most complex structures to be found anywhere in the Universe. In view of the accompanying consciousness which comes about at some level of complexity, it would seem that in physical terms what is more relevant than size is *degree of complexity*. As far as organized complexity is concerned, the Sun must count as an extraordinarily simple object compared to the human brain.

If the size aspect is to be discounted in favor of complexity and accompanying consciousness, then it is perhaps not so absurd after all that God would take a particular interest in us.

Our importance in relation to life elsewhere in the cosmos

We are, nevertheless, still faced with the vast number of other stars and planetary systems, and the possibility that they too sustain life. Here it is not being suggested that they are populated by humans – with two legs, two arms, two eyes, height between five and six feet, etc. As already mentioned, it is most unlikely that evolution would have traced out exactly the same steps there as it has done here on Earth. But many scientists believe that other planets are likely to be home to life forms that, although they may look nothing like us, are at least as advanced in intellectual terms as we are.

This is not a consensus view among scientists. As we shall see in Chapter 10, there were many hurdles to be overcome before evolution could produce us out of what was originally inanimate chemicals on the surface of Earth. It might be that the chances of life forms as advanced as ourselves emerging are exceedingly remote – even given the vast number of locations throughout the Universe where theoretically it could have happened. Indeed, it might have happened only once in the history of the Universe.

The only way to settle this issue is to make direct contact with alien civilizations. To this end searches are being made of the heavens under the SETI (Search for Extra-Terrestrial Intelligence) program for signs of intelligent radio signals being beamed at us – to date without success. Some would argue that there is unlikely to be intelligent life very close to us or we would have evidence of their having visited our planet – despite the fact that even our neighboring stars could hardly be called "very close." (Here I am discounting UFO claims, crop circles, alien abductions, and so on.)

My own view is that although, for all we know, intelligent life in the cosmos might be unique to planet Earth, that smacks of arrogance – the kind of arrogance that led us initially to think that we were at the center of the Universe. I am quite happy to accept that the cosmos is teeming with life forms as intelligent as we are – *as* intelligent, but probably not much more so (for reasons I shall be explaining later when we deal with evolution).

Proof of the existence of other intelligent life forms would somewhat downgrade one's own sense of significance in the grand scheme of things. But not especially so. One can already feel the sense of being lost in a crowd walking down Oxford Street in London. If, in ways unknown to us, God is able to take a personal interest in every man, woman, and child on Earth, then clearly God's mind does not work in the same way as ours; he is not subject to the same limitations. Granted he can perform this feat, it is hard to see what would set a limit on his ability to accord individual attention to everyone – including those living on other planets – no matter how astronomical the number might be.

That said, the thought that there might be lots more intelligent life forms out there in the cosmos is a sobering one. But then again, when did a little humility do any harm?

9

How It All Began

Having seen what the Universe is like, it is only natural to ask how it got to be like that. Where did it all come from? This is where our investigation turns the spotlight on God as the Creator of the world. We take a look at modern cosmology to see what insights it might provide on that particular aspect of God's supposed relationship to the world. In particular, we need to examine recent claims that the Universe could have originated itself spontaneously – of its own accord. Were that the case, would we need a Creator at all?

Evidence for the Big Bang

It is generally accepted that the Universe began with a Big Bang. I have already briefly pointed out the various types of evidence that led to that conclusion. Let us examine them in somewhat greater detail:

(i) *The recession of the galaxies.* On looking at distant clusters of galaxies, we note that they are receding from us. We can deduce this from the color of the light they give out. We find that it is systematically shifted toward the red end of the spectrum, i.e., toward light of lower frequencies. This is somewhat similar to the way the siren noise emitted by a speeding police car or ambulance is heard to have a lower pitch when the vehicle is receding from us than when it is stationary or approaching us. The lower pitch is due to the sound waves being stretched out by the vehicle's recessional speed from us, and stretched out waves correspond to lower frequencies. Light is subject to an equivalent effect: if a source of light is receding from us, then the frequencies will be reduced by a ratio dependent on the speed of recession – in other words, the light appears to be redder. And this is what we find with the light received from the stars belonging to distant galaxy clusters. It is known as the *cosmological red shift*.

Combining our knowledge of how far away the galaxy clusters are, with the estimate of recessional speed based on the measured red shift, we come across a remarkably simple relation: the red shift is proportional to distance. Thus, for example, a cluster that is ten times further away than another will be receding from us ten times faster. This proportionality of recession speed with distance is called *Hubble's Law* – after its discoverer, the American astronomer Edwin Hubble.

It is not difficult to see that a world obeying Hubble's Law has a remarkable feature: namely, that at some time in the past, all the contents of the Universe were together at the same point. To see this, imagine a video recording has been made of the movements of the galaxy clusters over time. We now play the tape backward. In doing so, we note all the clusters coming toward each other. One that is ten times farther away than another has ten times farther to go to reach us – but it is going at ten times the speed. This means it arrives at exactly the same time as the other. And the same holds for all the galaxies – they all arrive at the same time. Now playing the tape the correct way we find that all the contents of the Universe start out from the same place. Suddenly, it all expands away – the faster material traveling the farthest distance from us in any given time. And that is precisely what we find today – the clusters obeying Hubble's Law.

The recessional motion of the galaxies, with its characteristic dependence on distance, is therefore the first piece of evidence pointing to the violent beginning of the Universe.

(ii) *The cosmic microwave background radiation.* The second argument in favor of the Big Bang theory comes from another quarter. It was argued by the Russian-born physicist George Gamow that the violent Big Bang ought to have been accompanied by an intense burst of electromagnetic radiation (in much the same way as a nuclear explosion is accompanied by a blinding flash of light). Moreover that radiation should still be about in the Universe today – there being nowhere else for it to have gone. By now it would have cooled down and become a form of radiation our eyes cannot pick up – hence we do not get blinded by the light from the Big Bang every time we look up at the night sky. Nevertheless there are types of equipment capable of detecting it. Two American physicists, Arno Penzias and Robert Wilson, were the first to observe it. They did so with equipment developed for radio communication rather than as a device for investigating cosmology. It was a discovery made by accident. They found that, regardless of where they pointed the antenna in the sky, they were plagued by an annoying "background signal." This turned out to be Gamow's predicted radiation.

Indeed, to pick up this radiation it is not necessary to own the specialized type of equipment used by Penzias and Wilson. A domestic TV set makes a good "Big Bang detector." When not tuned to the dominant signal of a broadcast station, it displays the familiar "snowy" picture. One in 100 of those "snowflakes" is due to the TV aerial picking up the remnant of the Big Bang fireball. (That snowy picture could well be more interesting than some of the programs broadcast.) The radiation is now called the *cosmic microwave background radiation*.

(iii) *Primordial nuclear synthesis.* A further piece of evidence in favor of the Big Bang hypothesis comes from a study of the chemical composition of interstellar gas. In order to see how this comes about, let me begin by introducing some basic atomic physics:

An atom consists of a particle, the *nucleus*, surrounded by smaller particles, *electrons*, moving outside it. It is sometimes likened to a miniature Solar System with the nucleus taking the part of the Sun and the electrons being the planets. But that is not a particularly appropriate analogy; the electrons do not actually move in smooth continuous orbits like planets. Suffice it to say that they are situated outside the nucleus. The nucleus itself is made up of smaller particles: the *neutron* and the *proton*. These are very similar to each other, apart from the proton carrying a positive electric charge whereas the neutron has none – it is electrically neutral. It is the attraction between the positive electric charge on the protons and the negative electric charge on the electrons that keeps the electrons close to their nucleus rather than drifting off somewhere else.

The different kinds of atom in nature differ in two ways: the number of electrons they contain (hydrogen has one, helium two, carbon six, oxygen eight, etc.); and also the number of protons and neutrons in their nucleus (hydrogen has a single proton, helium two protons plus one or two neutrons, and so on).

Turning to the Big Bang, we note that, at an early stage in its development, conditions were exceedingly hot, with everything moving about fast and violent collisions taking place. Under those conditions, matter was in the form of isolated protons, neutrons, and electrons. No sooner did neutrons and protons fuse together to form a heavier nucleus than they were smashed apart in some subsequent collision. And of course there were no atoms as such because no sooner did an electron form an attachment to a particular proton than it too was sent flying by a later impact.

But eventually (meaning about one minute after the instant of the Big Bang) things cooled down somewhat. Protons and neutrons that fused together could now stay together – later impacts not being violent enough to disrupt them. The newly formed nucleus could then undergo further fusion, adding more protons and neutrons. In that way more complex nuclei could form.

But the synthesis of the heavier nuclei was a race against time. The temperature was continuing to decline. This meant that eventually a point would be reached where the newly formed light nuclei would have insufficient energy to overcome the repulsive force between the positive electric charges on their constituent protons – and so would not be able to get in close enough to form further fusions. Not only that, with the expansion of the Universe, the density of particles was declining, and the chance of coming into collision with another nucleus was reducing. For a combination of both these reasons, the fusion processes came to an end after about 20 minutes. This yielded what we call the *freeze-out mix* of nuclei.

Three hundred thousand years later, conditions had further cooled to the point where the delicate bonds between nuclei and electrons could be established, thus forming the first atoms. These were atoms corresponding to the nuclei that made up the freeze-out mix.

Now one of the remarkable features of Big Bang theory is that it is able to calculate what the freeze-out mix should have been. This comes from information gained in laboratory experiments about the different types of nuclear reactions, and from a knowledge of the average density of matter in the Universe today. The latter tells us what the density must have been at any past epoch, and in particular what the frequency of the collisions must have been during the period of time available for the nuclear fusions to take place. The calculations indicate that the final mix issuing from the Big Bang should have consisted of 77 percent hydrogen and 23 percent helium (by mass), with traces of heavier nuclei.

What is found in practice? Here we have to be a little careful because in addition to the nuclear synthesis we have been considering – the so-called *primordial nuclear synthesis* – there has subsequently been further nuclear synthesis occurring in stars. Some of the products from *stellar nuclear synthesis* have been recycled into interstellar space and so, for our present purposes, form a contaminant. Nevertheless, when care is taken to examine regions of space thought not to be significantly contaminated, one finds almost exact agreement with theory.

(iv) *Time development of the Universe.* Finally, we note that when we view a distant object through our telescopes, the light being received by us today was actually emitted a long time ago. The further away the object, the longer it has taken for the light to reach us, and the further back in time we are effectively looking. What we find is that the Universe has developed and changed in character over time; it has not always been as it is today. These observations are consistent with the Big Bang hypothesis.

So, summing up our findings we can say that on the basis of (i) the Hubble recession of the galaxies, (ii) the cosmic microwave background radiation, (iii) the primordial nuclear synthesis, and (iv) the time development of the Universe, the Big Bang hypothesis has gained universal acceptance. As was explained in Chapter 1, any one of these indications, considered in isolation, might not in itself have been regarded as clinching proof. Rather, it is the combination of different, independent forms of evidence that makes for the convincing case.

When did it happen?

How long ago did the Big Bang take place? Knowing how fast the galaxies are receding from us, and how far distant this motion has taken them from us, we can work out how long they must have been traveling to have reached that distance by now. This simple calculation yields a figure of about 15,000 million years. But such an estimate needs to be handled with caution. The mutual gravity acting between everything in the Universe tends to slow down the expansion. A distant galaxy will not be receding from us today as fast as it was in the past. And having traveled faster in the past, it would have taken less time to reach its current distance from us. That in turn leads to a lowering of the time to the Big Bang. A figure of about 12,000 million years is probably more realistic.

The Big Bang as the origin of the Universe

The Big Bang was such a cataclysmic event, it is natural to suppose that it marked the origin of the Universe – the moment when it all came into being.

But it does not have to be that way. I have just said how, under the influence of mutual gravity, the recessional motion of the galaxies is slowing down. It is possible that there is enough material in the Universe to bring it all to a halt one day. What would happen then? Gravity will still be operating, so now all the matter of the Universe will be drawn together – everything being squashed down to a point. We call this possibility a *Big Crunch*.

What happens after the Big Crunch is anyone's guess. The Universe might go out of existence. The alternative is that it rebounds – we get a *Big Bounce*. What we have so far been referring to as the Big Bang might in fact be no more than the most recent of the Big Bounces. The Bounces might have been going on for ever. In that case, the Big Bang would *not* have marked the origin of the Universe. In fact, such an oscillating Universe might never have had an origin – it might always have existed.

But as I said – for reasons that will become clearer later, we do not accept the oscillating Universe scenario (there is not enough material in the Universe to pull everything back together again). As for the Steady State theory – an alternative way of having a Universe that has always been in existence – we dismissed that possibility in Chapter 1. So it is we come to regard the instant of the Big Bang as marking the beginning of the Universe.

The cause of the Big Bang?

That being the case, it seems only reasonable to ask what *caused* the Big Bang.

The religious response is to say that God created the world. But, as indicated at the opening of this chapter, that is not the only possibility. There are those who argue that the world might have created itself – spontaneously. For this to have happened, two problems must be addressed:

(i) *How to get something for nothing.* This is not as difficult as one might at first think. Let me explain.

On looking at the world, we see many properties – electric charge, for example. We have seen how atoms are made of protons, neutrons, and electrons, and how every proton has positive electric charge and every electron negative electric charge. There is clearly an enormous amount of electric charge in the world. But there is no difficulty creating electric charge. In the kind of experiments I used to do at CERN (Europe's main laboratory for particle physics) in Geneva with the big particle accelerator there, electrically charged particles are created all the time. The trick is not to try and produce the particles one at a time; instead several are produced together. That way the newly created positive electric charge on certain of the particles can be balanced by an equal amount of new negative electric charge on the others. Thus, there is no *net* increase in charge.

This being so, when we look at the Universe, the question we ought to be asking is not so much "How much charge is there in the Universe?" as "How much *net* charge is there?" It is then one discovers that the answer

– very, very precisely – is *zero*. There is no net charge in the Universe.

Take another property: momentum. This is a property possessed of moving objects and crudely speaking is a measure of the ability of the object to barge other things out of its way. As such, the momentum of the object depends upon the speed at which it is traveling, and how heavy it is. Again there is no difficulty in creating momentum. Get out of your chair and start walking, and you possess momentum that you did not have when seated. This was gained by pushing with your feet against the floor. This action sent the Earth recoiling in the opposite sense with an equal and opposite momentum (not that one notices this, of course; the Earth being so much heavier than you, it does not need to acquire much speed to match your momentum). Again there has been no *net* change in momentum.

When we look at the cosmos, clearly there is a great deal of momentum out there – planets orbiting their stars, the stars orbiting the center of their swirling galaxy, the motion of the galaxies within their clusters, and the recessional speeds of the clusters themselves. But note that there is as much movement in one direction as in the opposite sense, so the net amount is again zero.

The same argument holds regarding angular momentum – a property of rotating objects. One notices that there are as many stars and galaxies rotating in one sense as in the opposite sense. Again, this yields a nil result for the net total.

What this shows is that one can have as much as one likes of any property, but it will still add up to nothing if there is an equal amount of its opposite.

But, you might be thinking: "Surely it is not possible to get rid of *everything* that way. What about this book I am reading; where is the 'negative book' to cancel out this positive one?"

Here we must draw on an insight from Einstein's theory of relativity. Energy comes in different guises: heat, electrical energy, gravitational energy, chemical energy, and so on. What Einstein showed was that matter itself is a form of energy. An object with a certain mass, denoted by m, carries within it a corresponding amount of energy, E. All this is embodied in the famous equation $E = mc^2$ (c is the speed of light, and is included simply to allow us to write mass in the same units as energy). The energy contained in the book you are reading is equivalent to that of a nuclear bomb. Fortunately it remains securely locked up. Only under special circumstances, like those giving rise to nuclear synthesis in the stars and in nuclear bombs, does a tiny fraction of the energy locked up in matter get released. In the present context, it is sufficient for us to recognize that matter – like this book – is just a form of energy.

Now an interesting characteristic of energy is that, like the other properties we have been talking about, it comes in negative as well as positive forms. Whenever two bodies are bound together, it takes an input of energy (positive energy) to separate them – to tear them apart. That energy goes toward canceling out the negative energy associated with the binding.

So how much *net* energy is there in the Universe? Obviously there is much positive energy – all that locked up in the mass of the stars, to say nothing of that associated with their motions. But we must recall that everything is attracting everything else with gravity, and that introduces negative energy. In any case, there is a certain ambiguity as to how one defines the zero level of energy. To some extent one is free to define it in any way to suit the problem being addressed. So, a plausible case can be made for claiming that the net amount of energy in the Universe – like the other net quantities we have considered – can be taken to be zero.

Summing up this line of argument we can infer that there is no difficulty in getting a Universe for nothing. Why? Because the Universe amounts to nothing – albeit an ingenious rearrangement of nothing!

Which brings us to the second main problem encountered by those who believe the Universe spontaneously created itself.

(ii) *How to bring about the ingenious rearrangement of nothing.* This too, so it is argued, need not be an insuperable difficulty. We see this in the following way.

In the days of classical Newtonian physics, it was thought that everything that happens has to have a cause. Cause is followed by effect. The effect in turn becomes the cause of the next effect down the causal chain. Thus, for example, boy throws stone (cause) leads to window breaking (effect); window breaks (cause) leads to boy sent to bed early (effect); boy sent to bed early (cause) leads to boy growing up resenting parents (effect), and so on. In Newtonian mechanics everything is predictable – at least in principle. Repeatedly setting up the identical causal event always yields exactly the same effect.

But as was mentioned in Chapter 4, with the advent of quantum theory all that changed. Thanks to Heisenberg's uncertainty relation, we now know that from a given state of affairs, one can predict only the relative *probabilities* of a whole variety of possible later states: for example, a 60 percent chance of one, a 30 percent chance of another, and a 10 percent chance of yet another. Repeatedly setting up the identical initial state will lead to *different* end results. For instance, a neutron that is not bound tightly in a nucleus – a free neutron – is an unstable particle. It changes, or decays, into a proton and an electron (plus another particle called a neutrino). It has a 50 percent chance of decaying within twelve minutes of its creation; a 25 percent chance of decaying between twelve and twenty-four minutes; a 12.5 percent chance of decaying between twenty-four and thirty-six minutes, etc. But for any particular neutron there is absolutely no way of determining in advance when exactly it will decay; one just has to wait and see. All one can deal in are relative probabilities of various possible outcomes.

This element of uncertainty – unpredictability – affects everything happening in the world. The fact that it is not obvious in everyday life is because the effects only become noticeable on the small scale. This generally means one has to be examining the behavior of individual atoms, or of sub-atomic particles like neutrons. But the uncertainty is always there. For example, it is present every time a golfer strikes a golf ball. On the scale of golf balls, however, the uncertainty relation indicates a quantum uncertainty that is tiny compared to the other vagaries involved in trying to strike the ball – even when the club is being handled by a professional.

With quantum uncertainty being the rule, some physicists have been led to propose that we can invoke it to account for the way the Universe came into being. Starting from a state of nothing, it is proposed that there could be a small but finite chance that this will be succeeded by a state consisting of a Universe (the rearranged nothing).

One has therefore only to wait around for this quantum fluctuation to occur.

But, it might be objected, we have said that quantum effects become significant only on the small scale – that associated with atoms and sub-atomic particles. The Universe is the *biggest* thing we know. Well, it is certainly big today, but according to the Big Bang theory it was not always so; it started out as an infinitesimal point – the smallest possible scale. In that condition, one might expect it to have been subject to pronounced quantum fluctuations. Thus it is envisaged that the Universe began as a minute-sized quantum event, which then promptly underwent violent expansion to become the Universe we know today.

In summary, therefore, the proposal is that we could get a Universe for nothing, via a spontaneous quantum fluctuation, without the need to invoke the active involvement of any Creator God.

The suggestion, at first sight at least, appears quite plausible. But it is not without its difficulties. For example, it is all very well talking of a quantum fluctuation, but what exactly is fluctuating if there really is nothing there to begin with? Not only that, but quantum theory was devised to account for the behavior of the component parts of the Universe. It does not by any means follow that one is justified in applying it to the Universe as a whole. Besides, the theory is intended to provide a way for an observer to order his/her measurements on that component part of the Universe. So, who in the present context is supposed to be the "observer" – an observer external to that which is being observed? Is this not by implication God once more?

A further difficulty is that if there is a finite probability of this Universe popping into existence at some point in time, why not other universes at other points in time? Is one not led to the conclusion of there being universes without number? That seems a rather extravagant claim – a costly way of getting rid of a Creator God. It is one of the characteristics of scientific investigation that one goes for the simpler, the more economical, of two rival hypotheses.

A further problem with this suggestion will arise in a short while when we come to the subject of *time*, and whether one is justified in thinking of there being a "cause" of any kind for the Big Bang.

The source of the laws

But setting aside for the moment these various objections, suppose for the sake of argument we were to concede that the world had its beginning in a quantum fluctuation; would that in fact undermine the idea of a Creator God?

I think not. It is all very well putting the Big Bang down to a quantum fluctuation, but why a *quantum fluctuation*? Why was it quantum physics that was in charge of the process rather than some other type of physics? After all, we can all dream up imaginary worlds run according to laws of nature different from our own. Science-fiction writers do it all the time. Where is quantum physics supposed to have come from? Would it not have taken a God to have set up the laws of physics in the first place – a God who *chose* the laws for bringing this world (and perhaps others) into existence?

This would put God at one step removed from the origin of the Universe. Instead of initiating the world by direct intervention, he created the law – the natural outworking of that law then being the agency for bringing the world into existence. But note: ultimate responsibility for the existence of the world would remain invested in God – the creator of the law.

Such argumentation stems from the general observation that we live in a world that is law-like – it is intelligible. It presumably did not have to be that way. It is easy enough to imagine a world that was entirely chaotic in its operation. Indeed, certain ancient creation stories describe the initial condition as being one of chaos. The Babylonian story for example describes how the god of Babylon, Marduk, had to subdue the chaos, but there remained the fear that everything was liable to revert once again to its natural chaotic condition.

Indeed, the everyday world we live in is so complex and varied that it is easy to imagine that almost anything goes. We look around us at the bewildering variety of nature: hundreds of thousands of different chemicals; vast numbers of species of animals – no two animals being exactly alike; the many patterns of movement, ever-changing, ever-evolving. It looks confused – without rhyme or reason.

It is only under close examination that this is shown not to be so. Behind this richness there lies breathtaking simplicity. For example, most of matter is made up from just a few constituent particles – neutrons, protons, and electrons. The neutrons and protons are themselves made up of quarks. The fundamental quarks and electrons are believed to have no size at all, and hence no internal structure – they couldn't be simpler.

There are a few forces: gravity; the electrical force; the magnetic force; a nuclear force for binding the nucleus together; and a weak force that causes, for instance, the neutron to decay radioactively. And that's all; except that it is not even that many forces. In the nineteenth century, Clerk Maxwell demonstrated that the electrical and magnetic forces were simply different manifestations of a single force – the electromagnetic force. And in our own time it has been shown that the weak radioactive force, like the electromagnetic force, is just a manifestation of a single force, now called the electro-weak force. So, currently, we are down to just three forces. Who knows, perhaps the time will come when we are able to recognize that these three can be whittled down to a single force. That would be very exciting and aesthetically pleasing.

Based on those few particles, with the few forces operating between them, there are a few laws of nature: conservation of momentum, conservation of angular momentum, conservation of energy, etc. Could it be that one day we shall discover that these are simply different manifestations of the operation of a single law? That would give the physicist the ultimate satisfaction.

Whether this proves to be the case or not, no one at present can say for certain. But anticipating that this is how things might indeed turn out, this law has been given a name – the Theory of Everything. I have my reservations about the use of such extravagant language – a language that seems to imply that scientists are likely one day to be able to answer all questions. Questions regarding physical behavior maybe – but not *all* questions. Nevertheless, I do share my fellow physicists' hope that perhaps the time will come when I might be able to go into class with the new intake of undergraduate physics students, write a single equation on the board and declare, "Right, that's it. Any questions? If not, file out and collect your degree."

But even if that situation were never to materialize, one thing is already certain: despite appearances, the world is run on remarkably simple lines. In other words, the world is intelligible; it just takes a bit of intelligence to recognize it.

That being so, I find myself impelled to go a step farther and ask: "If it takes intelligence to work it out, might it not have taken an Intelligence to have put it in place to begin with?"

In summary, it may well be that one can have the Universe spontaneously come into existence by itself, from nothing, via a quantum fluctuation. But a question mark remains as to:

(i) how we should interpret the intelligibility of the laws that govern the Universe's operation. Does this not point to an intelligent source?

(ii) how we should account for the laws being these particular laws, rather than some other set. Did it not take a supreme Intelligence to decide? In other words, the plain fact that the Universe is run according to a particular set of intelligible laws can, in itself, be interpreted in the context of our God experiment as evidence in favor of the existence of God. It is evidence under our very noses – and hence easily overlooked.

The origins of space

I wish now to turn to what I regard as the most intriguing aspect of the Big Bang. So far we have been speculating on what might have caused the Big Bang – a quantum fluctuation or God. But what I want to talk about now throws doubt on whether there was a cause *at all*.

In describing the Big Bang I have probably given you the idea that it was an explosion much like any other explosion – bigger, yes, but essentially the same. By that I mean that it takes place at a particular location in space. In the case of a bomb, it might be located in the left-luggage office of Euston Station in London. Following the detonation, the pieces of the bomb come flying out so as to fill up the rest of the station. But this is not how it was with the Big Bang. Not only was all of matter concentrated initially at a point, but also all of space. There was no surrounding space outside the Big Bang.

Perhaps an analogy will help. Imagine a rubber balloon. On to its surface are glued some quarters. The coins represent the galaxies. Now we blow air into the balloon. It expands. Suppose a fly were to alight on one of the coins; what would it see? All the other coins moving away from it – the further the coin, the faster it recedes into the distance. A coin twice as far away as another recedes twice as fast.

But that, of course, is the observed behavior of the galaxies – they too are receding from us in exactly that manner. So far we have thought of the galaxies as speeding away from us as they move through space. But with the balloon analogy in mind, we now have an alternative way of interpreting that motion. It is not so much the case of the galaxy moving *through* space, as the space between us and it *expanding*. The galaxy is being carried away from us on a tide of expanding space, just as the quarters are moving apart on account of the rubber in between them expanding. And just as there is no empty stretch of rubber surface "outside" the region where the coins are to be found (a region into which the coins progressively spread out), so there is no empty three-dimensional space outside where we and the other galaxies are to be found.

Note that with the particular kind of expansion we are considering, where the speed of recession is proportional to distance, the situation is the same from all vantage points. In the case of the balloon, it would not matter which particular coin the fly happened to alight upon; all the other coins are receding from it in exactly the same manner. All points on the surface are on the same footing; there is no point *in the surface* that can rightly be called the "center" of that surface. (The balloon itself does, of course, possess a center, but that is situated outside the two-dimensional space under consideration.)

Bearing in mind that this two-dimensional rubbery space is the analogue of our normal three-dimensional space, we can conclude that Hubble's Law will hold regardless of which galaxy is chosen as the point from which to measure distances, i.e., there is no point out there in three-dimensional space that can be regarded as the center of that 3-D space, i.e., the center of the Universe. There is no privileged location out there where one would be justified in erecting a blue heritage plaque announcing "The Big Bang occurred here." In truth, the Big Bang happened everywhere.

It is this interpretation of the recession of the galaxies that leads us to conclude that at the instant of the Big Bang, all the space we observe today was squashed down to an infinitesimal point. Because of this, it becomes natural to suppose that the Big Bang not only marked the origins of the contents of the Universe, it also saw *the coming into existence of space*. Space began as nothing, and has continued to grow ever since.

The origins of time

That in itself is a remarkable thought. But an even more extraordinary conclusion is in store for us. Here we have to anticipate one of the results of a subject we shall be tackling in Chapter 13. There we shall take a look at Einstein's theory of relativity. We shall discover that space and time are more alike than one would guess from the very different ways we perceive and measure them. We measure spatial distances with rulers, and intervals of time with a watch or clock. Yet despite these different approaches, there is an exceedingly close link between the two, to the extent that we speak today of time as the fourth dimension. We are all familiar with the three spatial dimensions, i.e., we can designate them as up-down, backwards-forwards, and left-right. In a way that will become clearer later, time has now to be added as the fourth dimension. For the present, it is sufficient for us to accept that space and time are as indissolubly welded together as the three spatial dimensions are to themselves. *One cannot have space without time, nor time without space.*

The reason I am telling you this now (rather than waiting until we get to Chapter 13) is because of what I said a little earlier about space itself coming into existence at the instant of the Big Bang. In the light of what I have now asserted about the indissoluble link between space and time, we can immediately proceed to the conclusion that the instant of the Big Bang must also have marked *the coming into existence of time*. This in turn means that there was no time before the Big Bang. Indeed, the very phrase "*before* the Big Bang" has no meaning. The word "before" necessarily implies a pre-existent time – but where the Big Bang is concerned, there was none.

Now, for those who seek a *cause* of the Big Bang – whether a Creator

God or some impersonal agency – there is a problem here. We have already spoken of the causal chain: cause followed by effect. Note the word "followed": it refers to a sequence of events in time – first the cause, then the effect. But in the present context we are regarding the Big Bang as the effect. For there to have been a cause of the Big Bang, it would have had to have existed prior to the Big Bang. But this we now think of as an impossibility.

Stephen Hawking has come up with an interesting variation on this. According to the above ideas, time comes into being instantaneously at the moment of the Big Bang. There is a precise instant at which the cosmic clock begins ticking. But Hawking has suggested that this might not be so. He envisages the possibility that as we imagine going back in time toward the Big Bang, we do *not* come to a sudden start to time. Instead, time in a sense "melts away." The farther back we go, the more like the other dimensions it becomes. Ultimately it becomes a dimension much like the other three spatial dimensions and one never encounters time zero.

This idea is little more than a speculation, at least for the present. But on the assumption that there is something to it, we cannot but note that this would do away with any clearly definable time marking the origin of the Universe. It was this that prompted Hawking in his bestseller *A Brief History of Time* to remark: "What place then for a creator?" – a sentence that is probably the most often quoted in the entire book.

Actually it is beside the point whether or not Hawking is right about the nature of time changing as we imagine going back toward the Big Bang. In either case, the important thing is that there is no time before the Big Bang. This alone is sufficient to get rid of the kind of Creator God that most people probably have in mind: a God who at first exists alone (or in the case of the Christian God, a God consisting of the three Persons: Father, Son, and Holy Spirit). Then at some point in time – note *in* time – God decides to create a world. The blue touch-paper is lit, there is a Big Bang, and we are on our way. God becomes the cause of the Big Bang. But as we have seen, without time before the Big Bang, there could not have been a cause in the usual sense of that word.

It has to be said that exactly the same problem confronts the alternative idea we have been discussing whereby the cause of the Big Bang is thought to have been a quantum fluctuation. According to that scheme, an initial state consisting of nothing was (thanks to the quantum fluctuation) "followed" by a world that promptly underwent the Big Bang. In the absence of any prior time, there could no more have been that kind of "initial" state (one that could undergo a quantum fluctuation), than there could have been a God. Indeed, the only kind of quantum fluctuations we know of are those that occur *in* space as well as *in* time. Prior to the Big Bang, there was neither.

So, where have we got to? Have these considerations dispensed with a Creator God? Before jumping to that conclusion, let us consider the following quotation:

> It is idle to look for time before creation, as if time can be found before time. If there were no motion of either a spiritual or corporeal creature by which the future, moving through the present, would succeed the past, there would be no time at all. . . .
> We should therefore say that time began with creation, rather than that creation began with time.

If the archaic expression "either a spiritual or corporeal creature" had been replaced by a more up-to-date one – such as "a physical object" – one could well have thought that the quote came from Hawking or some other modern cosmologist. In fact, those are the words of St. Augustine. (Modern cosmologists find it hard to come to terms with the fact that, where the beginning of time is concerned, it was a theologian who got there before they did – 1,500 years before!)

How did he do it – bearing in mind that St. Augustine obviously knew nothing of the Big Bang? He argued somewhat along the following lines.

How do we know that there is such a thing as time? It is because things change. Physical objects (for instance, the hands of a clock) occupy certain positions at one point in time, and move to other positions at another. If nothing moves (or in the past had ever moved), we would not be able to distinguish one point in time from another. There would be no way of working out what the word "time" was supposed to refer to; it would be a meaningless concept. *A fortiori*, if there were no objects at all, moving or stationary (because they had not been created), clearly there could be no such thing as time.

In this way, Augustine cleverly deduced that time was as much a property of the created world as anything else. And being a feature of that world, it needed to be created along with everything else. Thus it makes no sense to think of a time that existed before time began. In particular it makes no sense to think of a God capable of pre-dating the world.

The distinction between origins and creation

Despite this, Augustine remained one of the greatest Christian teachers of all time. His realization of the lack of time before creation clearly had no adverse effect on his religious beliefs. To understand why this should be so, we have to draw a distinction between the words "origins" and "creation." Whereas in normal everyday conversation we might use these terms interchangeably, in theology they acquire their own distinctive meanings.

So, for example, if one has in mind a question along the lines: "How did the world get started?" that is a question of origins. As such, it is a matter for scientists to decide, their current ideas pointing to the Big Bang description.

The creation question, on the other hand, is different. It is not particularly concerned with what happened at the beginning. Rather it is to do with: "Why is there something rather than nothing?" It is as much concerned with the present instant of time as any other. "Why are *we* here? To whom or to what do we owe our existence? What is keeping us in existence?" It is an entirely different type of question, one not concerned with the mechanics of the origin of the cosmos, but with *the underlying ground of all being.*

It is for this reason one finds that whenever theologians talk about God the Creator, they usually couple it with the idea of God the Sustainer. His creativity is not especially invested in that first instant of time (if there was one); it is to be found distributed throughout all time. We exist not because of some instantaneous action of God that happened long ago – an action that set in train all the events that have happened subsequently – an inexorable sequence requiring no further attention by God. We do not deal with a God who lights the blue touch – and *retires*. He is involved at first hand in *everything* that goes on.

As an analogy, consider a pile of books stacked one upon another on a table top. The table is in contact with just one book – the bottom one. It is this book that is being supported directly by the table. This first book then acts as the support for the second book; the second book supports the third, and so on. In the analogy, the sequence of books represents whatever exists at successive points in time, the bottom book representing the state of the world at the instant of the Big Bang. With the table representing God, this is how many people see the supporting action of God: he is directly involved only in that first instant; this is his only point of contact. With this picture in mind, it is not surprising that Hawking's suggestion that there is no first instant of time (no bottom book) sounds worrying.

But the picture presented here is *not* that of a theologian. To gain insight as to what it means to be dealing with a God who is a Sustainer as well as a Creator, we have to pick up the pile of books and lay it down on its side. Now the table directly supports each book; they are all on an equal footing. If Hawking wishes to remove the book at one end of the line, so be it; it has no effect on the others.

An atheistic response to this discussion would be to dismiss the "creation question" as meaningless. Why not simply accept the existence of the world as a brute fact? What is to be gained by saying that God created the world – that only raises in its turn the question of who created God.

This is to misunderstand how we are using the word "God." God is not an existent object. One cannot say that God exists in the same way as we say an apple exists. If that were the case, then postulating one more existent thing – God – would not be any real advance in understanding. No, the point is that God is the *source* of all existence. "God" is the name we give to whatever is responsible for the existence of things – including you and me.

So, strictly speaking, the question posed by our God experiment ought not to be "Does God exist?" but rather "What, if anything, can we meaningfully say about God, the source of all existence?" In particular, can we think of that source as being in any way personal or conscious? Does it have an interest in us, or is it rather some mindless, inanimate "force" (for want of a better word)?

A reason why many believers resist the idea of there being no God before the Big Bang is that this seems to imply that God too must have come into being at that instant. How could God have made himself?

The trouble with this is that one's conception of God is again too small. Not only are we once more mixing up existent things with the source of existence, here we are compounding the mistake by regarding God as an object confined within the limits of space and time; it assumes that God can exist only *in* time. But again that is not the traditional belief about God. Certainly God is to be found in time; we are interacting with God in time whenever we pray. But he is also *beyond* time – God *transcends* time. What I mean by this will become a little clearer when later we acquire a whole new perspective on the nature of time in the light of Einstein's theory of relativity.

Genesis creation accounts

A further concern believers might have as a result of our discussions relates to the Genesis creation story. To put it bluntly, has modern cosmology caught out the Bible with its account of the creation taking place over a period of six days? Not only does the Bible not mention anything about a Big Bang, it seems to have got its chronology hopelessly wrong. Printed on the back cover of an old family Bible I once possessed was an article by Archbishop Ussher entitled "A Chronological Index of the Years and Times from Adam unto Christ, Proved by Scripture." The author industriously adds up the ages of Adam's descendants, at the time they begat the next one in succession. He ends triumphantly with the conclusion:

> Whereupon we reckon that from Adam unto Christ are three thousand, nine hundred and seventy four years, six months and ten days.

So, adding on the 2,000 years that have occurred since Christ (and neglecting the odd ten days) we would have to conclude that the world came into existence some 6,000 years ago – rather than the 12,000 *million* years ago indicated by the recession of the galaxies.

All of this assumes that the Genesis creation account was intended as a literalistic, scientific description of the origins of the world. But was it? This seems most unlikely.

For a start we note that there is no such thing as *the* Genesis account of creation. As we saw in Chapter 6, there are two of them. They are quite different from each other; indeed, as literal accounts they would contradict each other. This in itself should be sufficient to assure us that they were never meant to be read that way.

This view is confirmed when we note that people in those days were not particularly interested in scientific questions; our modern way of describing things with literal scientific accuracy had no place in their culture. Instead, as we noted earlier, much use was made of myths. Here we need to be careful. Words have a nasty habit of changing their meaning over time. Today if we call something a "myth" we are dismissing it as untrue. In terms of Biblical criticism, the same word acquires a strictly technical meaning. It refers to an ancient narration or story, the purpose of which was to convey to future generations some deep timeless truth or truths. As such, the incidents in the story might not have taken place in exactly the way described; everyone accepted that, and it did not matter. The story was merely the vehicle for conveying the truths.

We shall be saying a good deal more about this in the next chapter when we come to consider the Adam and Eve myth in the context of the scientific account of our human origins based on the theory of evolution by natural selection. For the present, all we need to know is that we do not look to the Genesis creation stories for a rival scientific cosmology.

Nor is this some modern insight. It is *not* the case that there has had to be a retrospective reappraisal of how to read the Bible, the earlier one having been discredited by modern scientific developments. There had always been two schools of thought regarding how one should read the Bible. The first, based in Antioch, adopted a literalistic interpretation. The second, and more influential one, based in Alexandria, treated the Bible in a more allegorical manner. It included noted thinkers such as

Origen, Basil, Clement, and Gregory of Nyssa. In the fourth century BC, Gregory for instance declared:

> What man of sense would believe that there could have been a first, and a second, and a third day of creation, each with a morning and an evening, before the Sun had been created?

(The Sun was supposedly created on the fourth day.)

What kind of truths are contained in the creation myths? In the first place, the world needed to be created. It has not always existed and it need not have existed. In other words, the world is contingent; its existence is not necessary. This in itself is an important notion. The ancient Greek philosophers reckoned that everything could be worked out by pure thought. They did not have to look at the world to discover what it was like. With sufficient intelligence they ought to be able to work it all out from first principles, or from common sense. The world was the way it was because that is how it *had* to be; there was no other way for it to be.

The Judaeo-Christian starting-point was quite different. The world existed because God decided to make it. It was up to God whether there should be a world, and if so, what kind it should be. This in turn means that anyone who wishes to find out what the world consists of and how it operates has to *look* at it – or in modern terminology, has to carry out experimental investigations on it to see which type of world God decided to make. This is a totally different mind-set to that of the Greeks and of other ancient civilizations. For this reason there seems some justification in the view, often expressed these days, that the Judaeo-Christian religious mind-set was the necessary forerunner for modern science to get started. In other words, the reason why science took off in the West (whereas it had not done so to anything like the same extent in other civilizations – civilizations that were in other respects as highly cultured and advanced) was that the religion of the West pointed the way to a mode of thinking firmly rooted in experiment. Far from science and religion being in conflict with each other, it was religion that helped give birth to science. Certainly when one considers the early scientists – for example, those who originally founded the Royal Society (the leading professional body of scientists in the UK) – one is struck by the number who were prominent church people and devout believers. They clearly had no difficulty reconciling their religious beliefs with their scientific activities. And, as you will be aware by now, one of the main reasons for my writing this book is to refocus attention on the way theology, in common with science, rests on an experimental underpinning.

A second feature of the Genesis creation stories is how the world is pictured as an ordered one. Remember how the Babylonian creation story told of a world of chaos. The Judaeo-Christian belief in an inherently intelligible world acted as an additional spur for later scientists to try and enunciate that intelligibility. Because of this intelligibility, the kind of world attested to in Genesis is one where the decisions we humans make lead to *foreseeable* outcomes. We are therefore to be held *responsible* for our actions in a way that would not be the case if the world were chaotic and nothing was predictable.

A third feature of the myth is that God is pictured as a personal deity. God knows what he is doing.

Fourthly, God sees that the world is good. The Genesis story is an optimistic, positive account of creation. Despite the many disasters that befall us humans – volcanic eruptions, hurricanes, floods, earthquakes, famine, etc. – in a deep sense the world is good; it is good to be alive.

Which brings us to one final feature: we ourselves owe our existence to God. Our lives are not given to us to live in whatever way we fancy. God gave us life for a purpose, and we should live it the way he wants.

These then are some of the enduring insights contained in the Genesis myths. It is for conveying these kinds of truth that they were first formulated, and why they remain as relevant for us today as they ever did. The myths of creation complement the scientific accounts of our origins.

IO

Human Origins

So far we have concentrated on the Universe and how it had its origins in the Big Bang. But how is the Creator God supposed to have created ourselves – human beings?

Many would turn to the Bible for an answer – the Adam and Eve story. Adam, we are told, was formed by God out of the dust of the ground; Eve followed later, being fashioned from a rib taken from Adam's side. Recent polls held in the USA indicate that almost half those interviewed accept this as a literal account of our beginnings. One doubts that anything like that proportion would apply to the UK. Though it does have to be said that the part of the church that is growing fastest at the present time is that section where acceptance of the literal interpretation of Genesis figures prominently.

But the Genesis story, of course, bears little relation to the modern scientific account of our origins – that based on Darwin's theory of evolution by natural selection, as subsequently refined and developed by later workers.

The theory of evolution by natural selection

On a number of previous occasions, I have had cause to refer to this theory. Let us now examine it in closer detail.

It begins with the observation that offspring resemble their parents. The parental characteristics are encoded in the genes each parent contributes to the offspring at its conception. At the birth of a baby, the parents' relations debate endlessly whether the color of the baby's eyes or hair comes from their side of the family or the other – and which side should be blamed for the sticking-out ears. Later there will be arguments as to where the child's intelligence, musical ability, or temper have come from. To a large extent the child appears to be a mixture of the two parents' characteristics, plus others that appear to have more in common with those of the grandparents (we hear of characteristics that "skip a generation"), and yet others that are unique to the child. So, although offspring resemble their parents in various ways, there will also be differences between siblings.

We now have a good understanding as to how this comes about. Recapping from an earlier chapter, we note that the inherited characteristics are encoded in a molecule called the DNA molecule. It is in the form of a double helix – like two bedsprings enmeshed together. The long chain of this complex molecule is made up of an amalgamation of smaller molecules. It is the order in which these smaller molecules occur along the sequence that constitutes the code for determining the individual's physical characteristics. As the code has been copied from those of the parents, it is clear why there should be the similarities between parents and children. But in the copying process, mistakes sometimes occur; what is passed on to the child is not an exact replica of the parent's original. Thus new codes arise, and these in turn lead to novel physical characteristics. As we shall be seeing, these variants provide the all-important material on which the process of natural selection gets to work.

These considerations, of course, are not unique to humans. There are analogous similarities between parents and offspring throughout the animal kingdom. All animals have their characteristic DNA codes dictating the kind of animal they are to be. And as with humans, there will be mistakes in copying the DNA, leading to new physical characteristics.

In situations where food and shelter are in short supply, as is often the case, not all animals of a particular generation will be able to survive. Certain individuals will be fortunate in that their inherited characteristics confer upon them some survival advantage over their fellows. For example, a young cheetah that happens by chance to inherit a gene that endows it with an above-average ability to run fast, is the one more likely to catch and kill the scarce prey. Thus it has a better chance of surviving to an age where it can mate than some other cheetah that is less well endowed. In mating, the fortunate cheetah will pass on to its offspring the self-same advantageous "fast-running" gene that helped in its own survival. The less advantageous gene, on the other hand, tends to die out since the cheetah to whom it belonged has less chance of mating and passing it on. So we would expect the next generation of cheetahs to be somewhat faster runners on average than the previous one. And with each new generation, the process repeats itself once more, leading to yet faster-running cheetahs in each succeeding generation.

And what goes for fast running will hold for any characteristic that confers on its holder an edge in the competition to survive – sharp claws and teeth, strong jaws, powerful wings, a tough defensive skin or hard shell, greater intelligence, etc. In this way, over the course of time, we find that the cumulative changes become so great that, in effect, one type of animal has developed into another. In other words, one species of animals descends from another that was different from itself.

The fact that evolution has happened – to some extent – is indisputable. We know this because evolution is still taking place today all around us. An often quoted example is that of peppered moths (*Biston betularia*) living in industrial areas. Over the years their coloring has become darker. This is because the surfaces on which they habitually come to rest became progressively dirtier. Those moths that by chance had somewhat darker markings than the average had a greater chance of escaping the attention of predators; to some extent they were camouflaged. As a result, they had a good chance of surviving to the point where they could pass on the gene corresponding to that darker color to their offspring. The lighter-colored variety of moth, being more inclined to get killed before mating, had less chance of passing its gene on. Thus, over the years, the color of the species has progressively changed; it has evolved.

The evolution of humans

What about the evolution of humans? We descended from something like an ape. This ape-like creature in its turn had come from a small insectivorous mammal, that from a reptile, that from a fish, and so on, right back to a bacterium. Even that is not thought to be the beginning of the evolutionary trail. Most biologists today hold that evolution goes right back to inanimate matter – to chemicals or, if you like, to plain dirt or mud. They think of life emerging from some kind of primordial slime.

This suggestion as to our earliest origins receives some corroboration when one examines the composition of the gases and dust clouds to be found in the space between stars. They consist of many different kinds of molecule. Some of these are found to be exactly those that act as the basic building blocks of living creatures here on Earth. The raw materials for life are therefore spread throughout space. The scene appears to have been set from the earliest times for life to develop on planets like Earth.

Yet many people find it totally unbelievable that something as complicated as a human being could have evolved from inanimate primordial slime, without the intervention of an intelligent designer of some kind. The Argument from Design had long been held as an important way of arguing with skeptics that there has to be a God. After all, if one came across a watch lying on the beach, one could immediately infer that it must have been made by a watchmaker. Something as complicated and highly organized as that could not have arisen spontaneously. Thus, in similar vein, it was argued that everything about the bodies of humans, and of other animals, is so well suited to its function (with the possible exception of the appendix!) that it must have been deliberately designed by someone with that function in mind – and that someone must, of course, have been God. Hence one has to believe in God.

Even Darwin himself, in his book *The Origin of Species*, expressed a measure of concern as to how something as complicated as the eye could have evolved. And yet he was confident that it must have evolved somehow. It was not a matter of a fully formed eye suddenly appearing by chance. Rather, it had to be a case of a whole sequence of small changes being strung together, each small change conferring some incremental advantage. Over the course of time, the chain eventually added up to the eye as we know it today.

Even so, many still find it totally implausible that one could go all the way from slime to intelligent humans purely by chance occurrences. The answer to such objections is that although the mistakes in the copying of DNA do indeed take place purely at random, and these lead to random variations in physical characteristics, that is only half the story. One has also to take into account the selective manner in which the advantageous changes are preserved at the expense of the disadvantageous ones. This is not a random process; it is *systematic*.

Perhaps an analogy will help: In my garden I have a huge, 150-year-old oak tree. Normally I love the old thing. But in the autumn it is an absolute nuisance. It dumps a carpet of brown leaves over the entire garden. The leaves are spread out at random everywhere. It would of course be much more convenient for me if they came down in neat piles waiting for me to collect them up and put them on the compost. So what do I do? Do I immediately set to and rake over the whole area? No. There's no point in getting old if you don't get crafty with it. I leave them for a while. We are situated on the top of a hill. It can be very windy. The wind swirls in from all directions. Thus we have winds from random directions blowing leaves that have been dumped randomly. What happens? To a large extent they conveniently gather themselves into neat, organized piles ready for me to collect up! Order emerges out of chaos. How does this come about – without any help from an intelligent, purposive gardener? Simple: there are certain regions in my garden that are comparatively sheltered – odd corners next to the shed, or against the walls of the house – especially the angle between the studio extension and the living room. It is easy for a leaf to be blown into these areas but, once there, it is not subject to a wind that will blow it out again. Once it lands up there, that is where it will stay. One might say that, in a sense, that particular location for the leaf has "survival value." Thus, over time, more and more leaves accumulate in these preferred areas. Which is exactly what I want to happen – it makes life much easier for me.

So it is with evolution: it is no more likely that an advantageous gene will arise than a disadvantageous one (indeed, given the random nature of the process, it is much more likely that a change will have a deleterious effect – there generally being more ways of getting something wrong than there are of getting it right). But the process of natural selection operates in such a way that once an advantageous change does occur, it is likely to be perpetuated, whereas the disadvantageous ones, by their nature, have a tendency not to be retained. In this way it is wrong to object to evolution on the grounds that it is all down to chance. It is not.

The second factor to be taken into account when assessing the likelihood or otherwise of going from slime to humans is the enormous time-scale over which evolution has operated. From radioactive dating techniques it has been shown that the Earth, along with the rest of the Solar System, formed 4,600 million years ago (some 7,000 million years after the Big Bang). Exceedingly primitive life forms (bacteria) probably put in an appearance about 3,000 million years ago. Modern humans emerged from primitive ancestors only in the past 100,000 years.

To get that into perspective, we note that if the history of the Earth were in imagination reduced to one year, then our primitive ancestors came on the scene at about 10 p.m. on December 31, modern humans at 10 minutes to midnight, and you and I at half a second before midnight tolled the end of the year.

Compared to the evolution of humans, the changing of color of a moth is, of course, a very modest evolutionary change. But when it is realized that, on the reduced time-scale we have been considering, the moths achieved this transformation in no more than a fraction of a second, we begin to glimpse that unimaginably large changes could have occurred over the vast tracts of time that have been available to evolution.

Life from the non-living

But you might be asking, "How can life come from that which is not living?"

There are many who regard life as something so special that it is beyond the province of science to investigate at all. They would claim that scientists will never succeed in taking inanimate chemicals and converting them into something that is living – and this means it would be even less likely that this could have happened spontaneously in the past without intelligent intervention. Life, so it is held, is a special non-physical quality that is in the gift of God alone. But is it?

When it comes to drawing a distinction between living and non-living objects there is clearly no difficulty in classifying humans, cats, dogs, fish, and oak trees as living, and water, rocks, trains, and buildings as non-living. It is when we come to much simpler objects that problems can arise. Yeast, for instance, can be bought in shops as a powder in a packet, and yet it is alive. Viruses, such as a flu virus, can be made into inert crystalline preparations much like sugar or salt. But they also reproduce (after a fashion), this making it difficult for biologists to know quite how they should be classified.

There is in fact no single criterion for deciding what is living. Living objects usually have more than one characteristic in common. These distinguishing characteristics include *nutrition* (the ability of the body to take in substances from the environment and use them to promote growth and to provide energy for the body's activities); *growth*, with changes in shape as well as in size; *respiration* (the process of taking in substances, like oxygen, and using them as sources of energy); *excretion* (the ability to get rid of waste products); *responsiveness* (the characteristic of reacting to stimuli coming from the environment); and *reproduction*, whether that involves sex or otherwise.

Inanimate objects can exhibit one or more of these characteristics. A piece of iron, for instance, will react to a damp atmosphere by becoming rusty; ice crystals will grow by freezing the surrounding liquid water; a computer virus will reproduce itself on gaining access to another computer system. As I said, there is no single watertight criterion by which one can judge whether something is living or not. Rather it becomes a matter of looking for a cluster of criteria to be satisfied. Biologists cannot even agree on what exactly the set of criteria should be. The list given above is just one attempt to do this. Thus, it can become a genuine problem as to how to categorize something as simple as a virus. Strictly speaking, a virus cannot reproduce *itself*; what it has to do is infect an animal and get the animal to manufacture the virus material on its behalf. In this way it becomes a moot point whether the virus really has satisfied the relevant condition to do with reproduction.

Thus, there exist today uncertain gray areas, bridging the gap separating the clearly identifiable living from the clearly identifiable non-living. This surely makes it all the more reasonable to suppose that in the far-off evolutionary past, the world imperceptibly developed from an exclusively non-living environment, through a transitional phase containing something as simple as our current viruses (but *not* our actual modern viruses), to a state where the first clearly living plants and animals were present. Thus, the living evolved out of the non-living.

Evidence from the fossil record and from DNA sequencing

The clinching evidence for our evolutionary past could of course come only from a complete fossil record charting all the minute changes that have marked the development of the human species through its antecedent species, and back to the primordial slime. But the record has many gaps in it. Although the gaps are continually being narrowed with the making of ever more finds, it is unlikely ever to be complete. For instance, not all past primitive species are expected to have left fossils; and some of those that were left have subsequently been irrevocably destroyed. In this regard we have to bear in mind that the surface of the Earth is continually shifting and reforming itself. The surface of the Earth is made up of crustal "plates" floating on top of molten rock (rather like the skin on custard). The plates move about and collide with each other. Sometimes they buckle to form mountain ranges. Sometimes they get caught up with each other where their boundaries come into contact; the sudden release of the built-up tension is what causes earthquakes. In some locations, one plate is pushed under its neighbor, carrying every-thing on and near its surface – including any fossils – underground and into the molten rock beneath. For this reason we have to expect that some vital links in the fossil record will have been lost for ever.

An alternative approach is offered by the study of DNA sequencing. To some extent we can determine how close we are to other species by comparing our respective DNA. Thus, for example, quite independently of the fossil record allowing us to trace our ancestry back to primitive ancestors we have in common with chimpanzees and gorillas, we can note that 99 percent of our human DNA is identical to that of chimpanzees and gorillas. That alone is a measure of how closely related we are to them. And the fact that certain DNA sequences are common to *all* living animals and plants appears to be a clear sign that we all have a common ancestry in primitive life forms if we go back far enough.

Problems remaining

Having said this, I do not mean to gloss over the difficulties remaining.

It is hard to understand how, at various points along the evolutionary path leading up to humans, certain crucial steps were negotiated – for example, the formation of the first cell. There can also be disagree-ments about the way progress is made in evolution. For example, whether it is a matter of smooth, continual, steady change, or whether the changes occur in fairly rapid bursts, interspersed by rather lengthy periods of time when not much change is happening – the so-called "punctuated equilibrium" scenario. If it is the latter, then this will make it even more difficult to find the fossils relating to the brief transitional stages marking the change from one clearly defined species to its suc-cessor. This might be a contributory cause as to why there are so many crucial gaps in the record.

And yet, despite these reservations, I join with the vast majority of scientists in fully accepting that we humans, and the other species we have today, are the products of evolution by natural selection.

Biblical interpretation

But of course not everyone is happy to accept evolution. I mentioned at the outset the large number of people who continue to adhere to a lit-eral understanding of the Adam and Eve account. So it is now time to address this issue. How ought we in fact to interpret what we read in the Bible? I have already said a little about this, but now it is time to go into it in more depth.

The first thing one has to recognize about the Bible is that it is not a book, but a whole library of different types of writings: history, biogra-phy, songs, statements of law, poetry, theological reflection, collections of sayings and proverbs, and so on. Just as it would be foolish to enter a public library today, take books down from the shelves at random, and read them all in exactly the same frame of mind, regardless of whether one was reading a work of fiction, a history textbook, poetry, a science book, etc., so one should not expect to be able to open the Bible at random and just start reading without first considering what the intention of the author might have been. Finding that out is often no easy matter. We need to be guided by Biblical scholars who have made a lifelong study of the culture and practices of people living long ago.

Only when one has steeped oneself in the mind-set of those who lived 2,000 to 4,000 years ago, can one begin to appreciate what they were really trying to get across in their writings.

Does that mean, for example, if one has identified a piece of writing as setting out an episode in the history of the Jewish people, that one can immediately go ahead and read it, and judge it, as one would a piece of modern historical writing? No. The writers' approach to history was radically different from ours. Whereas we put great store on trying to get the facts right – what people actually did and said, where they did it and on what date – ancient writers would have been inclined to dismiss such an approach as irrelevant – a pointless exercise. What possible use could such a cold recitation of facts have? How boring. For them history was intended to be uplifting and inspiring. Great heroes of the past – such as Moses and David – were held up as examples to the young. If a little elaboration would make the account more effective in bringing about desirable attitudes in the readers, such as emulating worthy role models and having pride in one's nation, then why not? This process of enhancing figures of the past was so prevalent that it is nowadays wondered whether some of these people even existed – whether their supposed deeds and victories in battle were just an amalgam of various people's achievements. Such practices might strike our modern mind as exceedingly dubious, if not fraudulent. But surely it is not if everyone is aware of what is going on; if everyone knows what the underlying intention is.

Another aspect of Jewish historical writings we gleaned from Chapter 6 was that they were primarily concerned with the developing relationship between the Jewish people and their God. Historical fact and theological interpretation were inextricably intertwined in a way that would be most unusual in an historical account written today. Thus, even the identification of a piece of writing as being largely historical in character still leads to difficulties of interpretation for those unaware of the hidden agendas that make ancient historical writings so different from our own.

The role of story

So it is we come to the Adam and Eve account of our human origins. What kind of writing is that meant to be?

One kind it *cannot* be is a scientific treatise. Ancient civilizations simply did not think or reason in accordance with modern scientific practice. No, the Adam and Eve account is an example of myth. Earlier we discussed the subject of myth in connection with the two accounts of the creation of the world in the first two chapters in Genesis. There we used the word "myth" in its original, technical sense to refer to an ancient story that acted as a vehicle for conveying deep, timeless truths. Although myths described events that might not have actually happened as such – not in the literal manner described – that did not matter because a literal account had never been the intention behind them.

You might have been prompted to wonder why the ancients should have adopted such a procedure. Why not simply write down what they had to say in plain language which everyone could read and understand – without the need to *interpret* it? Why run the risk of causing confusion over readers mistaking the dividing line between the fictional story-line on the one hand, and the inner spiritual content on the other?

Here we have to recognize that for much of the time that these stories were in circulation, they were not written down, as the majority of people could neither read nor write. Whatever wisdom one wished to pass on from one generation to the next had to be done orally – by word of mouth.

But we all know how difficult it is to remember oral messages. Recall the game of "telephone" where a chain of children have progressively to pass on a certain message by whispering it into a neighbor's ear. A comparison is then made between the final version and the original, often with hilarious results (even in the absence of someone mischievously distorting the message on purpose).

We must not imagine that ancient people were as bad as we are today at remembering what we have been told. They made a point of training people in learning things by rote. We on the other hand, in accordance with modern educational thinking, tend to downplay such training. Nevertheless, despite their greater skills at rote learning, the ancients still had a problem transmitting information down through the ages without progressive distortions taking place.

In this respect they noted that there was one kind of narration the human mind was especially good at remembering – a *story*. There is something about a story-line that is particularly memorable – the way thinking about one event prompts the recollection of what happens next, which in turn prompts the recollection of the next incident, and so on. So there grew up the custom of passing on truths in story form – stories that translated abstract theological ideas into concrete analogies, using vivid imagery.

It was a custom that was to be perpetuated. We see this in the teachings of Jesus. There we don't refer to the stories as "myths" but as "parables." The tradition is continued in our own days. We have only to think of George Orwell's *Animal Farm* or William Golding's *Lord of the Flies*. In neither case does it matter whether the events described actually happened as such. (Animals talking!?) That was not their point. Both stories have powerful messages to convey about human nature.

The truths behind the Adam and Eve myth

What then are the timeless spiritual truths conveyed in the Genesis myth of Adam and Eve?

In the first place we note that the name Adam is no ordinary name – not like John or Paul, say. It means "man." So straight away we have the clue that what we are reading applies not to an individual but to humankind in general.

Adam is placed in the garden of Eden. He is not there to sit around having an easy time of it; he is there to tend it, to look after it. Perhaps one can see in this something of the modern Green message – a vision of stewardship we urgently need to recapture in our own times where, through the power that has come from scientific and technological advance, we now have the ability to transform for good or ill the garden we call planet Earth.

Eve is described as being made from a rib taken from Adam's side. This is pointing us to the nature of marriage – the idea that man is not complete without woman, nor woman complete without man. Again, as we see the institution of marriage – the idea of making a binding commitment to a partner – coming under increasing threat, this is another message as relevant for our own times as it was in the past.

Then we have the strange story of the taking of the forbidden fruit. The couple were expressly told not to eat of that particular tree. They had no need of it; they were amply provided with alternative food. And yet they rebelled against this injunction. Rather than do what God wanted of them, they decided they would please themselves regardless. They had no right to the fruit – it did not belong to them – and yet they greedily, selfishly took it. In the words of the song for which Frank Sinatra was most famous: "I did it *my* way."

What this is telling us is that humans are basically selfish and self-centered. No matter how perfect the surroundings in which we find ourselves, there is a mean streak in us that is bound to spoil that paradise. We read how Adam and Eve were banished from the garden of Eden, never to return. The same was to apply to their descendants – you and me. From that time, humankind was to be under a kind of curse. We are condemned never to be able to regain paradise on Earth. From the moment of conception we have built into us the seeds of selfishness; we are born self-centered rather than God-centered.

This idea is formulated in the religious notion of "original sin." While we might be inclined to assume that all babies are born perfect, and when they eventually fail to live up to that standard, the blame can be put down wholly to a bad environment or upbringing, Genesis says no. Even if it were possible for children to live a cocooned existence, protected from all undesirable external influences, they would still turn out to be sinful and self-centered. That is their basic make-up – their intrinsic nature from the moment of conception.

Original sin in the light of evolution

The doctrine of original sin has never been popular – for obvious reasons. But, with the insights that come from the modern understanding of our evolutionary origins, we can begin to appreciate how that doctrine does in fact make a lot of sense.

So far, we have seen how our physical make-up is determined by the codes to be found in our DNA molecule. But that is only part of the picture. In the evolutionary struggle it is no good for a cat to have sharp claws if it does not know what to do with them. A cat that has in addition a natural, unthinking, automatic tendency to hunt and use those claws to kill suitable prey has a clear advantage over another that has to reason everything out from the beginning each time it is faced with the opportunity of a meal. Accordingly, besides there being survival value in having certain inherited physical characteristics, there would also be survival value were certain inherent behavior traits to be passed on. And as we noted earlier, that is in fact what happens. Certain of the codes in the DNA are to do with behavior that is conducive to survival. In fact, it appears that a great deal of animal behavior is genetically influenced; it is behavior the individual did not have to learn from its own limited experience of life. As part of its inherited survival kit, the animal comes to some extent "pre-programmed." It instinctively operates in ways that assist it to survive to the point where it, in its turn, can pass that same genetically influenced behavior trait on to its own offspring.

Genetically influenced behavior helps us to understand much of what is going on in the animal kingdom. In Chapter 5, when we first introduced the subject, we noted the hunting behavior of today's domesticated cat, and the manner in which the baby kangaroo, on being born, instinctively heads up its mother's fur to the pouch awaiting it. These and many other behavior traits in animals were vital to the survival of their ancestors. Because the ancestors had these traits, today's animal also has them – even though, in the case of the domesticated cat, the hunting instinct is now no longer needed.

Once one accepts that we humans are also a form of animal – a product of the same evolutionary process – we can begin to learn things about ourselves by studying the behavior of other animals. If we find that their behavior is to some extent influenced by their genes, then we must expect the same to be true of ourselves. Genetically influenced behavior is something we earlier recognized to be connected to the Jungian idea of a collective unconscious. Given the nature of the evolutionary struggle, if there is survival value in selfishly grabbing limited food supplies for oneself, and for one's close kin, regardless of the consequences to others, that is a behavior trait that is likely to be preserved and passed on.

So, what we find is that the theory of evolution, far from discrediting the Adam and Eve story, actually backs up one of its important spiritual truths about ourselves: namely, that we must expect to find a measure of self-centeredness in us – from the moment of conception. Before the theory came along one just had to accept, as a matter of observation, that that was the way humans behaved. Now, thanks to evolutionary theory, we can understand the mechanism.

Competing interpretations of Genesis

Earlier, in connection with the creation myths, we saw how this non-literal way of interpreting the early Genesis writings was not new. Recall how St. Augustine had already worked out that there could have been no time before the world had been created. We noted that he must have had a quite sophisticated appreciation of what it meant to regard God as creator (God not being a pre-existent "cause").

St. Augustine also had a presentiment that Adam's arriving on the scene fully formed did not seem right. Indeed, he advocated that in the beginning there were only the germs or causes of the forms of life which were afterward to be developed in gradual course. It was an evolutionary theory – of a sort! Naturally, this should not be taken to imply that St. Augustine got there before Darwin. What he had in mind bore no relation to an evolutionary theory incorporating the mechanism of natural selection. But Augustine's views on the subject confirm what we noted in the last chapter, namely that one does need to exercise care over the interpretation of Genesis. One cannot simply take it at face value and read it with our modern scientifically conditioned mind-set; one must do a little probing to get back to the authors' original intentions.

This is the view of the majority of Biblical scholars. Yet it is a view not universally held. There remains today a strong literalistic school of thought. Repeated attempts continue to be made to have the teaching of evolution in US schools, if not banned, then downplayed, with the theory presented as no more than a speculative hypothesis. Coupled with this is the attempt to accord equal time to the teaching of so-called "creation science" – with the Adam and Eve story put across as a rival scientific account of our origins.

The advocates of this view are obviously well-intentioned; they act out of a deep sense of reverence for the Bible; and they sincerely believe they are defending the original interpretation of the Bible. What they do not seem to recognize is that the strictly literalistic interpretation of Genesis rose to prominence only as late as the sixteenth century – the time of the Reformation. How did this come about?

Disillusioned by the way power was being wielded in Rome, the Protestants, under the leadership of people like Martin Luther, broke away from the rule of the Pope. Their authority for taking such a step? The Bible. From now on, the ultimate authority rested with Holy Scripture, not with the Pope. Those remaining loyal to Rome, not to be outdone, reaffirmed that their respect for the Pope in no way diminished their acceptance of the authority of the Bible. One side vied with the other as to who most truly reverenced the Bible. In the process, it became more and more difficult to question any feature of the Bible: one's standing as a Christian depended on how much of the Bible one could accept unquestioningly. In the 1540s, the Roman Catholic church set up the Council of Trent primarily with the aim of clarifying its position on aspects of belief challenged by the Protestants. From this council a statement was issued to the effect that God was to be regarded as "the author" of the Bible – both the Old and New Testaments. The writings had been produced "at the dictation of the Holy Spirit." In other words writers such as Matthew, Mark, Luke, and John had simply acted as secretaries taking down dictation.

It is hard to understand how such an attitude toward Scripture could have come about. After all, when one gospel is compared to another, it is not difficult to find manifest contradictions – the type of discrepancies one would expect in comparing the recollections of different people some thirty or more years after the event (which is when the gospels were written). For example, did the disciples have to go to Galilee in order to meet Jesus after his Resurrection, as Matthew and Mark say, or did he appear to them in Jerusalem, as Luke and John would have us believe? A small point admittedly, but one we might expect God to have got right – if indeed the words had come directly from him. Not only are there these discrepancies, there are changes of writing style, and even examples, so I am told, of bad grammar.

It was this hard, uncompromising line the church had taken toward the Bible that did much to bring about the Galileo affair. In our earlier discussion of that episode we examined some of the background that had led to the notorious trial. It is relevant to add that the trial took place not long (some seventy years) after this shift in attitude toward the Bible. Martin Luther had already denounced the Copernican theory (that it was the Earth that went round the Sun rather than the reverse) by appealing to the Bible:

> This fool wishes to reverse the entire science of astronomy; but Sacred Scripture tells us that Joshua commanded the Sun to stand still, and not the Earth.

Given the prevailing climate of the time, where no one wished to be thought of as taking a casual attitude toward the Bible, one can appreciate that the situation needed especially careful handling – a sensitivity beyond the capability of the forthright Galileo.

Fortunately the Roman Church's attitude has been modified since those times. In 1965, at the Second Vatican Council, it was stressed that it was not the words themselves that had come directly from God, but rather it was a case of the writers of the words having been *inspired* by the Holy Spirit – they had written under the influence of God:

> . . . the interpreter of sacred Scripture, in order to see clearly what God wanted to communicate to us, should carefully investigate what meaning the sacred writers really intended, and what God wanted to manifest by means of their words.

Thus, we can see that when modern-day fundamentalists defend a literalistic interpretation of Genesis, it is not that they are getting back to the original understanding of Scripture, but one that gained the ascendancy in the Reformation – one more likely to be a *mis*interpretation.

To some extent one can appreciate the attraction of the literalistic interpretation. I know many fundamentalists; they live deeply religious lives and have a genuine relationship with God. Indeed, I sometimes find myself envying them their buoyant, joyful type of faith. (I myself probably agonize too much over my beliefs!) They show great love and respect for the Bible – which is only to be applauded. But I suspect that many of them fear that once they start to question some aspect of the

Bible – once they approach it in a *critical* sense, allowing for the possibility that some of it might not be true in the literal sense – then they are on a slippery slope. Where is one to draw the line? Is there not a danger the baby goes out with the bath water?

It is an understandable concern. Where interpretation is concerned there are bound to be differences of opinion. But a blanket literal approach to the Bible is itself an interpretation. The line *has* to be drawn somewhere, and I believe that the one place it cannot be drawn is where the literalists draw it.

Now you might respond to this by asking, "Does it matter what they think? If, as you say, they enjoy a genuine, joyful, loving relationship with God – if they are effective in attracting growing numbers of people into the church and into loving relationships with God with their simple, straightforward, uncomplicated beliefs – where's the harm?"

I think it is all very well pointing to those who are attracted by this approach to religious belief, but what of those who are *repelled* by it? I know that the attitudes toward religion of several of my academic colleagues in the biological sciences are significantly colored by their need to be constantly defending the integrity of their work from attacks by religious fundamentalists. If I as a physicist had been faced with attempts to pass a law that compelled me to downplay the convincing nature of the evidence for the Big Bang, and even worse, afford the six-day creation story as much time in the physics curriculum as is at present devoted to the Big Bang theory, it would have done nothing toward helping me to take religion seriously.

In summary, what I am saying is that there is absolutely no need to see religion and science on a collision course over the subject of human origins. To my mind the only course of action a religious believer can take – with intellectual integrity – is to accept that, with all its possible faults and deficiencies, evolution by natural selection is currently our best scientific description of our origins. We can regard it as God's way of bringing us into existence. It is then up to us to use that knowledge to discover more about ourselves and about God's ways of working.

Further Insights from Evolution

The Biblical Fall

We have already noted a correspondence between, on the one hand, self-centered genetically influenced behavior, and on the other, the religious notion of original sin contained in the Adam and Eve story. But what of the Fall? The Fall is the idea, contained in the same Biblical account, that initially all was well – Adam and Eve living a happy life in paradise. Only later did they spoil this sinless state when they ate the forbidden fruit. How does this ideal first state fit in with the theory of evolution?

In a nutshell, I don't think there ever was such a state. That certainly would not be part of the evolutionary scenario as we know it. But that is not to say that the Bible was wholly wrong on that count. There *was* a crucial stage of development that clearly delineated our present state from another that preceded it. I refer to the emergence of self-consciousness – that stage in our evolutionary history when for the first time a creature acquired a brain sufficiently complex for it to become consciously aware of itself.

How this came about we do not know. As we have had cause to note previously, the nature of the relationship between the physical brain and the mind remains a mystery. The activities of the brain are described in terms of electrical currents and chemical changes; those of the mind consist of thoughts and feelings. But whatever the nature of that relationship, we do know there must have been a point in the evolutionary past where there was some kind of crossing over from unthinking matter to mental beings.

Although one cannot be sure, it probably began with a mental awareness of feelings such as pain, fear, hunger, cold, satisfaction, etc. These were possessed by what we might regard as the first primitive animals. In time the thoughts became progressively more sophisticated and complex. No longer confined to simple automatic mental reactions to stimuli, they began to include powers of reasoning. In particular there would, at some stage or other, have developed an awareness of oneself as an entity in one's own right – as distinct from the environment. There would be the recognition that the environment was partly made up of creatures similar to oneself, but distinct from oneself. This was the acquisition of self-awareness.

Somewhere along the line would come the ability to make decisions – conscious decisions. Although the tendency to behave in certain pre-programmed ways according to the dictates of the genes would still be there, for the first time there would have arisen the ability consciously to decide to act differently from the dictates of one's inherited traits. Whereas the behavior of more primitive animals might be spoken of as genetically *determined*, now it was no longer the case. Genetically *influenced*, certainly; but no longer determined.

This coming into existence of an ability to act otherwise than in conformity with one's inborn instincts marked an important transition – one that I suggest can be seen as evolution's equivalent of the Biblical Fall. Up to this point, the world had indeed been *sinless*, as the Bible would have us believe. But this was not because everything had been perfect. It was because prior to this transition stage it would have been a misuse of the word to describe any action as "sinful." One can hardly speak of "sin" in the absence of any alternative choice of action. Exactly the same kind of situation would arise today were one to describe a domestic cat as "evil and wicked" when it kills innocent birds. How could it really be held culpable if it knew no other way of behaving?

The point in evolutionary development where it truly became possible for a creature consciously to decide to act in a moral manner, marked a watershed. From here on, "sin" became a *meaningful* concept. Sin entered the world, not as a dramatic change from a previous state of peace and harmony to the one we find ourselves in today, but when primitive humans were able for the first time to be held *accountable for their actions*.

The image of God

But that in turn raises another question: why should we in any case *wish* to act differently from what our genes would have us do?

This is where another Biblical insight comes to the fore: that not only were we fashioned out of the dust of the ground (in itself literally true if we think of "the dust" as being "the primordial slime"), but we are also spoken of as being made "in the image of God" – we have within us the potential to be God-like. One must stress the word *potential*, because being God-like does not happen as a matter of course. As the Christian rite of baptism affirms, we have to "repent and turn to Christ." We noted earlier that the word "repent" means more than simply feeling sorry for what one has done; it has much more to do with changing one's mind; having a change of heart; resolving to act differently in the future. Like the prodigal son, one has consciously to decide to "come home"; one has to *decide* to become God-centered rather than remain self-centered.

The idea of being made in the image of God implies that ultimately we cannot be *truly* fulfilled until we are at one with God. You will remember we talked of this in Chapter 5 in connection with Jungian psychology. Given the nature of that God – the good God who is the father of us all – that means not only being at one with God, but also with all our brothers and sisters. Hence the two great commandments: loving God and loving one's neighbor as oneself.

It is when we try to respond to the demand to live up to that second commandment – treating everyone equally as our brothers and sisters, sacrificing our own interests on their behalf if need be – that is when we are likely to have to make decisions as to whether or not to act differently from the promptings of our genes. And that is where decisions of a moral nature come in, and where it becomes meaningful to speak of sin and virtue.

Genetically based altruism?

One of the concerns you might have about what I have said so far is that we seem to have equated genetically influenced behavior *exclusively* with selfishness – an absorption with the self which readily leads us humans into morally reprehensible behavior. But what about other behavior traits – altruism, for example? Could there not be survival value for a species if there were to develop a genetic code that led to cooperation between members of the species? Could we not hold to a much more positive assessment of our likely genetic characteristics – one where everyone had a natural inborn tendency to look after each other's interests? That way one would not have to invoke a God as the source of our higher, more laudable motivations. This is an intriguing question with various ramifications.

For a start we noted earlier that mothers have a natural tendency to care for their young. They might have to put themselves to great inconvenience, all for the sake of their offspring. Indeed, one knows of situations where a mother bird, on seeing a predator, will leave the nest and make a great display, thereby attracting the predator's attention toward herself and away from the contents of the nest. She is prepared to sacrifice herself if necessary for her young. Such behavior is quite the opposite of what we would expect if a selfish concern for one's own interests were the whole story. Such self-sacrificing behavior in a human would be accounted most commendable.

But such instances have a simple explanation in terms of evolutionary theory. Instead of thinking primarily in terms of the survival of the *individual*, we perhaps ought to be concentrating our attention more on the selection and survival of the *gene*. In this context, the self-sacrificing, "altruistic" behavior of the mother bird makes perfect sense. The mother and her young share the same genes. If it becomes a case of either the mother or the young getting killed, the genes are more likely to be preserved for posterity if it is the young that survive. The mother bird, having done her job of passing the genes on to the next generation is now, in a sense, expendable. A gene that in effect says: "When you are a mother, be prepared to sacrifice yourself if necessary for your young" is more likely to get passed on and survive than one that says: "Under all circumstances put your own interest first." In this way the self-interest is a feature of the gene rather than of the individual – hence the commonly used term "the selfish gene." So it is we can expect a certain measure of altruistic behavior to be encoded in our genes as well as the selfish behavior we spoke of before.

But one should note that this type of self-sacrificing behavior would be expected only on behalf of close kin – those (like one's young) who in large measure share the same genetic material – including the "self-sacrificing" type of gene.

Altruism beyond close kin?

Having established the survival value (for the gene) of parents being altruistic toward their young and possibly other close family members, we must next ask whether there could be survival value for a gene that promoted altruism on behalf of the wider community.

For a time it was thought that there was a known example of this at work. It concerned the behavior of blackbirds. It was noted that on the approach of a hawk, a blackbird would immediately issue a cry to warn the rest of the flock of the approach of the predator. In so doing, it betrayed its own position to the hawk, placing itself in imminent danger for the good of others – many of whom would not be related particularly closely to the individual giving the warning. Laudable altruistic behavior on behalf of the community of blackbirds as a whole. Or was it?

Later workers noted that the warning cry emitted by the blackbird was pitched high. It is a characteristic of high-pitched sounds that their source is hard to locate. So, in truth, the bird had *not* given away its own position. And what was the consequence of issuing that cry? The rest of the flock had taken to the wing in alarm. But only one bird knew in which direction the hawk lay. So, on average, half the flock would be flying in the wrong direction toward the source of danger. In other words, the bird's act of so-called altruism had been nothing of the sort; its cry had successfully sent up into the air a flock of decoys that would effectively cover its own – selfish – escape! This example demonstrates just how careful one has to be when drawing conclusions about the motives at work in the animal kingdom.

In fact, there is a good theoretical reason why a gene concerned with the general welfare of the community might find it hard to get established. Such a gene would be of the general kind: "I'll scratch your back, if you scratch mine." As far as it goes there seems to be plenty of survival value in such a strategy, as much more can be achieved cooperatively rather than having everyone trying always to go it alone. The trouble is that the success of such a gene is likely to be undermined by the development of a further type of gene – one that in effect says: "I'll scratch your back, if you scratch mine (except that when it comes to my turn to do you the favor – I won't)." This is referred to as a "cheater" gene. The trouble is that the survival value of the cheater gene is likely to be greater than that of the non-cheating type. After all, it can only benefit from the arrangement, never having to put itself at risk. In the end there would only be the cheater genes left – in other words there would be no generalized altruism.

There is one caveat to make about this. This line of argument holds for communities where one does not know who the cheaters are. But in small closed communities where everyone gets to know everyone else rather well, it presumably could become known that certain individuals, having reaped the benefits of the reciprocal arrangement, never in fact put themselves out for others when it is their turn. They could then be excluded in future from the arrangement, and be at a survival disadvantage relative to the non-cheating types. That being so the cheater gene would not be able to gain the ascendancy.

So, in conclusion, has the case been made that, to some extent at least, there could be a genetic tendency toward altruism? As far as close kin are concerned, yes. The selfish gene concept allows for altruism between those sharing the self-same gene. In addition, within tightly knit closed communities one might expect altruism of the sort "you scratch my back, and I'll scratch yours." The mutual grooming of monkeys would be a (literal) example of that.

Altruism in humans

In the above discussion, we have to recognize that we have been using the word "altruism" in a rather specialized *biological* sense. It has to be said that a philosophy of "you scratch my back, and I'll scratch yours" falls far short of what *morally* we would regard as true altruism in humans. In fact, what we have been describing could perhaps more accurately be regarded as enlightened self-interest than altruism. True altruism – the type that figures in religious discussions – is one where one sacrifices oneself for another *without any thought of getting repaid*. Moreover, this is done for those beyond the circle of close kin. That is a type of altruism that does not seem to figure at all in the context of the selection of genes.

And yet such altruism does exist among humans, and in existing, raises the question of its source. According to the Bible, this is all bound up with the idea that, beyond the purely physical side of ourselves, in some sense we are made in the image of God.

A genetic basis for religion?

In our earlier discussion of Jungian psychology, we noted just how deeply embedded in the psyche is the sense of the religious. A tendency toward religious observance seems to be part and parcel of what it is to be human.

This raises the question whether it might have been genetically encoded in the same way as our species came to acquire other behavior traits. What we have in mind is that long ago there might have been a random change to the genes such that the resulting code corresponded to the individual acquiring a belief in a god – an imaginary god. Though the belief was wholly spurious and unfounded, if it conferred some survival advantage over those who did not have this code, then it could have been selected.

To some extent we have already examined this possibility. In Chapter 5, in our discussion of the origin of the religious archetype, we noted that such a belief might have encouraged those possessing the gene to act cooperatively. Working together, rather than as individuals, has undoubted advantages, as witness wolves hunting in packs, or ants living in a colony. But in that previous discussion we drew attention to the fact that it was hard to see how loyalty to an imaginary, invisible god would be effective when there were clearly much more tangible alternatives that might act as the focus for the shared loyalty.

However, a more severe weakness in this attempt to dismiss belief in God as a mere artifice thrown up by an evolutionary accident, comes from considering the *type* of God that is worshiped. As already noted, the most prominent characteristic that comes to mind in thinking about God is that of love. And this is not just love for people we like. Followers of the Christian God are to love their *enemies*. They must forgive to the point where, having been attacked, they are to turn the other cheek. This being so, one has to ask where the survival advantage in a strategy like that might lie. One suspects that a predator confronted by such a cooperative prey would simply think its luck was in. No, anyone acquiring a genetic code giving rise to such behavior would have been rapidly eliminated.

Thus, evolutionary theory seems unlikely to come up with any satisfactory explanation of the origins of the innate religious sense, and its accompanying characteristic of truly moral, self-sacrificing altruism. We must look elsewhere for its source. Many would claim that source to be self-evident; it is to be found in the God hypothesis. The innate moral sense certainly must be included in the data to be assessed in our God experiment.

The evolutionary tree and survival

In talking of evolution, it is common to have in mind a tree. The trunk represents our earliest common ancestors, emerging out of the ground – the primordial slime. Out of this common trunk grow various branches; these in their turn split up into side shoots; and these into individual twigs. The twigs represent all the different species of animal alive today. Being a tree, it has to have a topmost branch, and of course, it is natural for us to think of ourselves as being at the very top.

But this prompts us to ask: "Top, in what sense?" If what we have in mind is the ability to survive, then that distinction is hardly ours. Modern humans have been around for only about 100,000 years. How much longer does our species have? Given the ever-present threat of a nuclear bomb capability getting into the hands of an irresponsible world leader, or a nuclear holocaust being triggered accidentally, one might be hard-pressed to think that humans will be around for another 100,000 years. Even an optimist can surely not imagine that we shall be able to match the dinosaurs, who thrived for a thousand times longer than that. When it comes to surviving, humans have become too clever for their own good. *Tyrannosaurus rex* survived longer than we are likely to, not because it was better behaved, or more sensible than we are, but because it did not have as much potentially destructive power as our superior intelligence has given us.

The dinosaurs did, of course, eventually depart the scene. This, it is thought, was due to tremendous climatic changes brought about by the impact of a meteorite. This might also be the fate of the human race – if we have not already blown ourselves up in the meantime. Certainly destructive objects are still hurtling about space – witness the recent collision between a comet and Jupiter. No way could we, or other advanced forms of life, survive an impact of such magnitude were one to involve the Earth. The only types of life to stand any chance would be very small simple forms like bacteria. In fact, where survival is concerned, bacteria are the most successful. They were one of the first forms of life to appear, and they are still with us today. Indeed, there are more types of bacteria around today than at any previous time.

So, with regard to survival, humans don't rank at all.

The survival advantage of the human brain

If we are to regard ourselves as top of the evolutionary tree, we must specify which particular characteristic we have in mind when we make that claim. Humans have a number of particular advantages: they walk upright and this frees their front paws to operate as hands. These hands have developed great mobility, with a thumb that is set in opposition to the four fingers, so giving greater manipulative capability. We have developed good hand-to-eye coordination.

But our most important distinguishing asset is, of course, our brain. It is not that our brain is bigger than that of all other animals. Part of the brain is devoted to keeping the body functioning, and the bigger an animal's body, the larger the brain it needs simply to keep itself going. As far as intelligence is concerned, the crucial thing is not so much brain size, as how big the brain is in proportion to body size; in other words, how much brain capacity is left over for doing intelligent thinking after the ongoing needs of the body have been attended to. It is in this respect that humans have the advantage over other animals. But there is a price to be paid. Fortunately for us men, it is women who pay that price – at childbirth. They have to give birth to a baby whose brain size is relatively large compared to the size of the body of the mother giving birth to it; that is to say, the baby's head is large compared to the size of the hole it must pass through. Humans partially overcome this difficulty by seeing to it that, in a sense, their babies are all born prematurely – while the head is still small enough to get through. That is why human babies are so much less mature than the offspring of other animals. A newborn calf or foal, for example, is up and about, walking, in no time at all; a human baby on the other hand has to wait until he/she is older.

Somewhere along the line, the complexity of the brain would have become such as to make possible the use of speech. This was a great leap forward. Now it was no longer the case that one's understanding of the world had to be confined to whatever one had learned from one's own direct experience of life (plus the inherited information genetically encoded). Through speech one could learn from other people's experiences. One generation could build on the knowledge accumulated by former generations. This pooling of knowledge led to a vast explosion of understanding as to how the world operated. This in turn led to the ability to manipulate the environment for one's own ends. What need had humans for sharp claws, protective shells, powerful legs, etc., when the equivalents of all these could be had at will through sheer ingenuity?

The origins of the human spirit

In the evolutionary past a point was reached where the brain capacity became such as to permit the individual to think of more than just how to get shelter, the next meal, sex, etc. The first thoughts would have formed as to whether there might be something beyond what one could see and touch. This is where there opened up for the first time the possibility of entering into a conscious relationship with God. Here we have the birth of the first primitive spirit.

There would also have been a sharing and comparison of religious experiences. With the development of speech there would come the ability to articulate and further develop one's appreciation of God – opening up the possibility of a fuller, more enriching relationship with God. Indeed, where spirituality is concerned the first conscious thinking about God might not have happened before the development of speech.

The evolution of the spirit might strike some people as an odd idea, especially if they have been brought up to think that humans have a spirit and go to Heaven, while animals do not. In the light of evolutionary theory, it is hard to see how such a clear-cut distinction can be made. But why should it have to be all or nothing? To the extent that a dog or a dolphin today – or a primitive ancestor of our own in the distant past – has any capacity to think about why it might be here, and what the purpose of life might be, I don't see why they should not be accorded a rudimentary spirit. By this is meant the ability whereby they can experience to some small, superficial extent a relationship of sorts with God, and have a glimmer of appreciation of a life beyond death. But then again, perhaps this animal appreciation is so utterly rudimentary, it remains valid to reserve the word "spirit" to refer to something that, to all intents and purposes, is a distinctive characteristic of humans alone.

So, in summary I would say that when it comes to thinking of ourselves as being at the top of the evolutionary tree, this is specifically in regard to intelligence and spirituality.

The future evolution of the human species

So much for the evolutionary development that has taken place in the past. What of the future? Where might further evolution be taking the human race?

If evolution were to continue as it has done, then we might expect humans to develop into a super-intelligent species. But this is unlikely. The reason is that we have now entered a stage where the evolution of humans is being frustrated. Describing evolution by natural selection (very crudely) as "the survival of the fittest," we have only to look at the practice of modern medicine to realize that this is not happening any more. We are taking the most extraordinary measures to ensure that those who suffer from disabilities and ailments of all kinds should be preserved. Even with the comatose brain-dead, there is great reluctance to switch off the life-support system. Not only that, but people are living longer – well past the age where they have served their evolutionary usefulness in passing on their genes to the next generation. In evolutionary terms, once the young are able to stand on their own feet, the sooner the older generation dies and stops using up space and food the better. To some extent it can be argued that on average the more intelligent people are inclined to get the better-paid jobs (not always of course), and the higher the standard of living the *fewer* children they are inclined to have. In contrast, those in lower-paid jobs have somewhat bigger families. This is not conducive to raising the average IQ. In any case it is hard to see how, in today's society, the more intelligent have a better chance of surviving to the age where they have children. And without that, there will be no further selection in favor of greater intelligence.

All this makes it sound as though the human species is on a downward slide. And in terms of being a successful evolving animal, that is probably true. But I doubt that there would be many who would wish to withhold the benefits of modern medicine from those who need it, and exchange our present society for one that does not look after its weaker members – even though this might be storing up trouble for the future.

The Human Genome Project

So far in our discussion of where the human species might be heading, one factor has not been mentioned: the Human Genome Project, or as it is sometimes called, the Human Genome Initiative. It might completely turn the above argument on its head.

In speaking of our genes, we refer of course to our DNA. Looking at its structure in more detail, we note that DNA (short for *deoxyribonucleic acid*) contains two chains of smaller molecules (nucleotides) twisted around each other into a double helix. There is a link between each small molecule on one of these chains to a complementary molecule on the other strand. These linked pairs of molecules are called *base pairs*. There are some 3,000 million of them in the typical DNA molecule. It is the order in which the base pairs occur along the chains that constitutes the genetic code. One might regard the base pairs as the letters, and the genes as the meaningful sentences made up from those sequences of letters. Altogether in human DNA there are about 100,000 genes or coded messages. These govern our physical characteristics and also our genetically influenced behavior.

The aim of the Human Genome Project (HGP) has been to sequence all the base pairs. In 1987, the US government agreed to fund it at the rate of $200 million per year. This work was completed in 2000. The task of identifying which sequences make up which genes, and how the genes function continues. The purpose, as far as the scientists are concerned, is simply that of finding out what is there. But there are potentially great pay-offs. For example, it is thought that 4,000 human diseases are caused one way or another by genes. These include Huntington's chorea, cystic fibrosis, Alzheimer's, etc. There are hopes of locating a gene responsible for most forms of breast cancer. If this is achieved, then it opens up the possibility that, through genetic engineering, the harmful gene might be eliminated, leaving future generations free of this kind of disease. This would be a contribution to the overall aim of genetically engineering a healthier human species.

In the same way one might find a genetic link with intelligence. If so, not only could we produce a healthier species, but a more intelligent one. Indeed, what of other characteristics such as strength and longevity? And if that is thought desirable, how about a taste for blue eyes and blond hair? Could we be on the way to producing the perfect child?

At this point, one is likely to experience a vague unease. All this smacks of *Brave New World* and past attempts to breed super-races. Where is the line to be drawn as to what is thought desirable and what not? Are imperfect humans ever likely to be able to manufacture humans that are perfect? What about all the people who are unable to afford the expensive, customized genetic engineering of their offspring?

These concerns apart, one thing is certain: in a few years we shall have the ability, should we so wish, to give a helping hand to evolution. We shall be able to direct it down paths of our own choosing. No longer shall we need to wait for changes in the coding to happen at random – changes caused by mistakes in the process whereby the parents DNA is copied to provide that of the offspring. From here on we shall, in principle, be able deliberately to direct the course that evolution shall take.

I say "in principle" because this presupposes that one is able to anticipate all the side-effects and consequences of "playing God" in this manner. Perhaps there are some unforeseen and unpleasant surprises in store for the unwary.

What I find particularly worrying is that there seems little or no control over the process. Who is to make the decisions as to which manipulations should be made to the DNA. According to what criteria are these decisions to be made, and in whose interest? It looks at the moment as though there is no responsible overall supervision in place, and that decisions are being made on an ad hoc basis, with only the commercial interests of mainly pharmaceutical companies at stake.

There are further ramifications. If a person is revealed to have a defective gene that increases the chance of later developing some illness or disability, should an insurance company have the right to demand access to such information before agreeing to issue a policy?

The genes and human responsibility

The implications of the HGP go deeper still. There have been reports of the identification of genes to do with behavior traits that can lead, for example, to a certain type of alcoholism, to a certain kind of homosexuality, and to aggression. Does this mean that someone with an innate aggressive streak can claim that they were not really responsible for having carried out an act of, say, grievous bodily harm? ("It wasn't me, m'lud; it was me genes wot dun it!") Is it not unfair to expect the same standard of behavior from someone who has a genetic tendency making it more difficult for them?

It is an interesting question, but not one I think that introduces any fundamentally new challenge. It has always been recognized that we are all "born different." We know for instance that some men have much stronger sex drives than others; that presumably makes them more liable to succumb to the temptation to commit rape. Some exhibit violent tempers; they are the ones more likely to commit crimes of violence. All the genetic information is doing is helping us to localize the source of these traits.

The fact that life is not fair also manifests itself, of course, on the "nurture" side of the argument as well as the "nature" side. If one is brought up in a bad home, or in a bad neighborhood where one cannot avoid unsavory company and influences, then again one's chances of running foul of the law are greater than if one has had a comparatively sheltered upbringing.

In both cases, whether one is thinking of unfortunate genes or unfortunate environment, the important thing is that we are not blind victims of our fate – we have the power of choice and are expected to exercise that choice and shoulder responsibility for our actions. Recall how we are genetically *influenced* rather than genetically *determined*. At least where humans are concerned, there is the ability (our free will) deliberately and consciously to go against one's natural inclinations where necessary. And that is what society, and religion, require of us. We are expected to take responsibility for our actions.

But you might be thinking, in a world where one seeks justice – and God is supposed to be a God of Justice – is it not unfair that some people begin life with the cards stacked against them? From the moment they acquire their genes they find it harder than others to live up to the standards of acceptable behavior.

It would be unfair only if God expected the same standards of behavior from everyone regardless of individual circumstances. The fact that this is unlikely to be the case is manifestly demonstrated by the Biblical warnings that we ourselves should refrain from judging others – "Judge not, that ye be not judged." This implies that true judgment is not a matter of simply comparing one person's behavior with that of another. If that had been the case we would all be in a position to judge. No, we are to refrain from judging because we are not in possession of all the relevant facts.

The role of death

One further interesting question that will be thrown into sharp relief by the HGP is the role of death. The prospect is held before us that we might soon understand a great deal about the genetics of ageing and the onset of death. To what extent is longevity to be prized?

Whether it is a good thing or not is likely to depend in large measure on one's state of health. If one is constantly fighting for breath, or in pain, or crippled with arthritis, or one's mind has gone, then there seems little point in prolonging that state indefinitely. But suppose it were possible to alter the genes in such a way as to slow down the age-ing process. Suppose one could live to 150 or 200 years of age with the body of a 40-year-old; what then?

This raises a serious question: Are we to regard ageing as a natural process that ought not to be interfered with, or as a disease which like other diseases ought to be attended to once this becomes possible? What would be the effects on society if people lived twice or three times longer than they do now? Many ambitious young people already feel frustrated at not being promoted as fast as they would like because the senior positions are still occupied by older staff. Can we psycholog-ically adjust ourselves to a working life extending to 100 or 150 years before we become eligible for a pension? Do we really have to try and sustain the excitement of sex in our marriage over *that* span of time? Or in our leisure time, how many *Monday Night Football* games can we bear watching before it finally palls? In short, is our psychological make-up capable of coping with a significantly extended life span?

This brings us to the subject of death. It is important for us to accept that in evolutionary theory, death has an important part to play. Evolu-tionary change can only come about if each generation at some point gets out of the way, thereby making room for the next. This applies not only to those individuals with disadvantageous characteristics (the ones that need to be weeded out before they mate), but also to those with the advantageous characteristics – once they have successfully mated and passed the advantageous gene on to the next generation. Death is such an integral feature of the successful species that it might well be that there is a specific gene in our DNA responsible for seeing to it that we do not hang around too long. The "eventual-death-of-the-individual" gene would then have to be regarded, somewhat paradoxi-cally, as an integral part of the survival kit of the species as a whole. That being so, should we be tampering with it?

Such a discussion quickly highlights the need to adopt a construc-tive attitude toward death. Too easily it comes to be regarded as an evil to be resisted in almost all circumstances. Only in extreme old age, and in the throes of unremitting pain and disability, might it be spoken of as "a merciful release." But why? For those of us with a belief in a life beyond death, might not death be a merciful release in *all* cases? Perhaps from the vantage point of Heaven it will be those who live to a ripe old age who will be aggrieved because they were left down here so long while those who died young had longer to enjoy Heaven.

The HGP undoubtedly raises a host of questions, promises, and problems. It is good to note that, from the outset, 5 percent of all its funds have been set aside for the study of the ethical, legal, and social implications of the project.

The human species and the Son of God

Let us return to the prospect of further evolution of the human species. If this were to happen in the natural course of events (despite the apparent frustration of the process of natural selection at present), or if it were to happen as a result of directed evolution through the controlled manipulation of our genes, a religious question arises for Christians. It comes about in the following way: Christians hold that the eternal Son of God took on human form as Jesus. But if we present-day humans are merely a staging post on the way to some superhuman species, that later species will doubtless look back at us and regard us as primitive – in much the same way as we regard our ape-like ancestors as primitive. Thus the question arises as to why the Son of God took on the "primitive" form of a human, rather than waiting for the superhuman species to come on to the scene.

By way of an answer, one might begin by saying that by the term "superhuman" one presumably has in mind a species that has greater intelligence. But intelligence does not necessarily equate with spirituality. A highly intelligent person might have no conscious relationship with God, whereas someone with a low IQ might enjoy a deep and sincere love of God, and have a keen sense of the presence of God. Inasmuch as we take the term "spirit" to refer to the immortal spirit that is in active communion with God, the first person might be a spiritual little person, the latter a giant.

The heart of the spiritual life is the depth of one's love for God. The measure of love is the extent to which the lover is prepared to sacrifice his or her own interests in favor of those of the beloved. The supreme loving sacrifice is that one be prepared to lay down one's life for the other. Jesus did precisely that on the cross, and since that time there have been countless martyrs who have also voluntarily given everything they had in order to be true to their faith in God. It is in fact impossible to imagine greater acts of self-sacrifice than those that have been offered out of love of God. While it might be possible for some future superhuman species to have deeper spiritual insights and knowledge, and more intense religious experiences than we, in *practical* terms they would be incapable of demonstrating greater loyalty to God than many humans have already done, and others would be prepared to do if faced with similar circumstances. That being so, it does indeed make sense that the Son of God should come in human form, even though those endowed with superior intelligence might still be to come. The point is that no one can be *spiritually* more mature and advanced than we are.

Evolution elsewhere in the Universe

One final point before we close this discussion of evolution. What of evolution elsewhere in the Universe?

Whether life has evolved on any other planets in the cosmos, we do not yet know. Given the vast number of stars (each one a sun like our own Sun), and the knowledge that a significant proportion of them have planets going round them, and many of those will be at the right kind of distance from their star to have a temperate climate, it strikes me as highly unlikely that the Earth is the unique home of life in the cosmos. There are some who would be inclined to the opposite view. They hold that the evolutionary path from slime to intelligent life is so beset with difficult steps that it might well have happened only the once. But suppose my guess is right and life has evolved elsewhere, what are the implications for religious belief?

If I were to meet aliens from outer space, I suppose one of my first questions would be to find out whether they believed in God, and if so what their ideas were on the subject. I would suspect that they would indeed have a religion. I would also suspect that if they have evolved in the same kind of way as we have, through evolution by natural selection, their behavior will be to some extent genetically influenced, and like us they will be inclined to self-centeredness – they would be subject to original sin. Like us they will be in need of a savior.

So how does the Son of God fit in here? Are we to regard the Jesus who lived here on Earth as the unique saviour of all intelligent forms of life throughout the cosmos? I personally shouldn't have thought so. Any belief that implies that we humans are uniquely privileged is liable to run the risk of being arrogant. I see no problem with the idea that the Son of God should visit each planet. He would not do so in human form, of course, but in whatever form was appropriate to the life to be found there.

We have spoken of the possibility of humans developing into a species of super-intelligent beings. Might this not already have happened on other planets in the cosmos? Because of the relatively short time over which we ourselves have evolved from markedly more primitive ancestors (100,000 years compared to the 12,000-million-year history of the Universe) a civilization would have to be only fractionally out-of-step with us for there to be a marked difference in intelligence between us and them. Thus one might expect there to be many alien civilizations ahead of our own.

But this leaves out of account one important factor. In the development of intelligence there comes the stage where language emerges. From then on, there is an explosion of knowledge arising out of the sharing and accumulation of experiences. This leads to the knowledge, among other things, of nuclear power. Just as the basically sinful nature of humans is liable to bring about their destruction here on Earth in a relatively short time (speaking in terms of evolutionary epochs), so it might well be that the pattern repeats itself endlessly throughout the cosmos. Each advanced civilization reaches the point where it has the intellectual capacity to engage in science, and through religion establish contact with God, but then soon afterward – because old, genetically encoded habits die hard – destroys itself.

A sober thought perhaps. But even if that scenario were roughly correct (and of course it might well be wide of the mark for some hitherto unknown reason), there is a crumb of comfort I can offer. It would mean that not only were humans the most intelligent creatures here on Earth, but our intelligence would be on a par with the best there is in the entire Universe!

In summary, I would say that evolutionary theory has many insights to offer concerning the nature and status of human beings – where we have come from, why we are the way we are, and where we might be heading. At no stage does it come up with any evidence that is contrary to the findings of our religious investigation. Indeed it can offer fascinating glimpses into the method God has adopted for working out his creative purposes. We understand now, for example, how it incorporates an element of chance. This leaves the world free to do its own thing – a very subtle form of freedom, embodying as it does a systematic selection procedure ensuring that, one way or another, creatures consciously able to relate to God will somehow emerge, thus fulfilling the overall Divine intention.

12

A Case of Over-design?

Toward the end of Steven Weinberg's popular introduction to Big Bang cosmology, *The First Three Minutes*, the author concludes: "The more the Universe seems comprehensible, the more it also seems pointless." A little earlier, he dismisses human life as "a more-or-less farcical outcome of a chain of accidents."

It is not difficult to understand how Weinberg arrives at such gloomy assessments. Take, for example, the size of the Universe. Are we really expected to believe that God designed it as a home for humans? It appears somewhat excessive – a case of over-design, perhaps.

Here we come across seemingly powerful evidence against the fundamental religious notion that we humans are important to God. If God's prime purpose in creating the world was to bring into existence creatures that could respond to him in a loving relationship, then we would expect the world to look as though it had been designed with that end in mind. Weinberg clearly thinks it does not. This is not something our God experiment can ignore.

In Chapter 8 we made a start on this question by recognizing that size was not everything – one must also take into account the role of consciousness (Pascal's thinking reed). We also noted that we did not have to regard the Universe as solely a home for humans here on Earth; there could be additional forms of life elsewhere in the Universe just as precious to God. But we are still led to ask: is the type of Universe revealed to us by modern cosmology and astronomy one that can be regarded as an *appropriate* home for life? Or rather is the character of the world such that life – *any* kind of life – could only be regarded as an accidental by-product?

A world hostile to life?

Most places in the Universe are hostile to life. The depths of space are incredibly cold; that is why most planets are freezing. To be warm a planet needs to be close to a star. But get too close – like Mercury and Venus – and they become too hot. And of course the most prominent objects in the sky, the Sun and the other stars, are in themselves balls of fire and hence not suitable places to find life. Planets tend to be without atmospheres, or if they do have one, it is unlikely to be the right sort for sustaining life.

For much of the past history of the Universe there was no intelligent life. Looking to the future, we expect after a further 5,000 million years our Sun will swell up to become a star of a type known as a *red giant*. Though it is unlikely that its fiery surface will reach out far enough to engulf the Earth, our planet will become unbearably hot – to the extent that all life will be burned up. Indeed, life might already have been eliminated long before then through the violent impact of a meteorite.

And what of the long-term future of the Universe and of life elsewhere? We have spoken much about the *origins* of the Universe in the Big Bang, but what of its *end*?

We have seen how the Universe is expanding. The distant galaxies of stars are still receding in the aftermath of the Big Bang. But as they rush off into the distance, they are slowing down. This is due to gravity, each galaxy exerting an attraction on every other one. Keep this up, and eventually the galaxies will be brought to a halt. Except that we have to remember that the force of gravity reduces with increasing distance. It goes down as the inverse square of the distance. Galaxies that are twice as far away exert only a quarter of the force on each other; three times further away, 1/9 the force; 10 times further away, 1/100 the force. . . . So, with the galaxies receding to ever greater distances from each other, the slowing down force is steadily reducing with time.

The big question then is whether gravity in the Universe is strong enough to stop the galaxies before it has essentially vanished to nothing, or alternatively the speeds of the galaxies are sufficiently great for them to succeed in escaping the pull of gravity. We are thus presented with two alternatives:

(i) *Big Crunch scenario.* If gravity is strong enough, then the galaxies will one day come to a halt. From then on they will be drawn back toward each other. All their separations will reduce until eventually everything comes piling back in at the same instant of time. This prospect is called the *Big Crunch*.

What would happen after that is anybody's guess. As with the Big Bang itself, one has here an instant in time where all the contents of the Universe are contained within a volume having no size, i.e., the density is infinite. Our understanding of physics is unable to handle that. It could be that this marks the end of everything; the Universe goes out of existence. On the other hand, it might rebound – a *Big Bounce*. The expansion of the Universe would then happen all over again. Perhaps this is how it has always been: a constant repetition of expansions and contractions – what we call an *oscillating Universe*. According to this scenario, what we have been calling the Big Bang would merely have been the most recent of the Big Bounces. It would mean that the Big Bang did *not* mark the origin of the Universe. It would mean that all that discussion in Chapter 9 about the Big Bang marking the beginning of time would also be wrong; there *was* time before the Big Bang – the time needed to accommodate the previous oscillations. It could be that we are dealing with a Universe that has *no* beginning, nor any end.

By way of an aside: would *that* get rid of the Creator God? Previously we were discussing this question in connection with the assumption that there was no time before the Big Bang – and hence no time to accommodate a God lighting the blue touch-paper. A Universe that had no origins *at all* would – superficially – be an alternative way of getting rid of him. Except that it is not. You will recall how earlier we made a distinction between the word "origins" and the word "creation." Whether the world had a beginning or not – an origin – we are still left with the creation question as to why there is something rather than nothing – a question to which the religious answer is God.

So that, then, is one possible scenario: the clusters of galaxies will one day come to a halt and thereafter come back together in a Big

Crunch. Were that to be the case, there would clearly be an end to life not only here on Earth but everywhere throughout the cosmos.

(ii) *Unending expansion scenario.* The alternative is that gravity is too weak to stop the galaxies, and they will continue flying apart for ever. What would be the significance of that for life in the cosmos?

Each star has only a limited amount of fuel. Eventually its fire must go out. For a medium-sized star like the Sun that would take about 10,000 million years. More massive stars have greater supplies of fuel, but they achieve higher temperatures and burn their fuel faster – so much faster they might live for only one million years. What happens to the star as it runs out of fuel depends critically on how massive it is. The Sun, having swollen up to become a tenuous red giant, will shed some of its outer layers before sinking back to become a compact *white dwarf* star. This in turn will continue to radiate away its heat until it becomes a cold, black cinder.

What of more massive stars? In order for a star to remain a stable size, it relies on all the vigorous jiggling motion of its atomic particles to counteract the inward pull of its own gravity. But as the fuel runs out and the star begins to cool, the movements become less vigorous and the outer parts of the star no longer experience the same resistance to being pulled in closer to the center. The star shrinks. The more closely packed, the stronger becomes the mutual gravity between its component parts, and hence the greater the tendency to become even more tightly packed. For a star several times heavier than the Sun, the situation suddenly becomes unstable. In no more than a second, the massive star undergoes catastrophic collapse. In the process, some of the material is blasted out. The star goes out with a bang – literally; it is called a *supernova.* This is one of the most spectacular occurrences in the cosmos. For a few days, a supernova will shine as brightly as a whole galaxy – as brightly as 100,000 million stars. As for the rest of the star's material – the bulk of it – it collapses down to a super-dense ball, a few miles across, called a *neutron star.* It has a density equivalent to that of an atomic nucleus; one teaspoon of the stuff would weigh as much as 10,000 melted down aircraft carriers!

Even something as rigid as an atomic nucleus, however, might not be sufficient to withstand the intense gravity force for an even heavier star. In fact, given enough mass, nothing at all can withstand the force of gravity, so the heaviest stars collapse down to a point – what we call a *black hole*. In the immediate vicinity of this point – within a distance called "the event horizon" – the gravity is so strong there is no escape; even light itself is unable to drag itself away – hence the adjective "black." A black hole emits no light of its own, nor does it reflect any light that falls on it. If we can't see it, how do we know it is there? From the way it continues to drag in any other material that passes too close to it, and from the way it might leave companion bodies still orbiting it at a safe distance.

But whether a star ends up as a cooled down white dwarf, a neutron star, or a black hole, the end result is the same – it becomes cold and no longer able to keep companion planets warm enough to sustain life.

As one generation of stars dies out in this manner, so new stars continue to form. A star is created when the hydrogen and helium gases that were emitted originally from the Big Bang collect together under the influence of their mutual gravity. The gas squashes down, heating up as it does so (in the same way as air squashed down in a bicycle pump gets hot). If enough gas is collected, the temperature rise becomes sufficient at the center to ignite nuclear fusion. In a very hot gas, the atomic nuclei are moving about so fast they can fuse together to form heavier nuclei. These heavier nuclei are so efficiently packed together that they are able to release unwanted energy – the energy of nuclear fusion. (The modest heat of the squashed-down gas acts merely as a trigger to get the much more energetic nuclear fusion reactions going. This is similar to the way we light a domestic coal fire by first setting light to some rolled-up paper and sticks of wood – the small output of heat from this being the trigger to get the coal burning.)

Not all the gas from the Big Bang was used up in producing the first generation of stars. Our own Sun was one of those formed at a later stage. Still more stars are to be seen today in the very earliest phases of getting underway. But it is clear that this is not something that can go on indefinitely. At some stage, *all* the hydrogen and helium gas will have been drawn together to form stars, or will have been dispersed so thinly as never to be incorporated into a star. From then on the last stars live out their active lives, and die. Everything cools down, and we are left with the *Heat Death* of the Universe.

So what we find is that if we are dealing with a Universe where the expansion goes on for ever, there will come a point when there can be no further life. One is then left with an ever-dispersing, lifeless Universe for an infinity of time.

So, Big Crunch or Heat Death – either way, the future for life is bleak. Yes, it is easy to see how Weinberg was led to the conclusion that the Universe seems pointless, and life but an accidental by-product of no significance.

The Anthropic Principle

But are we being too hasty? Let us change tack and introduce some reflections on the cosmos of a very different nature. These have surfaced only recently – in the past couple of decades. They go under the general heading: *The Anthropic Principle*.

To see what it is about, I want you to imagine that you have the responsibility of designing a universe. You have freedom to choose the laws of nature and the conditions under which this imaginary universe is to operate. The aim is to produce a universe tailor-made for the development of life – the kind of universe God presumably *ought* to have created if it really were intended primarily as a home for life. There are various decisions you have to make:

(i) *The violence of the Big Bang.* Assuming that you will start off your universe with a Big Bang, how violent will you make it? You might feel, for example, that the actual Big Bang was somewhat excessive if the aim was simply to produce some life forms.

It turns out that if you make the violence of your Big Bang somewhat less – only a little less – then the mutual gravity operating between the galaxies will get such a secure grip that the galaxies will slow down to a halt; they will thereafter be brought together in a Big Crunch. That in itself need not be a problem. The difficulty is in ensuring that the crunch does not happen too quickly – in a time shorter than the 12,000 million years needed for evolution to produce us. Turn the Big Bang wick down too much, and there is insufficient time for intelligent life to develop.

This danger might prompt you to err on the other side: you turn the wick up a little, i.e., make your Big Bang just a little *more* violent than the actual one. What happens now is that the gases come out of the Big Bang so fast that they do not have time to collect together to form embryo stars before they are dispersed into the depths of space. There being no stars, there is no life.

In fact it turns out that as far as the Big Bang violence is concerned, the window of opportunity is exceedingly narrow. If you are to get life in your universe, the thrust must be just right – as it happens to be with our actual Universe.

(ii) *The strength of gravity.* The next point to consider is the force of gravity. We have already seen that the force between two objects varies inversely as the square of the distance between them. But that just determines the *relative* values of the force for different separations. What of the intrinsic strength of the force? This depends on one of the physical constants of nature – one represented by the symbol G in the relevant equations. How big will you make G in your imaginary universe? If you make it a little less than it actually is, the strength of all gravity forces in your universe will be correspondingly less. You now run the risk of a universe that has no stars. Although the gas from the Big Bang collects together to form dense clouds, the mutual gravity force is not strong enough to collect the amount needed to produce a temperature rise sufficient to light the nuclear fires. Out there in space are objects called *brown dwarf stars.* It's a misnomer because they are not proper stars. They are collections of gas that become warm at their centers as the gas is squashed together, but they do not heat up sufficiently to trigger the nuclear fusions. Without access to the main source of energy, they just peter out after a while. In our own Solar System, the planet Jupiter is, or was, a brown dwarf. It is a globe of hydrogen and helium gases which is warm at its center. If it had originally collected about seventy times as much gas as it actually did, it would have caught fire properly and become a companion star to our Sun. So, if you decide on a gravity a little weaker than it really is, you will have a universe that has only brown dwarfs – and that means no life.

On the other hand, you must be careful not to have your gravity too strong. That way you would get only the very massive types of star. Recall how massive stars burn themselves out quickly – perhaps in only one million years. For evolution to take place you must have a steady source of energy for 5,000 million years – you need a medium-sized star like the Sun.

Indeed when you come to think of it, the Sun is a remarkable phenomenon. After all, what is a star? It is a nuclear bomb going off SLOWLY. In practice this is very difficult to achieve. I recall soon after the Second World War hearing a talk extolling the virtues of unlimited cheap supplies of nuclear power to be obtained from the fusion of the heavy hydrogen found in abundance in the oceans. How long would it take for this to be a commercial proposition? Fifty years, we were told. Since then, at regular intervals, I have heard talks updating us on progress in harnessing the power of hydrogen fusion. Always someone in the audience asks the question: "How long will it take for this to become a commercial proposition?" And the answer is always the same: "Fifty years." The past decades of research, costing countless millions of dollars, must surely have brought us somewhat closer to the goal – but sometimes it does not seem so. Not surprising really. It is incredibly difficult to contain fuel at temperatures reckoned in millions of degrees, and to persuade this bomb to go off in a controlled manner. Yet the amazing thing is that the Sun does all this – for nothing! The secret is the way the force of gravity in the Sun conspires to feed the new fuel into the nuclear furnace at just the right rate for the nuclear fires (governed by the nuclear force – an entirely different force from that of gravity) to consume it at a steady rate extending over a period of 10,000 million years.

Thus, in order for there to be life, the gravitational constant, G, must lie within a very narrow range of possible values. The gravity of the actual Universe does just that.

(iii) *Raw materials for making the bodies of living creatures*. Next you must turn your attention to the materials from which you wish to build the bodies of living creatures. This is no small matter. All that is emitted from the Big Bang are the two lightest gases – hydrogen and helium – and precious little besides. And it *has* to be that way. Remember you need a violent Big Bang to stop your Universe from collapsing back in on itself prematurely. And because of that violence, only the lightest atomic nuclei could survive the collisions occurring at that time – anything bigger getting smashed up again soon after its formation. But one can't make interesting objects like living bodies out of just hydrogen and helium. So the extra nuclei – those that go to make up the ninety-two different elements (i.e., types of atom) found on Earth – must be manufactured somehow *after* the Big Bang.

That's where the stars have another important role to play. Not only do they provide a steady source of warmth to energize the processes of evolution, they first serve as furnaces for taking light nuclei and fusing them into the heavy ones that will later be needed for producing the bodies of the evolving creatures. Again, it is a case of no stars – no life.

(iv) *The special problem of carbon synthesis.* But we are not home and dry yet. Perhaps the most important element for the making of life is carbon. In a sense it has an especially "sticky" kind of atom – good at cementing together the large molecules of biological interest. But forming a nucleus of carbon is by no means easy. Essentially it requires the fusion of three helium nuclei. Whereas it is relatively easy to get two billiard balls to collide with each other (a two-particle collision), to get three colliding all at the same instant (a three-particle collision) is an entirely different matter. The same goes for the three helium nuclei. Common sense would say that this simply is not going to happen in stars. Yet somehow it does – obviously (otherwise we wouldn't be here). But how? In the first place, when two helium nuclei collide they momentarily stick together to form a beryllium nucleus. That would make it easier for the third nucleus to collide a little later – it does not have to collide with the other two helium nuclei at *exactly* the same instant as they do. First the two helium nuclei collide to form beryllium, and then in a separate (two-particle collision) the third helium nucleus joins them. Unfortunately the first two stick together so briefly, this is but a small improvement – not enough to make any substantial difference.

This is where the most extraordinary coincidence emerges. To understand how it comes about, you must first know that a collision between nuclei is not the same as that between billiard balls. How big one nucleus looks to another depends on how fast they approach each other. This is obviously not true of macroscopic objects like billiard balls, but it is true of sub-atomic particles. Now, it just so happens that at certain special approach speeds, one nucleus can look absolutely enormous to the other – they can hardly avoid banging into each other. We call it a *nuclear resonance*. And that is what happens inside stars. By a most extraordinary chance, at the speeds characteristic of the nuclei moving about in stars, the beryllium nucleus (made of the first two helium nuclei briefly attached to each other) looks absolutely enormous to the approaching third helium nucleus. They hit each other, fuse together, and produce the desired carbon.

It is hard for a lay person to appreciate the sheer unlikeliness of this. It was the physicist Fred Hoyle who first made this seemingly outrageous suggestion. He knew that carbon had somehow to be made in the stars and was led to make this brilliant deduction that it must be due to a resonance. His suggestion was at first greeted with skepticism. But in response to his persistence, a laboratory experiment was mounted to reproduce the conditions in a star. The resonance was found just where Hoyle had predicted it would be. It was a great triumph for him.

In his younger days, Hoyle had been a noted and militant atheist. I well recall the outrage he caused in the 1950s when he used one of his Reith Lectures on BBC radio to attack religious belief in a Creator God. Some time after his unraveling of the mystery of carbon synthesis, I was to hear him deliver a talk about this resonance. In the course of it, he spoke of "He who fixed it." In a private conversation I had with him afterward, it was clear that his discovery had had a profound effect on him. While still disavowing any association with "organized religion," Hoyle nevertheless felt the "coincidence" was so way out, it could not have been due to mere chance.

So you have your precious carbon. Collisions between some of these carbon nuclei and further helium nuclei yield oxygen – another vital ingredient for life – and so on. Thus you must be sure in your imaginary universe to incorporate that fortuitous nuclear resonance!

(v) *Escape from a star*. Does this mean that the stage is now set for evolution to take over, converting these raw materials into human beings?

Not so. You have your materials, but they are in the center of a star at a temperature of about 10 million degrees – hardly an environment conducive to life. The materials have to be got out. But how, in your imaginary universe, are you going to arrange for that? After all, we know how difficult it is to lift something off the surface of the Earth and out into space; a rocket is needed. Your stars have no rockets, and the gravity forces at the surface of stars are in any case stronger.

What happens in this actual Universe is that a proportion of the newly synthesized material is ejected by supernova explosions. As we noted above, these occur when a massive old star collapses in on itself. But that raises a new problem. How can an *im*plosion produce an *ex*plosion? This was a conundrum that exercised the minds of astrophysicists for many years. In the event the mechanism turned out to be the strangest imaginable. The material is blasted out by *neutrinos*. Like the quarks that make up the neutrons and protons of nuclei, and the electrons that attach themselves to nuclei to form atoms, neutrinos are one of the fundamental particles of nature. They are produced, for example, when the protons of a star absorb electrons to convert into neutrons as they collapse down to form the neutron star remnant. Perhaps the best-known feature of neutrinos is that, unlike the other fundamental particles, they hardly interact with anything. As you sit reading this book, millions upon millions of neutrinos coming from the Sun are passing through you every second and yet you are unaware of this. Indeed, one could pass a neutrino through the center of the Earth to Australia 100,000 million times before it had a 50:50 chance of hitting anything. They are incredibly slippery. And yet it is the neutrinos coming from the region of the newly forming neutron core at the center of the collapsing star that blasts out the precious stardust. So, in your imaginary universe, make your neutrinos slippery if you wish, but be sure not to overdo it – otherwise you will not get life.

(vi) *Last-second synthesis*. A further provision you need to allow for is that not all the nuclear materials for forming living bodies are produced in the steady nuclear synthesis taking place in stars prior to catastrophic collapse. Those heavier than iron don't exist up to that point. So, where do *they* come from? They are manufactured in the extraordinarily short-lived conditions of the supernova explosion itself. It is as though someone has had an afterthought and said, "Whoops. No bromine, cobalt, copper, iodine, or zinc; they'll be needing those as trace elements. I'd better make some double-quick." They are made in the few seconds of the explosion itself (making use of the exceptionally high density of neutrons flying about at that time).

(vii) *Further requirements?* The material is now out among the interstellar gases. In time, this collects together to form a dense cloud, which squashes down to form a new star. Outside the star there can be secondary eddies that settle down to form planets. It is now possible for some of these planets to be of the rocky kind, like Earth, Mercury, Venus, and Mars. For the first generation of stars this had not been so; at that stage there had only been hydrogen and helium around. Given a rocky planet at a reasonable distance from the star for a temperate climate to prevail, one has now at last a chance of life evolving from the primordial slime.

How likely this is to happen is not known. If one is a physicist like myself, one tends to be impressed by the vast number of planets there must be out there – in other words how many attempts there have been to produce intelligent life. On this assessment, there is almost certainly life out there. If, on the other hand, one is a biologist, one might be more impressed by the size of the hurdles that have still to be negotiated on the way to intelligent life – like for example the formation of the first cell. This might require yet more "coincidences" – biological ones this time rather than the physical ones we have been considering.

Inferences to be drawn from the Anthropic Principle

It is impossible to put a hard figure on the likelihood of getting life from simply throwing together a bunch of physical laws at random – laws incorporating arbitrary values for the various physical constants. In talking, for example, about the strength of gravity having to lie within a narrow range, it is impossible to be more quantitative unless there is some way of specifying a permissible range of values that the strength could conceivably take on. If it could be *any value whatsoever*, then the finite range compatible with the production of life would be divided by infinity – and the chances would be virtually zero. Whatever the true odds are, it is probably fair to say that to have a universe that, purely by chance, satisfies all the requirements appropriate to the development of life is less likely than winning first prize in the State Lottery.

All of this goes under the name of the Anthropic Principle. It calls for an explanation of some sort – though to hear some people talk one might think it doesn't. What they say is this: "Of course, the world has to be suitable for the development of life – otherwise we wouldn't be here asking these questions." There is a certain element of truth in this. Given that we are here, we *must* find ourselves in such a universe. But that still doesn't address the question of *why* we should be here in the first place. Richard Swinburne puts it nicely when he describes a prisoner facing a firing squad. There are ten marksmen; they have never been known to miss. But on this occasion all ten miss the target. The prisoner, when interviewed afterward about his miraculous deliverance, is quite unimpressed. "There's no mystery," he declares. "Of course they missed, otherwise I wouldn't be here talking to you about it."

No, we have to face the fact that we are presented with a Universe that, although at first sight appeared somewhat hostile to life, on closer examination is found to be exceptionally fine-tuned for the development of life. Thus, for instance, we began thinking that the immensity of the Universe was far in excess of requirements, but now we recognize that if the galaxies are to continue receding at high speed for the 12,000 million years of evolutionary history, a life-bearing Universe cannot be any smaller.

Such then are the experimental data before us. Now comes the interpretation. What might be the explanation of the mysterious appropriateness of the Universe? There are essentially three alternatives:

(i) *Science will one day come up with an answer.* The first is to pin one's faith on science, and assert that in the end a natural explanation of it all will be forthcoming. From that vantage point we shall be able to realize that there was no mystery – no need to invoke coincidences.

To a limited extent, this explaining away of the coincidences appears to have begun already – at least in respect of getting the thrust of the Big Bang right. Recall that there are two broad scenarios: a Big Crunch or expansion for ever. Which one do we think it will actually be? As indicated before, that depends upon whether gravity is strong enough one day to halt the expansion. And that in turn depends upon how much matter there is in the Universe acting as the source of the gravity. If one imagines all the matter bound up in galaxies to be uniformly spread throughout space, that would give us an average density of the Universe. The greater this average density, the greater will be the slowing down effect of the gravity. Indeed, there will be a certain value for the density that marks the borderline between the two scenarios; this is called the *critical density*. If the density is a little greater than critical then we get a Big Crunch; a little less and we get expansion for ever.

So, what is it to be? If we count up all the matter we can see – that bound up in stars, planets, and interstellar gas clouds, then it adds up to no more than 0.3 percent of the critical value. That would indicate expansion for ever. But we must not be hasty. The stars are gathered into rotating galaxies. They are held there by their gravitational attraction for each other. Except that the galaxies rotate so fast, no way can the gravity between stars hold them together; they ought to come flying out like a child on a fast-rotating roundabout who does not hold on tightly enough. The conclusion is that there must be more matter in the galaxy than we can see. It is called *dark matter*, and it is the added gravity coming from the dark matter that holds the galaxy together. How much dark matter is needed? At least ten times as much as the matter we can see.

Nor is that the end. The galaxies are gathered together into clusters of galaxies. They move about within their cluster, but are held by their mutual gravity so as not to move too far from each other. Except that again there does not seem to be enough matter around to stop this random motion from tearing the cluster apart. The dynamics are such that one must postulate that not only is there dark matter within each galaxy, there must be yet more dark matter in between the galaxies belonging to a cluster. And who knows, there might be yet more on the scale of superclusters. Currently it is thought that the density of matter is within a factor of 2 of the critical value.

What the dark matter consists of is the subject of much conjecture. At present there is no consensus – which is rather embarrassing, because it means we are completely in the dark about 99 percent of the Universe's contents!

Of all the conceivable values the density could presumably have taken on, it appears most odd that it should come out to be so close to critical. This is especially so as it can be shown that any slight deviation from criticality in the early stages of the Big Bang would have become enormously magnified by now. To get this close to critical today, the initial density must have departed from critical by no more than one part in a million billion billion billion billion billion billion. (It is rather like standing a pencil on its point. Only if it starts out *absolutely* vertical can it maintain its upright position. The slightest initial deviation from the vertical rapidly becomes magnified as it falls flat.) The only way the density of the Universe could be close to critical today is if it started out spot-on the critical density initially.

This is where a new theory called *inflation theory* comes into the reckoning. It is all to do with what happened a tiny fraction of a second after the instant of the Big Bang when the dropping temperature passed through a particularly crucial value. At this temperature the behavior of the particles underwent a radical change. It is called a phase change. A phase change we are all familiar with in everyday life is the freezing of water as the temperature drops below 0°C. Suddenly the liquid crystallizes out as solid ice. In doing so, it expands a little (which is why ice is less dense than water and floats, and why water pipes burst). According to the inflation idea, the most spectacular effect of the phase change that occurred in the early history of the cosmos was that it gave rise to a special period of superfast expansion. It took place 10^{-34} second after the instant of the Big Bang – that is to say:

$$\frac{1}{10,000,000,000,000,000,000,000,000,000,000,000} \text{ second}$$

and it lasted 10^{-32} second. Although it was all over so quickly, what happened during that brief interval of time sealed the subsequent fate of the Universe. This was because the very nature of the inflation mechanism drives the density toward the critical value. No matter what the density might have been before the onset of inflation, it assumes the critical value by the end. After the inflation period, the Universe then undergoes the familiar Hubble-type expansion, with the density remaining critical.

How inflation comes about is a complicated matter. For our purposes it is sufficient to know that cosmologists have come up with this plausible mechanism for explaining why the density should be critical. That being so, we can predict that the long-term future of the Universe is one in which the expansion will continue for ever, slowing down to the point where the recession velocities of the galaxies approach zero – but only in the infinite future.

This affects our discussion of the Anthropic Principle in that inflation ensures that the Universe will never undergo a Big Crunch. It therefore becomes impossible to turn the violence of the Big Bang down to a level where the Universe comes to an end before there has been time for evolution to have given rise to intelligent life. So that is half the problem of the Big Bang thrust solved. Of course, we could now start to worry about what a coincidence it was that the Universe had such a mechanism built into it to prevent collapse. Who ordered *that*?! We also still have the problem as to how the violence was not too great to prevent the dispersal of the gases before it could collect together prior to the formation of stars. But it is perhaps not surprising that inflation theory has been a source of encouragement to those who hold to the belief that one day science will come up with naturalistic explanations of all the so-called coincidences. For what it is worth, I am personally very dubious that this will prove to be the case.

(ii) *The possibility of our Universe being one of many.* The second way of addressing the puzzle posed by the Anthropic Principle is to assert that our Universe is not alone. There are a great many universes – perhaps an infinite number of them – and they are all run on different lines with their own laws of nature. The vast majority of them have no life in them because one or other of the conditions was not met. In a few – perhaps in only this one – all the conditions happen by chance to be satisfied and there life is able to get a hold. The probability of a universe being of this type is exceedingly small, but with there being so many attempts, it is no longer surprising that it should have happened. As a form of life ourselves, we must, of course, find ourselves in one of these freak universes.

This is a suggestion that has been put forward by some scientists, but that does not make it a scientific explanation. For one thing, the other universes are not part of our Universe and so by definition cannot be contacted. There is therefore no way to prove or disprove their existence. Not only that but the suggestion goes against the conventional way scientific development has tended to go. As pointed out previously (in Chapter 9), scientists are in the business of trying to explain things as economically as possible. Describing the enormous variety of materials in the world in terms of just a few quarks and electrons, or the collapsing down of the various forces of nature into ever fewer types of force is all part of this process of going for ever-simpler explanations. This being so, to postulate the existence of an infinite number of universes all run according to their own laws of nature is to go as far in the opposite direction as is imaginable. Which is not in itself to say that the idea of an infinite number of universes is necessarily wrong – merely that it does not count as science.

In fact this idea of many universes has gained a measure of support from the inflation theory we were dealing with just now. You recall how I described the phase change in the early history of the Universe as somewhat analogous to the phase change of water becoming ice. Well, the analogy can be taken further. A crystal of ice has certain well-defined axes. The directions in which they set are purely a matter of chance, the original liquid water having no preference for any particular direction. If ice starts to form at different positions, there is no reason why the separate crystals should have their axes aligned. Each crystal will grow until it comes up against the boundary of some other crystal.

In the same way, it is believed that the phase change in the early history of the Universe started out from various independent locations. One of the effects of inflation is that, not only should there be a period of superfast expansion, and not only should it produce critical density, but this is the point in the history of the cosmos when the various physical constants (those appearing in the laws of nature – such as the magnitude of the electric charge on the electron) took on the values we find them to have today. The values they assumed were to some extent arbitrary. That being the case, there was no reason why the same values should have materialized in the various independent domains. What this means is that we should end up today with a Universe divided up into domains where the laws of physics are somewhat different from each other. What we know as "the Universe" – or more strictly speaking "our observable Universe" is but one tiny section of one of these domains. Hence the laws seem to us to be the same everywhere. But according to inflation theory, there might well be other domains of the overall Universe that are very different from ours. These other domains are not exactly "different universes," but their laws of nature will be somewhat different. This idea therefore makes more plausible the suggestion that there might have been many attempts at getting the conditions right for the development of life, so it is not surprising that our part of the overall Universe is the way it is.

This is getting us part of the way toward a scientific explanation of the Anthropic Principle, in that it is an inference drawn from what we know about our world and how those laws might plausibly be extended into other realms. However, we are never likely to get experimental evidence one way or another about the existence of those other domains. This is because they are believed to be so incredibly larger than our known observable Universe that it is unlikely we shall ever be able to observe the boundary between our domain and its neighbor. This in turn denies us confirmation of the existence of those other domains.

So, an infinite number of universes, or other domains of the one Universe, is the second way of accounting for the Anthropic Principle.

(iii) *A Universe designed for life*. The third alternative is simply to accept that the Universe is a put-up job; it was designed for life, and the designer is God.

When it comes to arguments about God based on Design, we need to be cautious. We saw in Chapter 10 how the original Argument from Design held that everything about our bodies, and those of other animals, is so beautifully fitted to fulfill its function that it must have been designed that way – the designer being God – and therefore you must believe in God. The rug was pulled from under that argument by Darwin's theory of evolution by natural selection – at least in terms of it being a knock-down proof of God's existence – one aimed at convincing the skeptic.

Bearing that in mind, I would advise religious believers today against making too much of this new Argument from Design – one based this time on physics and cosmology rather than biology. God can neither be proved nor disproved on the basis of such reasoning. Someone inclined to reject the idea of God can do so in the expectation that science will one day show how the coincidences are not really coincidences, or on the basis of there being many attempts at different universes, or domains of this Universe.

On the other hand, for religious believers, the simplest explanation is in terms of a Designer God. The Anthropic Principle therefore plays an important part in building up the cumulative case for the God hypothesis. It is further persuasive evidence to be taken on board by the God experiment.

The cosmos as a reflection of God's nature

Accepting God as the Creator of the world opens up the possibility of learning more about him from the study of that world. After all, if we look at human creations – for instance, a disturbing painting by Francis Bacon of a screaming Pope with his face horribly distorted, and compare that with the serenity of a saint painted by Fra Angelico – one can hardly escape the conclusion that the painting reveals something of the artist as well as the subject. Or, to use another analogy – one that takes note of the feminine attributes of God – one might think of the world as being born from the womb of God. Again, one would be looking for similarities between the originator and that which is produced. Thus we come to expect that the cosmos ought to hold clues as to God's own nature.

For instance, take the size of the cosmos. Though one's first reaction was to think of one's own insignificance in the face of such vastness, perhaps it would be more appropriate to think of it as reflecting the unimaginable glory and the sheer power of God. In which case, with such a powerful God taking a personal interest in each and every one of us, that can only *enhance* our own sense of significance.

Then there are the vast aeons of time over which God has worked, through evolution, to bring us into being. Surely this bears testimony to long-sightedness and patience. It puts a different perspective on our own petty annoyances at things not being sorted out immediately to our liking. One of the difficulties of life is always that of keeping things in perspective – God's perspective.

We see in nature the way God is prepared to employ an element of randomness. We have already noted how God allows the chance processes of evolution by natural selection to give rise to intelligent life forms. Before that he might have used inflation theory to throw up many differing domains of the overall Universe, allowing chance to give rise to those that were to be capable of sustaining life. There is an openness to creation; God is the kind of god who allows the Universe to be itself, knowing that in broad terms at least, his will for the world will be accomplished.

There is an orderliness to the way the world runs – it is not chaotic. It is beautiful; there is a lovely use of symmetry; there is breathtaking simplicity and economy in the basic building blocks of matter and the interactions between them – and yet these are able in ingenious ways to give rise to unlimited richness and variety. Is this not saying something about the way the mind of God works?

One final thought about the cosmos

In discussing the Anthropic Principle we have focused attention on the nature of the cosmos as seen in relation to the life it contains. In this context it is to be seen as "a vale of soul-making." In the cut and thrust of day-to-day living, our spiritual selves take form. According to Christian belief, these then live on in some other embodiment when this present physical body is discarded at death. Eventually, the cosmos, having acted as the mold from which this store of spiritual beings has been shaped, is then itself to be discarded as having outlived its usefulness.

But, as has been mentioned before, there is no reason to think of the cosmos as having but the one function – a receptacle for transitory life. After all, in most regions of space there is no life. For much of the Universe's past history there was no intelligent life anywhere within it. An infinity of time lies ahead after the Heat Death when again there will be no life. If inflation theory is correct, the vast majority of the domains of the overall Universe will *never* house life. Are we to regard this as a waste? Not necessarily. God's interest might not be narrowly confined to life. That is why I suggest that God might take delight in the physical world for its *own* sake. Who knows, perhaps the making of the physical cosmos was God's primary intention. Perhaps God took so much pleasure from what he had made that he wanted others to share some of it – and that is at least part of the reason why we are here!

13

God and Time

God in relation to time

The God experiment not only examines evidence relating to whether God exists or not, but aims also to find out something of the nature of the supposed God. Chapter 6 was devoted to tracing out the development of ideas as regards God's personal qualities – culminating in the all-powerful God of love, justice, and mercy. How about the way God is thought to relate to time and space?

It has long been recognized that God's relation to time could be different from our own. Although we interact with God *in* time – for example, when we engage in prayer, perhaps asking for some future favor – it is also believed that God is, in a sense, *beyond* time – transcendent, unchanging. But this raises a difficulty: if God never changes, our request will not change his mind, so what is the point of asking for anything?

And that is not the only problem over God and time. It is held by Christians that God has foreknowledge. But how is this possible? How can God know the future before we ourselves, for instance, have made up our own minds as to what we shall do? Surely God could only have such knowledge if humans were nothing more than totally predictable automatons. What then of our supposed free will? It is understandable that many people – including those theologians called "process" theologians – reject this claim. They regard it as a logical impossibility for there to be knowledge of a future that does not yet exist. And as we noted before, even God cannot be expected to do things that are logically impossible.

And yet, God's foreknowledge is part and parcel of orthodox Christian belief. It is what gives believers added confidence in the assurances from God that all in the end will be well for those who love him. It is not a case of God having a better judgment as to what the future *might* contain; he actually *knows* the future – so it is claimed.

This is not the first encounter we have had with the subject of time. We noted earlier how time appeared to have had its origin at the instant of the Big Bang. This led us to reconsider what exactly was meant by the term "God the Creator." If we are now somehow to accommodate these strange ideas about God's foreknowledge, then our common-sense notions about time need to be shaken. That, as I hope to show, is what modern physics does.

Common-sense notions of time and space

Time is divided into past, present, and future. The past consists of all those events that have happened. These happenings might well have left memories and other lasting effects, but the past events themselves no longer exist. As for the future, by that we mean all those events that will one day happen, but as yet do not exist. The present is that instant in time we label "now." It divides the past from the future. We live in the present. All that exists is what belongs to the present – what is happening right *now*.

Time moves on. We are being swept toward the future. What lies in the future becomes the present, and is then left behind in the past. What will be becomes an actuality, before passing once more out of existence in the past. We call this the "flow of time," or the "passing of time." We might disagree about how fast time flows (it seems to speed up with old age), but we are all agreed that time does indeed pass.

The future is open, uncertain. Through what we do now, we can affect the future. The past on the other hand is fixed. We might not agree on what happened then; memories can play tricks, or we might put different interpretations on past events. But whatever it was that happened, we have no power to change it now.

The future differs from the past in another sense. This is summed up in the Second Law of Thermodynamics – a topic briefly mentioned in Chapter 2. The First Law is to do with conservation of energy; the Second draws attention to the way disorder tends to increase with time.

For example, one might have a glass of water with an ice-cube in it. This is an ordered situation in that all the "cold" water molecules are together in one location (vibrating gently in the ice-cube), while the warmer molecules are on the outside (moving about in the liquid water). But after a while the heat is randomized, leading to the ice melting and the water cooling. Now the slow- and the fast-moving molecules are all jumbled up together.

Another example of the Second Law at work is to consider a tall chimney. Put a stick of dynamite to its base and it collapses into a heap of bricks. If, in contrast, one starts with a heap of bricks lying on the ground, one is unlikely to find the rubble spontaneously coming together to form an intact chimney (with a stick of unused dynamite at its base). This means if one were to be shown a photograph of a chimney, and another of the same chimney felled, it would not be difficult to decide which came first in time. The same with photos of the ice-cube in the glass of water, and of the same glass but with the ice melted. This shows that the time axis is not symmetric; there is more disorder toward the end labeled "future" than there is toward the end labeled "past."

We exist in time; we also exist in space. But space and time are very different from each other. We measure distances in space using a ruler; we measure intervals of time on a watch. There is just the one three-dimensional space, and the one one-dimensional time, and both are common to us all. Thus we can all agree as to the order in which events occur – whether one occurs before the other, or they happen simultaneously.

These then are some of our commonly shared ideas about time. In fact, as we shall be seeing, most of them are *wrong*.

Undermining the arrow of time

We begin with the idea that one can tell the direction of time from the increase in disorder. Suppose you are shown a film of rubble lying on the ground. Suddenly, all the pieces of brick come together to form an upright chimney. Immediately you would know something was wrong. Play the film the other way round – chimney collapses – that's fine. You conclude that, at the first showing, the film was being played backward. In other words, you can distinguish the correct direction in time.

But in fact, there is something odd going on here. The scene we have been considering was made up of atoms and their movements. One type of atomic movement is a vibration. But if you saw a film of an atom vibrating, you would not be able to tell whether the film was being shown the right way or the reverse; either way looks normal – in the same way as a film of the swing of the pendulum of a grandfather clock would look the same whether it was played backward or forward. Another type of movement consists of atoms moving through space and colliding with each other. Again, a film of that event would look equally plausible whichever way it was shown – in the same way as a film shot from above a billiard table showing a ball coming in from the east and another from the west, colliding and going out north and south respectively, would look just as likely as balls coming in north and south and going out east and west.

These examples show that with a film dealing with individual atoms, or individual collisions between atoms, it is *impossible* to tell the direction of time. And yet with the film of the chimney and the rubble, one *could* tell that one way of showing the film was "wrong" – despite the fact that the scene was exclusively made up of atoms vibrating and colliding! How can one put together a whole lot of movements, none of which carries the slightest clue as to the direction of time, and yet one ends up knowing the right direction of time?

The answer to this conundrum comes from studying the way the individual events are *related* to each other. We have already established that a collision – a *single* collision – between billiard balls says nothing about the direction of time. But what if you saw a film in which *many* pairs of balls collide? Suppose you observed them coming in from random directions, but always going out after the collision in exactly the east and west directions. That would appear distinctly odd. What a coincidence, you might think. It is almost as though there was something sucking the balls out in the east-west directions. That doesn't happen in practice. Next, you are shown the same film, but running the sequence in the opposite sense. All the balls now enter from the east and west, and leave in random directions. Is that any better? Obviously, yes. You conclude there must be two players, situated just out of shot, one to the east, the other to the west. They each have a pile of balls which they propel toward each other, allowing them to bounce off in random directions. This second sequence is wholly plausible and easy to set up; it requires no wild coincidences.

Thus, it is the *relationships* between collisions (how the directions of the balls in one collision relate to those of the others) that provide the information on the direction of time. But note – and this is important – although one way of showing that film is more probable than the other, the reverse sense is not impossible. It *cannot* be impossible because each of the individual collisions could occur equally well either way round.

Now, you might be wondering what this might have to do with the film sequence of the chimney and the rubble. Simply this: the whole sequence of events was made up of vibrating and colliding atoms. None of these atomic events, in themselves individually, carries any information about the direction of time. Physicists call this *time-reversal invariance*. But put a lot of atomic events together and you *can* tell the direction of time – from the way the individual events relate to each other. The "chimney collapse" version of the sequence is much more likely than the "spontaneous chimney-making" version of the sequence. But, as with the balls on the pool table, although the reverse sequence is less probable (overwhelmingly so), it is *not* impossible – it cannot be impossible because each of the individual atomic events making up the sequence *could* have occurred either way.

But you might be wondering how. How, for instance, could the bricks leap off the ground into the air?! I refer you back to our previous discussion (in Chapter 2) of the cup that spontaneously leapt up from the kitchen floor: The heat vibrations of the atoms making up the ground generally occur in random directions. However, it is conceivable – just conceivable – to imagine them all by chance momentarily moving in the same direction – the upward direction. It would require an incredible coincidence, of course, but if it were to happen, a brick, or cup, or any other object that happened to be lying on the ground, would be flung up into the air.

And this does not just apply to cups and bricks falling to the ground or leaping up off the ground; everything happening around us could conceivably happen in precisely the opposite sense. And that does mean *everything*: Cars, for example, could end their journey with more gas in the tank than they had when they started out; people could rise out of their graves and live a life where they gradually got younger –

the "tomb-to-womb scenario." These occurrences of course do not happen – in practice. But this is not because they are impossible; it is simply that they are less likely.

What this means is that the firm distinction between past and future appears not to be as surely based as one might have thought.

Einstein's theory of relativity

This undermining of the distinction between past and future is taken a stage further by Einstein's theory of relativity. But first a word of reassurance: it is *not* my intention to put you through a crash course on relativity theory! It is sufficient for our purposes merely to point out some of the theory's more startling consequences – consequences which I hasten to assure you have been fully vindicated by experiment.

Let us imagine an astronaut in a high-speed spacecraft, and a mission controller at Houston. The astronaut leaves Earth at a speed of nine-tenths the speed of light. (The speed of light is 300,000 kilometers per second, so such a rocket engine is clearly not a practical possibility. However, it is more striking to illustrate the effects with somewhat exaggerated examples!) Relativity theory is able to show that the astronaut and mission controller, being in relative motion, do not agree on the distance the craft has to travel to reach a distant planet. At the particular speed we have chosen, the astronaut calculates the journey distance to be about half that estimated by the mission controller.

Nor is this the only effect of their relative speed. The two not only disagree over their estimates of distance, but also of the time the journey takes. According to the controller, time for the astronaut is passing at about half the rate it does for himself. Thus, everything happening in the spacecraft – the ticking of the clocks, the astronaut's breathing rate, her heartbeats, her ageing processes – everything has slowed down by a factor of a half. Not that the astronaut will be aware of this; a slow clock looked at by a brain in which the thinking processes have been slowed down by the same factor appears perfectly normal.

Which of the two observers is right in their assessments of distance and time? It is impossible to say. But why? Won't the astronaut realize that something must be wrong with her observations when, because of her slowed-down clock, she arrives at her destination in half the time she should have taken? No. Remember, she thinks the journey distance is only half that which the controller claims it to be. Both the astronaut and the mission controller have sets of measurements that are entirely self-consistent.

But, it might be argued, the mission controller is stationary, whereas the astronaut is traveling at high speed; perhaps the speed of the astronaut is making her measurements unreliable in some way – and so one should place greater weight on those of the stationary observer. This is to lose sight of the fact that the mission controller is *not* stationary – he is on the Earth's surface, and the Earth is spinning; the Earth goes in orbit around the Sun; the Sun goes in orbit around the center of the Galaxy; the Galaxy is moving in its cluster of galaxies.... How does one define a "stationary observer"? All uniform motion is relative; the two observers are in relative motion, and that is all we can say – hence the name "relativity theory." There are no grounds for according preference to the measurements of one observer over those of the other.

Confusing? It certainly appears that way when one comes across the ideas of relativity theory for the first time. We are so accustomed to thinking in terms of us all inhabiting the one space and the one time, that it requires a severe mental wrench to conceive of something radically different: namely, that we each inhabit our own space and our own time, and these will differ from each other if we are in relative motion. The reason most people go through life unaware of this is that for most everyday purposes, the differences between our various estimates of distance and of time are so small as to make no practical difference. For example, those who decide to drive express trains all their working lives, age less quickly than those who opt instead for sedentary office jobs. The effect of the train's motion is to increase the driver's life expectancy by one millionth of a second – hardly a factor worth taking into account when deciding careers. (The effect is that small because even the speed of an express train is negligible compared to that of light.)

Four-dimensional space-time

How are we to understand these differing spatial and temporal measurements? Let me give you an analogy:

A lecturer holds up a pen. What do the students see? They all see something slightly different – some a long shape, others a short one. Confusing? No. We think nothing of such differing observations. We realize that what each student sees is merely a two-dimensional projection of what in reality extends in three dimensions. The two-dimensional projection is at right angles to the line of sight, and this line of sight will vary depending on where the student observer is seated relative to the pencil. We are unperturbed by the different observations because we know that when each observer makes due allowance for how the pencil extends along his or her line of sight, they come up with identical results for the true length of the pencil. Thus, for example, someone who sees a short-looking pencil (the projected length is small) compensates by having a large value for the length along the line of sight. On the other hand, someone who sees a big-looking pencil has only a small contribution coming from the direction along the line of sight.

The situation just described can be used as an analogy for the case of the astronaut and the mission controller. Just as the students in the lecture theater had differing perceptions as to the length of the lecturer's pen, so the astronaut and the mission controller have differing perceptions of the distance to be traveled to the distant planet, and also of the time the journey takes. The solution is to regard both the spatial distance covered by the journey, and the time taken for the journey, as mere *projections*. We are *not* dealing with a three-dimensional space and a separate one-dimensional time – two separate realities. Instead, we are dealing with a combined *four-dimensional reality* in which three dimensions of space and one dimension closely related to time are inextricably mixed together. We call this combination *space-time*. The astronaut and mission controller are observing the contents of this 4-D reality from differing viewpoints. And that is why they are confronted with different appearances. Each is dealing with an alternative set of projections.

What kind of "object" do we find in this 4-D space-time? Firstly, it must be characterized by a value for each of the three spatial dimensions, i.e., it must have a location in 3-D space; secondly, it must be characterized by a value along the time axis, i.e., it must occur at a point in time. This means we are dealing with *events*. An example of an event might be the launch of the spacecraft from Earth (which defines its spatial location) at noon on January 3 (which is its location in time). Another would be the arrival of the spacecraft at a distant planet at some later time.

What does it mean to observe this 4-D reality from "different viewpoints"? Because of the way space-time mixes up space and time, a "different viewpoint" means more than just being at a different position in space (like those students in the lecture theater). One has to be at different positions in space at different points in time – in other words one observer has to be moving relative to the other observer. Two observers in relative motion (like our astronaut and mission controller) have differing perspectives on space-time by virtue of that motion.

If we are to regard the direct measurements made by the astronaut and controller as mere 3-D spatial projections and 1-D temporal projections of the "space-time distance" between the events marking the beginning and end of the spacecraft's journey, then it does not matter in the least that both their spatial distances and their time intervals are different. The important thing is that when they each plug into the relevant equation their *own* measurements for the spatial and the temporal projections, they obtain identically the *same* value for the 4-D space-time separation. Thus, for instance, the astronaut regarded the distance covered by the journey as being shorter than that determined by the controller. But she also regarded the time of the journey as being shorter. Combining the two projections in the appropriate mathematical way, it turns out the two effects cancel out, and she ends up with the same overall result for the 4-D separation as the controller. And what goes for the astronaut and mission controller holds for anyone else observing that interplanetary journey. The four-dimensional separation is the one thing they can all agree upon. It is for this reason one is led to the conclusion that what really counts is not the individual estimates of spatial distance or temporal interval but the four-dimensional space-time separation. Einstein himself once declared that henceforth we must deal with "a four-dimensional existence instead of, hitherto, the evolution of a three-dimensional existence."

It is an extraordinary conception. There is little point in trying to visualize four dimensions – one just gets a headache. The best one can do is to stretch out the thumb and three of the fingers on one hand. (Hold them out such that each is as far from the other three as you can make it.) The thumb represents the time axis; the three fingers the three spatial axes. Reality is more like that than having three fingers up on one hand (representing 3-D space), and one finger up on the other hand (representing time as a separate reality). But even then it is an inadequate analogy for space-time. Strictly speaking the thumb and three fingers ought all to be mutually at right angles. That is a physical impossibility to demonstrate (and it always hurts to try and do impossible contortions – so don't try). But if one does not pay too much attention to the wrong angles, this is the best one can do by way of visualizing the situation.

Actually, the preferred course of action among professional physicists is to ignore such visual aids, and just allow oneself to be guided by the mathematics. Mathematically speaking one can handle any number of dimensions.

But there is no doubt that the thumb-and-three-fingers approach does have its merits. For example, it reinforces the idea that the time dimension is welded on to the spatial ones; they are inseparable. We have already come across a consequence of this. Recall how when dealing with the Big Bang, I stated that the expansion of space, carrying the galaxies apart, was an indication that space itself started out from a point – from nothing; space was created at the instant of the Big Bang. I then went on to assert that if space was created then, so also must time have been created in that event; the Big Bang was the instant at which the great cosmic clock began ticking. With the thumb-and-three-fingers analogy in mind, you are now in a better position to understand how one arrives at that conclusion. There can be no space without time, nor time without space.

The block universe idea

We have already noted how one must stop thinking of events in three-dimensional space evolving in a separate time reality. One must additionally not get lured into thinking of events in four-dimensional space-time evolving in a separate time reality. Time is *already* incorporated into the 4-D reality as the fourth dimension. What that means is that four-dimensional space-time does not change. Something can only change *in time*. But space-time is not in time; on the contrary, time is in space-time. In our analogy, the instant at which you picked up this book to start reading it can be represented by one point along the thumb denoting time, the present instant can be represented by another, and the instant at which you will eventually lay the book aside (and reach for the aspirin bottle) by a third point along the thumb. It is all there along the thumb: *past, present, and future*. Space-time is static. We call it a *block universe*.

We are accustomed to think that all of space exists at each point of time. So, for example, at this instant in time there exists not only the location where you happen to be, but also New York, Hong Kong, planet Jupiter, and distant galaxies. We have no difficulty getting our mind around the idea that all of space exists at each point in time. What the block universe idea is saying is that likewise *all of time exists at each point in space*. That means, for instance, at this point of space here – where you are seated – all of time exists: the instant you started reading the book, this present instant, the instant you lay the book aside, the day the building you are sitting in gets demolished and replaced by something else, the day the site gets burned up when the Sun becomes a red giant, and the endless aeons of the eventual Heat Death of the Universe. In some sense, it all *exists*.

What exactly do I mean when I say "in some sense"? I don't know; I cannot say more. It is a sense that defies the imagination. All I can say is that the thumb (or if one prefers, the mathematics) implies that this is so. We must simply allow the analogy, or the mathematics, to be our guide.

According to this viewpoint, there is nothing special about the particular instant we choose to label "now." All points in time are on an *equal* footing. The future in itself is *not* uncertain. We might not *know* what the future holds. But that is only because the sum total of the information to which we have access (at this point in time) is too limited to permit such a deduction of what lies ahead. This is in contrast to the type of information we have at the present instant concerning past events. This is often of a kind that does indeed allow us to be reasonably sure of what exists in the past. But regardless of the inadequate nature of our knowledge of future events, our modern understanding of time would seem to indicate that whatever the future holds, in some sense it is there, fixed, waiting for us to come upon it.

This is so counterintuitive that many people – including several noted and highly respected physicists – find it quite impossible to accept. But as far as I am concerned, I think the conclusion is forced upon us for the following reason.

The loss of simultaneity

So far, I have indicated that our astronaut and mission controller do not agree about the time the interplanetary journey took. That is not their only disagreement about time. Relativity theory has a further surprise for us. It concerns the simultaneity of events. There is no problem about events occurring at the same location. For instance, if a stone is hurled at a window, everyone can agree that the event known as "ball arrives at window" is simultaneous with the event known as "window breaks." But what if we are talking about events occurring at *different* locations? Relativity theory shows that two observers in relative motion do *not* agree about the simultaneity of events that occur at a distance from each other.

For instance, at Houston it is 12 noon exactly. The controller is wondering what the astronaut is doing at this precise moment in time far out in space. He cannot know immediately; it takes time for information to travel at the speed of light from the spacecraft to the base. (It is another consequence of the theory of relativity that nothing can travel faster than light. This is a speed limit that requires no speed cameras for enforcement.) Eventually the controller receives the requisite signals from the spacecraft. Knowing the distance of the craft from Houston at any time, and making allowance for the time taken for each of the signals to travel from the craft, he is able to work out which event must have occurred in the craft at 12 noon Houston time. These calculations reveal that the astronaut had just started to do a series of exercises on her bicycle machine. Thus, according to the controller, he now knows that the astronaut started her exercises at the instant the Houston clock had indicated noon. So much for what the controller concludes.

The astronaut has likewise been thinking. She longingly wonders what has been happening back at Houston. She receives signals from home, and carries out analogous calculations to those that were done by the controller. She concludes that at the instant she had begun her exercises, the clock at Houston had been reading 12:10. There is a disagreement. Whereas the controller concluded that the event marking the start of the astronaut's exercises was simultaneous with the Houston clock showing 12 noon; the astronaut is equally convinced that the start of her exercises was simultaneous with the Houston clock showing 12:10.

The fact that they disagree is perhaps not all that surprising. Their conclusions can be arrived at only after calculation, and as we have already seen, they do not agree about the values of the distances and times to be put into the calculation.

The loss of agreement over simultaneity for events separated by a distance has serious repercussions for those anxious to retain the idea that only the events that occur *now* can truly be thought to exist (prior events no longer existing, and future ones not yet existing). In speaking of such contemporary events, one presumably needs to include those events occurring "now" in locations other than where one happens to be oneself. But in the example just given, there is no agreement as to which event in the control room at Houston existed at the same time – the "now" – as that which marked the astronaut commencing her exercises on the craft – the clock reading 12:00 or the clock reading 12:10. Indeed, there is no need to confine the possibilities to these two. Depending on one's speed relative to Houston, there can be any number of possibilities. There is no way to decide between them. In relativity theory, no one takes precedence.

For many of us physicists, it seems that the natural way of understanding this (perhaps the *only* way) is to regard each observer as taking a different slice through four-dimensional space-time – through the all-existent block universe. Accordingly, along with the bicycle-mounting event happening in the craft, *all* events in Houston exist – the clock saying 12:00, the clock saying 12:10; the clock saying 11:50; the clock saying anything at all. The disagreement is not over which event *exists* in

Houston, but merely over which event happens to share the same time coordinate (the same "now") as the event in the craft.

It is the fact that there is no agreement over what happens "now" that forces us to abandon the notion that existence is something *exclusively confined* to events that occur "now."

Mental time as distinct from physical time

But, you might be wondering, if physics does not pick out any special instant in time to be called "now," where does the concept of "now" come from? And if nothing is changing (the block universe idea), what about the flow of time – where does that come in? Not only that, if the future already exists, where do we get the notion of the future being uncertain and open to being affected by what we do now? What does this do for our free will? Are we not reduced to the level of automata?

Here we touch on one of the truly great mysteries: the fact that we have *two entirely different approaches to the concept of "time."* So far I have spoken of time exclusively in the way the concept is addressed in physics. We must now examine how this same word "time" is used in a different context – the description of what it is to be a thinking human being – a *mental* being.

On examining the contents of the conscious mind, we find mental experiences – sensory experiences, feelings, decisions, etc. These occur in sequence. What separates one experience from the next? We call it "time." We are able to estimate and compare these separations or intervals of time. This might be done through noting the extent to which the memory of a past experience has faded – the greater the separation in time, the greater the degree of fading. (Here we take it that one is not constantly recalling that experience and keeping it vivid, for then one is more likely now to be recalling the most recent earlier recall rather than the memory of the original experience itself.) So the fading of the memory is one way of estimating how long ago that experience was.

In addition there might be an indication of the time interval based on the number of other notable experiences we have had subsequent to the one in question. If this is the case, then it might give us a clue as to why time seems to speed up as we get older. When one is young and inexperienced, everything is new and catches the attention – one is laying down memories at a furious rate. As one gets older and more worldly-wise – or dare one say, jaded – most experiences are so familiar they are liable to pass us by without being recorded as faithfully as in the past. So, if one is using a time estimate based on the number of notable experiences one has had since the one in question, it will seem that not much has happened since that event, and hence, presumably, not much time has elapsed – a conclusion contradicted by the calendar.

The precise mechanism by which we subjectively assess time intervals is not at all well understood. The most we can say is that we do appear to have our own internal, mental way of doing it – semi-quantitatively at least.

For each mental experience there are other experiences on either side of it along the sequence, with one exception – the experience that marks the end of that sequence. This end point of the sequence we designate "now." It is only in consciousness that the "now" acquires its special status.

Although we use the word "time" to describe the separation between our mental experiences, it does not follow that this is the same "time" as is used in the description of what is going on in the physical world. For one thing, mental states occur in time but not in space. (It would be absurd to ask how much space a big decision like getting married takes up, compared to a small decision such as which tie to wear today.) And yet we know how indissoluble is the link between physical time and physical space.

Only through the recognition that we use the word "time" in two distinct ways can it make sense to say that all of time, including the future, exists now. What this means is that all of *physical* time exists at the instant of *mental* time called "now" – and indeed at every other instant of mental time.

It is perhaps unfortunate that the same word "time" is used in two such dissimilar contexts. The reason it is, of course, has to do with the fact that, despite the distinctiveness of physical and mental time, there is a close correspondence between them. A sensory experience which is part of the mental sequence (e.g., the hearing of a shot now) is correlated to a feature of space-time (the firing of a gun at a particular point in space-time). The "now" of mental time is correlated to a particular instant of physical time. Although, as I have said, *all* of physical time exists now, consciousness (not physics) singles out one particular instant as having special significance for the "now" of mental time.

A short while later (according to mental time, that is) the "now" correlates to a different physical time. The difference between the two physical times, judged on a clock, when compared with the perceived lapse in mental time, gives rise to a "flow" of time. Note that unless there were two types of time, there could be no flow. A flow is a change of something in a given time. The flow of water from a hose-pipe, for instance, is the amount of water emitted in a given time. But what possible meaning could be given to the phrase "a flow of time"? The amount of time passing in a given time? That means nothing – not unless we are talking of *two* different times. When the bored reader of this book complains that time is passing slowly, she means that, based on her subjective mental assessment of how much time separates her from the beginning of her reading, the physical time, registered by the hands of her watch, is not what she reckons it ought to be. There is too little physical time corresponding to the perceived span of mental time.

Earlier we noted that, in dealing with a physical time that was seamlessly welded to the three spatial dimensions to form a four-dimensional existence, one should not fall into the trap of thinking of this four-dimensional world as evolving in time – as though time were still somehow separate. That is true as far as *physical* time is concerned. Four-dimensional reality never changes. And yet, as far as we conscious human beings are concerned, there *is* change. Physical time might be integrally part of that four-dimensional existence, but mental time does appear stand outside it. It focuses conscious attention and mental experience on one particular instant of physical time, and temporarily correlates it with the mental "now." That conscious focus then appears to move steadily along the time axis in the direction labeled "future." But it is important to understand that this so-called movement is not out there in the physical world itself; *it is a feature only of our conscious experience of that physical world.*

In passing, I should perhaps mention that some people find the idea of the non-changing physical world puzzling in the light of the Second

Law of Thermodynamics. This is often stated in the form that disorder increases with time. So, does that not imply the dynamic passage of time? No. All the Second Law tells us is that there is more disorder toward one end of the time axis (that labeled "later," and having, by convention, the higher values of the time coordinates), than there is toward the other end (the one labeled "earlier," and having the lower values). But that in itself does not say that we mentally experience events sequentially in the direction toward the end labeled "later," rather than the reverse. The Second Law is solely concerned with describing the physics of the situation, not how a conscious being might perceive it.

God's foreknowledge and transcendence

Why have we gone into this lengthy discussion of time? Partly because it is a fascinating subject in its own right. But it also has an impact on religious belief. Once it is accepted that in some mysterious sense, it is possible to assert that the future "exists" – on the same footing as the present – this must surely go some way toward adding plausibility to the idea that God might have knowledge of it. According to the block universe idea, it is all out there; it is fixed. All God has to do is find a way of looking at it. I would not have thought that would be too difficult for a god! We saw with the analogy of the outstretched thumb and three fingers representing four-dimensional reality, we ourselves could look at it from outside. In a similar way, one suspects that God has the ability somehow to take in the whole of four-dimensional reality from some "external point" of view lying beyond the confines of that four-dimensional world. This is what we mean when we speak of God as being *transcendent*. That is not to imply that God is to be found located in yet more physical dimensions – a fifth, sixth, etc. But he is "in some sense" (to use an overworked phrase) *beyond* space-time.

God in time as well as beyond

But there is another aspect to this. Religious believers accept that God is a *personal* god. We might have difficulty over the lack of a suitable inclusive pronoun, and are not sure whether to refer to God as a "he" or a "she," but one thing God is not; God is not an "it." In thinking of God we have in mind attributes such as love, justice, and mercy; we think of God as having a purpose. None of this makes sense except in personal terms.

So, in the same way as we interact with other persons, we expect to be able to interact personally with God. We expect to be able to speak with God. Partly this is in order to ask him for things as a child would ask a parent – in anticipation that we shall receive an answer. We expect on occasion to find that our asking has had an influence on what later transpires. Such interpersonal actions take place *in* time. Thus, God has to be *in* time as well as *beyond* it.

But you might be wondering: how can my asking God for anything in time affect the outcome when the future, in physical terms, is fixed – set in concrete? As I see it, there is no difficulty in that future outcome already having built into it the effects of one's prayer to God at an earlier time. Indeed, I and certain others of my acquaintance, think nothing of praying for events that have already happened, but about which we do not as yet know the outcome. (It might have been through some oversight that we did not pray about it beforehand, or we might not have had prior knowledge of the situation as being one requiring prayer.) We offer up these after-the-event prayers confident that an all-knowing God will be aware that we will be doing this, and will be able to take our prayers into account in determining the outcome. As you see, thoughts stemming out of the idea of a block universe really transform one's thinking about what can and cannot be done!

A compromised free will?

One concern you might have about all this is the extent to which one's free will might be compromised. How can one be truly free if the future is already known – not known to us, but known to God?

Perhaps another analogy will help: Without your knowing, you have been caught on videotape. A security guard has been following your movements. He has monitored you walking down the street, entering the building, going to the lifts, deciding which one to take. On entering your chosen lift, another camera took over and recorded the button you pressed. It also caught you in the act of picking your nose when you thought no one could see you. Yet more cameras tracked your movements along the corridors of the upper floor, until you reached the door of the office you were seeking. The security guard has seen the tapes. In fact, he has now seen them so often he knows them by heart. Show him any incident, and he knows exactly what happens next. There is nothing you do on those videotapes that he doesn't know about. There is no element of surprise for him. So, what does that mean? Does it mean the guard is looking at a recording of an automaton – a predetermined robot that has no free will? Obviously, no. The tapes are a record of the actions of a free person making free-will decisions. The fact that when the guard plays the tape, he knows ahead of time the outcome of each of your decisions, does not in any way detract from them being your freely made decisions.

In that analogy, the guard, of course, is playing the role of God – the transcendent God. Just as he is outside the confines of the videotape and is able to view any part of it at will, so God lies beyond this four-dimensional world, etched as it is with the record of our lives.

But the analogy is closer. That videotape shows not only you, but also the guard himself. He is the man who greeted you as you entered the building; he is the one who answered your question as to which floor you needed. The tape incorporates a record of the guard interacting with you. He doesn't just watch these tapes at the end of the working day; he also takes part in them at first hand. So it is with God; when he surveys the four-dimensional world with its record of our lives, he sees in it himself relating to and interacting with us. If you like, the world is not a video he has rented from the video store; it is God's own home video.

So ends our discussion of the fascinating – but difficult – topic of time. If you feel you haven't quite grasped it all, be assured that that is exactly how it *should* be! *Nobody* truly understands time. Ultimately, it is a mystery. Here, as on previous occasions, we use the word "mystery" not to mean a puzzle – something that future scientists and thinkers are likely to get sorted out eventually. We mean something which, by its very nature, lies beyond the full grasp of the human mind, and will always remain that way. All we can ever hope to do is skirt around its edges, grateful for the occasional flicker of insight.

What I hope to have shown is that our modern understanding of the subject goes some way toward adding plausibility to the ideas of God's transcendence and foreknowledge. It helps confirm the insights of early religious thinkers.

14

The Ultimate Nature of God

The God behind the relationships

Throughout this book we have talked much about God, but always in terms of *relationships*. First, we examined how God relates to the physical world:

- His role as Creator/Sustainer; he is the source of all existence.

- The Divine Intelligence is the source of the intelligibility of the laws of nature.

- God is the reason why, seemingly against all the odds, that set of laws provides just the right conditions for nurturing life.

- Just as we ourselves, operating within that law-like structure, nevertheless affect the world through our free-will decisions, so God too exercises a continuing influence on the world in conformity to those laws.

- But they are *his* laws; he need not always abide by them, should he choose to act otherwise. Nor do such occurrences have to be regarded as "violations" of the laws; such miraculous interventions might be seen as having a natural place within a hierarchy of laws, of which the physical laws are but a sub-set.

- We have seen how God relates to the world both within space and time, and transcendentally from beyond it.

Secondly, there are God's relationships with us at the personal level:

- There is the meeting of minds when we engage in the various forms of prayer that are open to us. In prayer we are confronted by a presence – the sense of the numinous. Unexpected thoughts come into the mind which appear to have come from outside ourselves –

thoughts that seem to be the guidance one has been seeking.

• There are those who have experience of answers to prayers for the sick – the kind of response that the prayer experiment is trying to illuminate.

• We have the voice of conscience – the moral law within.

• There is the experience of trying to put the teachings of the great spiritual teachers into practice – giving rather than receiving, loving your enemies rather than taking revenge, turning the other cheek – very strange teachings that seem to fly in the face of common sense and the dictates of our own genetically influenced behavior traits. Inasmuch as they do appear to lead to deep inner contentment and fulfillment in a way that nothing else does, one has to ask who or what the source of this strange wisdom might be.

• God meets us in our contemplation of the beauty of nature and of the splendor of the heavens.

• He is to be found in the working out of history and in the way our own personal lives develop a purposeful pattern once they have been surrendered to him.

• He relates to us through the lives of the saints – those of the past as set down in Scripture, and those we meet today.

• Above all, for the Christian, God makes himself known to us through his Son, Jesus.

Those, therefore, are some of the ways in which God impacts upon the world and upon ourselves. They are the data of our God experiment.

But note that this is all we have ever talked about – God's interactions with the physical world, or with ourselves. At no time have we said anything about who or what God is *in himself*. Before we conclude, we are bound to address this one last issue.

The Bible informs us:

God is spirit, and those who worship him must worship in spirit and in truth.

(John 4:24)

But what exactly is meant by the word "spirit"? We all have direct experience of what is meant when something is spoken of as "physical" or "mental" – but what is the word "spiritual" supposed to convey?

It is here some people see a crucial difference between our religious quest – the God experiment – and *true* science, or *real* experimentation. In science we are dealing with something tangible; we all understand the intrinsic nature of what is under investigation. When it comes to spiritual matters, however, as soon as attention becomes focused on the supposed intrinsic nature of this spiritual world, the discussion becomes vague, obscure, and unsatisfactory.

This is taken by some to be an indication that there is, in fact, no such thing as an objective spiritual realm. God in himself does not exist. Religion is purely a subjective matter. "God is what man does religiously," as Don Cupitt once put it. The inference to be drawn from this presumably being that if no one is acting in a religious manner, the word "God" refers to nothing. It also implies that there has been no God during most of the time the Universe has been in existence – because intelligent life had not yet evolved. Nor will there be a God once the stars have exhausted their fuel and become cold cinders, and the so-called Heat Death of the Universe expunges all life.

But for most of us, God is more than just our subjective religious experiences. God has a reality independent of ourselves. He was there before we existed; he will be there long after we have ceased to exist. It is God who gives *us* existence, not we who give *God* existence.

All of which raises the question of how we *know* he is there as an independent reality. In short, how are we to reach beyond our various types of religious experience and get at the true nature of the objective God who allegedly lies behind them?

The quantum world

Before tackling that question I'd like us to look at what would appear to be a less contentious issue: knowledge of the physical world. What do we know of the physical world in itself?

In case you are thinking this must surely be a very straightforward question, allow me to point out that many physicists would say that the answer to that question is – nothing! We know absolutely nothing at all about the physical world – a world existing independently of our interactions with it. If they are right, then that does not augur well for what we might be able to say about God – a God existing independently of our relationship with him. Perhaps the demand to be more specific about what we mean by "the spiritual world" can be shown to be wholly unreasonable. So it is we ask: how *do* these physicists arrive at such a seemingly outrageous conclusion about the physical world?

It has long been recognized that in order to describe the world, one has to observe it. As we noted earlier, science began in earnest in the West with the rise of experimental observation. The world is contingent – it did not *have* to exist. The job of the scientist is that of describing whatever world we happen to have been presented with. And to do that, one has to look at it – one has to interact with it.

But what exactly do we mean by "interact with it"? To answer that, we must turn to the insights afforded by quantum physics. Again, let me hasten to say that, just as in the case of relativity theory in the last chapter, it is not my intention to give a crash course on quantum physics. I need simply to draw your attention to some of its implications.

We begin by noting that at this present moment you are physically interacting with this book. As far as you are concerned, it is part of the physical world you are observing. How are you doing it? Light from the page enters your eye and hits the retina – the surface at the back of the eye. What is it like for the retina to be hit by light? If we were to examine this in great detail we would find point-like exchanges of energy and momentum. Point-like: You are not viewing the page continuously. The situation is rather similar to being in a cinema. There one has the illusion of seeing the scene in uninterrupted fashion. But, of course, it is an illusion. What one actually sees is a series of individual pictures. If each of these pictures is slightly different from its predecessor, then one gets the further illusion of movement – continuous movement. Thus when you look at this page, or at any other scene, at the back of your eye there is a series of isolated, intermittent events – what we call "quantum interactions." I repeat: you are *not* presented with a continuous image.

In addition to seeing the physical world, you can also hear it. When you do so, your eardrum is being bombarded by vibrations in the air.

As we know, air is made up of molecules; molecules are made of atoms; atoms are made of electrons and nuclei; nuclei are made of neutrons and protons; neutrons and protons are made of quarks. So, ultimately air – and all matter – is made up of electrons and quarks. How do these interact? Again, in point-like fashion. If we were to examine very closely how the energy of the sound was being transferred to your eardrum, it would be seen to be taking place as a series of pinpricks. Yet the impression we get is that of continuous sound.

This point-like behavior is universal. Even when we have a macroscopic situation like, for example, you sitting in this chair, although it appears that your body is being subjected to a steady upward push (resisting the steady downward pull of gravity), in truth it is not. As far as quantum physics is concerned, we are again talking about point-like interactions – billions upon billions of them. Averaged out over time they give the illusion of a steady push.

Bearing in mind this point-like behavior, we now ask, "What is light?" or "What is an electron, or a quark?" The answers seem obvious: they are particles; tiny, localized particles. The light striking your retina hits it like a hail of gunfire. Indeed we are able to measure the energy contained in each bullet-like packet of energy: it is proportional to the frequency of the light. A packet of blue light, for example, has roughly twice the energy of a packet of lower-frequency red light.

But that is only half the story. There is more to this than meets the eye – literally. So far we have asked how light interacts and gives up its energy on striking a surface. But suppose we were now to ask a different question: "*Where* will this interaction take place?" In order to answer that, we note that before the light reaches the retina at the back of the eye, it has first to pass through the opening at the front – the pupil. How does light pass through an opening – through a hole?

If it were truly made up of a stream of tiny particles, we would expect it to produce a sharp shadow of the hole when it falls on a distant screen. It would be like the sharp shadow one gets on the wall when one sprays paint on it through a hole cut in a sheet of cardboard – the paint being made up of tiny droplets (or particles). But that is *not* how light behaves. The shadow is not sharp. The light beam, on emerging through the hole spreads out; it encroaches upon the geometrical shadow. This spreading-out effect is called *diffraction*. It is a characteristic of waves. Waves – not particles. Diffraction occurs every time a wave passes through a hole in a screen, or a gap in a barrier. It becomes especially noticeable when the dimensions of the gap are small enough to be comparable to the wavelength of the light – the characteristic distance between successive humps or troughs in the wave. When this is so, the smaller the hole, the more pronounced the spreading-out effect becomes.

In this way we get a marked contrast between the behavior expected of a beam of particles and that expected of waves. In the first case, a reduction in the size of the hole should always lead to a diminution of the size of the beam on the far side of the hole; in the second case, once the dimensions of the hole are comparable to the wavelength of the wave, further reduction in the size of the hole will lead to an *increase* in the size of the transmitted beam. And, as I have said, light behaves in this second manner – the manner expected of waves.

This is not the only indication of the wave-like behavior of light. There is refraction. This refers to the way a light beam can alter direction as it passes from one medium to another (from air to glass, or from water to air, say). When taking a bath, you have probably noticed that when your leg is partly in, and partly out, of the water, it appears to develop a kink at the surface of the water. This is because of the way the light from the submerged part of your leg gets bent, or refracted, on emerging out of the water – giving the impression it has come from some other direction. This bending of light is a characteristic of lenses, such as the lens in the eye. Refraction can be explained in terms of light behaving as a wave.

As yet further evidence of wave behavior, we have Polaroid sunglasses. Light normally vibrates in all directions at right angles to the direction in which it is moving. Polaroid glasses have the characteristic of cutting out all vibrations except those in a given direction. They would not function in the absence of vibrations – in other words, if light were not behaving as a vibrating, undulating wave.

Now this, of course, is very puzzling. Earlier we had clear-cut evidence for the particle-like behavior of light – the manner in which light interacts with a surface. The particles were tiny; indeed, they appeared to have no size at all – no extension. But now we have equally convincing evidence that light behaves like a wave. And waves, by the very fact that they are characterized by a wavelength, must have size; they must extend over a distance at least comparable to that of the wavelength. So, we are faced with a dilemma: how can something have no size, and yet it *does* have size?

It is a paradox – an apparent contradiction. Moreover, it is a paradox not confined to light. The same schizophrenic behavior afflicts electrons too. Electrons, when they interact, behave like point particles – as I indicated earlier. The picture one sees on a TV screen is made up of scintillations given out as individual electrons bombard the screen – as a hail of gunfire – clear evidence of particle-like behavior. But just as in the case of light, once one switches attention from the question of *how* electrons interact, to that of *where* they will interact, one has to treat them as a beam of waves. For example, a beam of electrons passing through an aperture will be diffracted. The beam will be characterized by a well-defined wavelength. The degree of spreading out into the geometric shadow will be governed by the ratio of that wavelength to the dimensions of the aperture – just as for light.

The connection between the particle nature and the wave nature of electrons is that the wavelength of the wave is inversely proportional to the momentum of the particle. The greater the momentum, the smaller the wavelength. And the smaller the wavelength, the more difficult it becomes to see the diffraction of the beam as it passes through the hole. With a very tiny wavelength, there is little deviation – little encroachment of the beam into the geometric shadow of the hole; the beam behaves like the paint spray, casting a sharp shadow.

Wave/particle duality affects not just light and electrons, but *absolutely everything* – including droplets of paint. The only reason we do not notice droplets of paint behaving like waves is that they are so much heavier than electrons; their momentum is always so much greater than that characteristic of electrons, and hence their wavelength is microscopic compared to the dimensions of any hole they are likely to pass through. The droplets do encroach somewhat into the geometric shadow on account of diffraction, but the extent of the overlap is too small to notice.

Even large objects – like you and I – have a wave nature. When, for example, you eventually stop reading and get up and leave the room, on passing through the doorway you will get diffracted; ever so slightly you will be deflected sideways. How much will depend on how fast you amble through, and how heavy you are (the two factors governing your momentum and hence your wavelength). I hasten to say it is a small effect – a *very* small effect. Having gone through the door, if you were then to continue in a straight line, by the time you reached the end of the observable Universe you would find that you were likely to have been deflected to a point about one millimeter from where you would otherwise have ended up. As I said, not a big effect – but nevertheless it's interesting to know that it is there.

In summary, therefore, quantum theory leads to the conclusion that everything has a wave and a particle character. And that in turn raises a big, big question: How can something be, at one and the same time, both a point-like particle of no extension, and also a wave spread throughout space?

As far as *interactions* are concerned, there is no problem. If we are asking: "*How* will it interact?" the answer is in terms of particles – point-like exchanges of energy. If, on the other hand, we are asking: "*Where* will it interact?" the answer is in terms of waves. The diffraction pattern one gets on a screen the other side of a hole gives the relative intensity of the beam falling on different areas of the screen, and hence the number of point-like interactions one will get in different regions. So, as far as interactions are concerned, we are either asking *how* it will interact (particle), or *where* it will interact (wave). We cannot be asking both questions at the same time, so we never need to use both the particle and the wave aspects at the same time. In terms of interactions, the two concepts are kept separate.

The trouble comes when we try to go *beyond* the interaction and talk about the electron, or the light, or whatever, *as it is in itself* – as it is divorced from the context of an interaction.

Let us suppose there is an electron out there in space – on its own. No one is looking at it. It is not hitting into anything. It is just sitting there. We are not asking how it interacts, or where it interacts; it is not interacting at all. Under *those* circumstances – what is it? Is it to be described as a particle, or as a wave?

This is a problem that was posed in the early 1930s. It exercised the minds of the world's greatest physicists of the time: Einstein, Bohr, Heisenberg, de Broglie, Schrödinger, Born, and others. There was no agreement then; there is no agreement today. All possibilities were tried. Some held that the electron was really a particle; it simply had a wave associated with it to guide it around. Others said no; the electron was really a wave; it just appeared to be a bit gritty at times. Really a particle; really a wave. Each had its advocates.

Then there were those who felt that this was the wrong approach altogether; it was not a case of either/or. This wave/particle duality, as it was called, was highlighting the need for a more thorough-going change in thinking. This revolution in thought went something along the following lines: all along we have been supposing that the task of science was to describe and understand the physical world. To do that one had to interact with it; observe it, experiment on it. But having performed those observational acts, what one wrote down in the physics books was a description of the way the world was and how it operated, regardless of whether it was still being observed.

Of course, in writing down that description one had to take account of any disturbance one's act of observation might itself have had. For example, we are all familiar with the idea that if we take the temperature of a beaker of liquid, the fact that the thermometer has to take up some of the heat to adjust itself to the temperature of the liquid will affect the temperature it is trying to measure. But this effect can, in principle, be allowed for and a correction made to arrive at what the temperature would have been without the disturbance caused by the measurement.

In the same way it was recognized that *all* observation affects that which is observed – even when the only thing we do is *look* at something. The act of looking seems harmless enough, except of course, it does involve shining a light on the object. According to quantum physics, that means the object is being hit by a hail of tiny bullets conveying energy and momentum. If what one is looking at is very small – say, an electron – it will recoil away under the impact of the quantum, or particle, of light hitting it. At first one might think that it should be a straightforward matter to make due allowance for the impact; to work out what the electron was doing before it was hit – before it was observed. But this proves extraordinarily difficult – in fact, it proves to be impossible. In order to be able to make the correction to the behavior of the electron, one would need precise information on both the momentum and the position of the light quantum hitting it. Unfortunately, the wave/particle duality of the illuminating light prevents one from gaining such information. It is denied to us by Heisenberg's Uncertainty Relation – something we briefly alluded to in Chapter 4.

Thus we find that we are denied complete knowledge of what is happening out there in the physical world in itself. Indeed, each time we try to talk about what is going on there we get enmeshed in impenetrable paradoxes – such as how something can be confined to one point in space, and at the same time be spread out over space.

Some physicists pin their hopes on this being but a temporary restriction. They claim quantum theory to be but a staging-post on the way to a fuller, more complete understanding of the world. Although admittedly at the present time our descriptions are on a firm footing only when it comes to accounting for the where and the how of our interactions with the world, one day, so they claim, we shall achieve what we always regarded as being the goal of science: namely, a description of the world as it is in itself, divorced from whether anyone happens to be observing and interacting with it. Such an optimistic stance was in fact the one adopted by Einstein himself. It might be correct. But one does have to say that it is now over sixty years since discussions on these matters were initiated, and we seem no closer to getting such a theory of the world in itself – a theory free of paradox. And as each year goes by, and still there is no complete theory of what might be going on out there, attention becomes more and more concentrated on a further possibility.

It was one advocated by Niels Bohr and his supporters in the great debates of the 1930s. Bohr proposed that the job of science is *not* to describe the world in itself – a world isolated from the observer. Such a description is impossible – *intrinsically* impossible. We were wrong ever to suppose that what we had written down in our physics textbooks was a description of the world we had observed. Instead it is *a description of ourselves observing the world* – and that is all we shall ever get. The observer, and that which is observed, are inextricably welded together.

Accordingly, none of the concepts we use in physical description applies to the world in itself. It is wrong to think (as we did earlier) of an electron sitting out there with a well-defined position and velocity, and that it is just our clumsy measuring techniques that deny us completely precise estimates as to what that position and velocity are (the operation of the uncertainty relation). Bohr claimed that terms such as "position," "velocity," "momentum," and "energy" were coined specifically to help us explain the results of our measurements of, or our interactions with, the world. As such they apply *solely* to the act of observation. It is *a misuse of language* to apply those concepts to what is supposedly happening in between the interactions. Recall how our interactions are discontinuous and point-like, these discrete observations being punctuated by periods where the world is not being observed. The concepts we use have relevance only to the discrete acts of observation – not to the gaps in between.

If this is the first time you have come across this sort of argument, I can well appreciate your reaction. It demands an enormous shift in thinking to recognize that all we ever talk about is *behavior* (how something interacts, or where something interacts); we never, never talk about what something *is* (what it is in itself). It is a difficult idea to swallow because in our ordinary, everyday language we appear to be talking about what things *are* all the time.

For example, I might hold up an object and say, "This object is blue." In doing so, I appear to have said something about what the object *is*. But have I? Suppose I were to hold it up under a yellow street light, would it appear blue? No. It would appear black. So, why not say, "This object is black"? Because we assume that one is not doing anything so silly as holding it up to a yellow light; it ought to be looked at in white light – light that contains some blue light that can be reflected.

All right, suppose I now heat up the object so that it is red hot. Why not say, "This object is red"? The answer is that it is tacitly assumed that one is not heating the object to ridiculous temperatures.

What this reveals is that, when I say, "This object is blue," what I *actually* mean to say is: "When I expose this object to white light, at normal room temperature, it will absorb all the colors of the white light except blue, which it reflects." In other words, it is a statement of behavior – how the object will interact, under a given set of circumstances. But, of course, that is such a long-winded statement that it is not surprising we come up with a shorthand way of putting it: "This object is blue." But we must not allow ourselves to be misled. The fact that we use the word "is" in that shorthand statement does not mean we have said anything about what the object is in itself; the statement merely describes how something interacts under a given set of circumstances.

And what is true of that statement is true of *all* statements that appear at first sight to be specifying what something is. When one takes the trouble to unpack what the statement actually means, it will come down to a statement about interactions.

If you are having difficulty with this (and who doesn't?), I don't think I can do better than quote a passage from a favorite book of mine. It has nothing to do with quantum physics, but it nevertheless accurately portrays the "feel" of what I am trying to get across. I refer to John Hull's book *On Sight and Insight*. It describes his experiences as he comes to terms with having gone completely blind.

> I heard the footsteps of passers-by, many different kinds of footsteps. . . . From the next bench, there was the rustle of a newspaper and the murmur of conversation. Further out, to the right behind me, there was the car park. Cars were stopping and starting, arriving and departing, doors were being slammed. Far over to the left, there was the main road. I heard the steady deep roar of the through traffic, the buses and the trucks. In front of me was the lake. It was full of wild fowl. The ducks were quacking, the geese honking. . . . There was the splash of paddle boats, the cries of children, and the bump as two boats collided. . . . Over this whole scene was the wind. The trees behind me were murmuring, the shrubs and bushes along the side of the paths rustled, leaves and scraps of paper were blown along the path. I leant back and drank it all in. . . .
>
> The strange thing about it, however, is that it was a world of nothing but action. Every sound was a point of activity. Where nothing was happening, there was silence. That little part of the

world had died, disappeared. The ducks were silent. Had they gone or was something holding their rapt attention? The boat came to rest. Were people leaning on the oars, or had they tied it to the edge and gone away? Nobody was walking past me just now. This meant that the footpath itself had disappeared. . . . Even the traffic on the main road had paused. Were the lights red? When there is rest, everything else passes out of existence. To rest is not to be. To do is to be. Mine is not a world of being; it is a world of becoming. The world of being, the silent, still world where things simply are, that does not exist. . . . The acoustic world is one in which things pass in and out of existence.*

What is true of the acoustic world of the blind is true of each of us. We all live in a world of action – interaction and observation. And that is all our science deals with.

John Hull in that passage talks about things going in and out of existence. He is talking in a rather poetic vein there, of course. But there are some physicists who regard that as *literally* true of the physical world. In between our intermittent observations of it, the world goes out of existence. The only physical reality is the reality of observations. Such a position reminds us of the philosopher Berkeley posing the question of whether or not the tree in the college quadrangle went out of existence whenever it was not being observed by anyone.

That seems to me to be an extreme position, and one that is hardly tenable. But what is not to be denied is that, if there is a real physical world in itself, in between our intermittent observations of it, then there are great difficulties in saying anything sensible about it. Heisenberg came to the view that it was, in fact, quite meaningless to try and talk about it.

The mental world

From knowledge of physical reality, let us now turn – very briefly – to knowledge of mental reality.

As was the case with physical reality, the mental domain is one where, at first, there appears to be no difficulty knowing exactly what we are talking about. We can be pardoned for thinking that there surely can be nothing more transparently straightforward than the contents of our own minds. Yet it is not so. An exactly similar revolution has occurred in the philosophy of mind as that which has occurred in physics.

Suppose I were to ask: "What exists in your mind at the present instant?" An unconsidered reply might list such things as a mental picture of this page you are reading; the sounds of traffic or birdsong coming into the room from outside; a memory (hazy or otherwise) of what you have read earlier in the book; and so on.

But there is a problem: if there is a visual picture of this page in your mind, with what are you looking at it? The mind's eye? What does that mean? Where is this inner eye? As for the sounds in your mind, with what are you listening to them? A mental kind of ear? And what of the memories of the earlier part of this book? Are they still in the form of mental pictures of the words you have read? Are they too being looked at by the supposed inner eye?

When one stops to think about it, none of this makes sense. Since the time Gilbert Ryle wrote *The Concept of Mind*, philosophers of the mind have come to recognize that when one searches the mind's contents, one does not find pictures and sounds and memories sitting there. Instead, one finds *experiences*. That is all; dynamic experiences – experiences involving the ego (the center of consciousness): an experience of seeing the page; an experience of hearing the sounds; an experience of recollecting what you have previously read. One is aware of conscious mental experiences – that and nothing else.

Perhaps you found that stuff on quantum physics just now rather heavy-going. You might have dozed off for a while. Did you dream? Dreams are believed to stem from the mind's unconscious. But all we find in the mind is the conscious experience of dreaming. The idea that this is the work of an unconscious part of the mind – a part of the mind lying beyond the mental domain of conscious experience – must be an hypothesis. We cannot consciously and directly note the contents of the unconscious, for they would then, by definition, become an aspect of the conscious part of the mind.

So we find that, on turning from the physical to the mental domain, we encounter the same kind of two-level knowledge structure. First comes the dynamic experience or interaction – whether we are thinking of physical observation and experiment, or mental experience. At this level we have good solid knowledge. Beyond that we have the cause of the experience – whatever it is we are interacting with – whether that be a paradoxical physical world-in-itself, or an unconscious part of the mind-in-itself consisting of unconscious processes, repressed past experiences to which no conscious attention is currently being paid, and other memories. Here we are on less certain ground.

The spiritual world

What has this to do with God – knowledge of God? Simply this: Faced with such difficulties over saying anything meaningful about a physical world-in-itself lying beyond our physical experiences, to say nothing of the difficulties attendant on accounting for the nature of the mind-in-itself lying beyond our mental experiences, is it reasonable to expect a clear unambiguous account of the nature of a spiritual realm lying beyond our religious experiences? If nobody can provide a satisfactory answer to the question: "What is an electron – in itself?" can one really expect an answer to the question: "What is God – in himself?" In the same way, if nobody can explain what the unconscious mind is through some "direct" route into it that bypasses subjective conscious mental experience, can one really expect to get a direct route into knowledge of God that somehow bypasses our experience of him?

As with the physical and the mental domains, when we enter the spiritual domain of knowledge we must pay heed to its two-level structure. First there is the level of interaction and observation – our experience of God. I listed some of these at the start of this chapter. These – the data of our God experiment – are the equivalent of the scientists' observations and experiments on nature. But, of course, some will argue that none of this amounts to *proof* of the independent existence of God – the supposed second level of knowledge lying beyond the first; all we have to go on are the so-called "interactions with God." True. But that is also how it is with the physical realm. As we have noted, some physicists think that the domain of physical interactions, or observations, is the *only* physical reality and that the independent world is an unsubstantiated hypothesis – a convenient fiction. Others say that there might or might not be a world in itself, but we shall never be able to say anything meaningful about it, so why worry our heads over it. Yet others believe that those interactions possess an "otherness" about them – an "otherness" indicative of an existence lying *beyond* the interaction.

What do I mean by "otherness"? I mean this: to some extent the scientist controls the observation to be made. The decision might be to ask how the quantum interacts. The fact that that is the kind of question chosen dictates that the answer will be in terms of particle-type behavior. On the other hand, if the decision is to ask where the interactions are likely to take place, then the answer will be of the wave-type. To that extent the scientist controls the situation. But it is not absolute control. The decision to ask where the interaction will be does not in itself dictate the actual location subsequently found. That is an input into the interaction that the scientist does not supply. It comes from some other source. What source? A plausible answer appears to be that it is some feature of a physical domain – a domain lying over against, and distinct from, the scientist.

In a similar way, a person can decide to go to sleep – a decision entailing the possibility of having a dream. But that does not mean the sleeper can consciously decide what to dream about. The subject matter of the dream (if there is to be a dream at all) comes unexpectedly; it is unanticipated. It is this "otherness" of the dream that points to some other source – an unconscious aspect of the mind.

So it is with the spiritual domain. With all the religious experiences I listed, there can be an otherness to them too. And it is that which leads to the inference that there is a spiritual being beyond those interactions – something or someone other than oneself that is inputting that unexpected quality of otherness.

If one accepts that there is indeed such an objective God lying behind the religious experience, what can be said about him? Not a lot. Indeed with the Christian conception of God, when one does try to talk about the nature of the Divine, one quickly becomes enmeshed in paradox. Here of course I refer to the doctrine of the Trinity. Part of that doctrine is the idea of there being one God. As we saw in our out-line of the historical development of the idea of God, the insight into monotheism was hard-won, and it is firmly incorporated into the Christian conception. But we cannot just leave it at that. Christians believe that Jesus was so special that to encounter him is to encounter God. He is fully divine. Not only that, but God dwells inside us in the form of the Holy Spirit. Thus, we have three main ways of encounter-ing God: God the Father (God over us); God the Son (God with us); and God the Holy Spirit (God within us). As far as the interactions are concerned, no problem; there are three ways of interacting with, or relating to, God. The problem comes when we try to go beyond those interactions and talk of who or what God *is* – in himself. Three in one; one in three. What does that mean? It is hard to say. It is a paradox.

And it is not the only paradox to be found in Christianity. Who was Jesus? We have said that he was the Son of God – fully divine. But it is also held that he was fully human. He was not a God merely pretend-ing to be human. Nor was he a human with aspirations to be God-like. He was fully both. But how is that possible? A human is limited in understanding and in power; God is not. A human is localized to one point in space and time; God is everywhere all the time. It begins to sound a little like the wave/particle duality that required the electron to be both a localized point-like particle, and a spread-out wave.

The similarity is not surprising because we are doing the same kind of thing in both cases. We have gone beyond the interaction-with-God and are trying to say something about who or what God is, or who or what Jesus is – in himself. This is exactly analogous to how earlier we tried to go beyond our observations of the electron to state what an electron is – in itself. We encountered paradox in the physical realm; we encounter it again here in the spiritual realm.

Personally, I find this fascinating. The same kind of thinking involved in trying to understand the created world is to be used in try-ing to understand the Creator of that world.

And note the precedence. It was not a case of theologians hastily having to readjust their thinking about God in order to make it con-form with the new quantum type of thinking. They were thinking in these terms around the fourth century – when they were putting together the Christian creeds. Indeed, if anything, the cross-fertilization between science and religion has been in the opposite direction. It is known that Niels Bohr, one of the great architects of the new quantum approach, was an avid reader of the Danish philosopher Søren Kierkegaard. Kierkegaard wrote extensively about the Trinity, maintaining that when the truth viewed objectively appeared to be a paradox, then this was an indication that subjectivity was the truth – meaning that the truth had to involve one's own active participation. This theological insight might indeed have been the trigger for Bohr to concentrate his attention on the observer's involvement, and backing off from the problematic paradoxes that arose whenever one tried to speak of the physical world in an objective, detached way – independent of the act of observation.

The fact that one must expect difficulties in trying to speak of God in himself goes back even further than Christian times. Philo, the Jewish philosopher (c. 20 BC–45 AD), drew a distinction between the "essence" of God, which is absolutely unknowable, and his activities in the world, his "energies." We could comprehend the energies because that was God revealing himself to us, but not his essence – what we have been calling God-in-himself. Augustine took up the same theme in the fourth century when he said that we could not expect to know the name of the substance of God. And Gregory Palamas, the fourteenth-century Archbishop of Thessalonica, who had a strong influence on the development of thought in the Eastern Orthodox Church, expressed similar views, as did Martin Luther later still.

Concluding thoughts

The recognition of the need to take into account our own involvement in whatever it is we are trying to understand – whether it be God or the physical world – is not the first time theologians have beaten scientists to the punch. In Chapter 9, we saw how Augustine arrived at the conclusion that there could have been no time before the world was created, long before modern cosmologists got there on the basis of their understanding of the nature of the Big Bang. These instances serve to illustrate how the two-way relationship between the religious and scientific enterprises sometimes gives precedence to the one, sometimes to the other. Here it was a case of theology leading the way; earlier we came across instances where science highlighted a need to refine and adjust one's understanding of God and of our relationship to him.

For example, the vast scale of the Universe revealed by modern astronomy and cosmology, with the possibility of teeming life forms out there, cannot help but force a reassessment of the sheer scale on which God works, and our own relatively humble position in the overall scheme of things. In similar vein, our modern understanding of the law-like nature of the world makes us much more cautious these days when it comes to accepting claims for miracles; it encourages us to work out what alternative ways God might adopt in order to have an effect on the world. It is only right and proper that the God experiment should embrace these, and whatever other new data come to hand through science, in order to promote progress in theology toward an ever-improved understanding of God and his ways.

On yet other occasions, it is more a case of science coming up with evidence that serves to confirm long-standing theological insights. Here we think of the role of genetically influenced behavior in connection with the doctrine of original sin, or the interpretation of relativistic theory that holds that the future in some sense exists – thus making more plausible the idea that God could indeed have foreknowledge, as has long been thought to be the case.

I would not myself go so far as to claim theology to be a science just like the physical sciences. Nevertheless, it has to be said that the two-way mutual interchange between theology and science could only take place if the approaches adopted in these two enterprises had much in common. By this I mean they are both based ultimately on the outcomes of practical experience, and both are open to modifying their assumptions in the light of that experience. In this regard, one should not be taken in either by dogmatic religious people, or by triumphal scientists when they claim to have once-and-for-all absolute knowledge and truth. The majority of theologians and scientists are content to accept that their respective theories are fallible and always open to improvement in the light of new evidence. Certainly, the developmental histories of theology and science provide ample confirmation that both are willing to change. Hence I do not feel it inappropriate to have called this investigation into the evidence for God the "God experiment."

And the conclusion to be drawn from that experiment? The types of evidence considered were listed at the start of this chapter. None on its own was adequate to provide clinching proof of God's existence. But as became clear early on, from our analysis of possible outcomes of that carefully controlled prayer experiment, this was not to be expected. It is unreasonable to demand such proof. The question is rather whether the *totality* of the various types of evidence surveyed in this book makes better coherent sense under the assumption that there is a God, or whether such an assumption is unhelpful. As far as I am concerned at least, the case has been made.

Note
*John M. Hull *On Sight and Insight: A Journey into the World of Blindness*, Oxford, Oneworld, 1997, p. 72.

Afterword

To end with, you might like to know that the thoughts presented in this book were based on the two series of Gifford Lectures I delivered at Aberdeen University in Scotland during 1997 and 1998.

On receiving the invitation to give those talks, I believed I knew what was expected of me. Judging from books based on previous Gifford Lecture series, I assumed they were to be given at an advanced level, to an audience of knowledgeable academics. But I thought I had better check. So I consulted the terms of Lord Gifford's will. I was in for a surprise. The will makes clear that the lectures were originally intended for the *public*; they were to be directed to "the whole population." It states: "The lectures shall be public and popular, that is, open not only to students of the universities, but to the whole community without matriculation."

How had that early vision become obscured? According to Stanley Jaki's book *A Hundred Years of Gifford Lectures*, the trouble can be traced to the size of the bequest. Each lecturer was to deliver two series of lectures, the fee for each series being equivalent to a professor's salary for two years! As Otto Pfleiderer, the third Gifford Lecturer at Edinburgh, was to remark: "The honour is not great, but the honorarium is colossal." With such generous resources at their disposal, the appointment committees set up by the four participating universities, Edinburgh, Glasgow, St. Andrew's, and Aberdeen, were able to attract the leading academic figures. Over the years they vied with each other as to how eminent a figure they could appoint – regardless of whether the speaker had any ability at communicating with the public. Thus, the needs of the public came to be discounted. The distinguished list of lecturers grew; the honor of being selected as a Gifford Lecturer increased accordingly. By the late 1960s, as Sir Malcolm Knox commented, it had become a widely expressed view that the honor of being selected as a Gifford Lecturer came second only to winning the Nobel Prize. (Meanwhile, I hasten to add, a hundred years of inflation had reduced the "colossal honorarium" to a much more modest figure!)

Having discovered this, I decided that for my two series of lectures, I would break with what had become established custom; I would return to Lord Gifford's original intention. My target audience would be the general public. And it is to that same general public that this book, based on those lectures, has been addressed.

In order to cover a wide spectrum of topics, and provide sufficient explanation of the many difficult underlying ideas, something had to be omitted. That was the historical background. Not that this was meant in any way to downplay the importance and interest of studies into the historical development of ideas. Several scholars in that field have given distinguished Gifford Lecture series in the past. The historical approach is one way of addressing the subject; my concern, however, was more with the contemporary situation, and how that might be made accessible to a general audience. Whether I succeeded is, of course, for you to decide!

Index